PRIVATE INVESTIGATIONS

The Novels of
Dashiell Hammett

Sinda Gregory

Southern Illinois University Press
Carbondale and Edwardsville

Grateful acknowledgment is made to Random House, Inc., and Alfred A. Knopf, Inc., for permission to quote from the novels of Dashiell Hammett: *The Dain Curse*, copyright 1928, 1929 by Alfred A. Knopf, Inc., copyright renewed 1957 by Dashiell Hammett; *The Glass Key*, copyright 1931 by Alfred A. Knopf, Inc., copyright renewed 1959 by Dashiell Hammett; *The Maltese Falcon*, copyright 1929, 1930 by Alfred A. Knopf, Inc., copyright renewed 1957, 1958 by Dashiell Hammett; *Red Harvest*, copyright 1927, 1929 by Alfred A. Knopf, copyright renewed 1957 by Dashiell Hammett; *The Thin Man*, copyright 1933, 1934 by Alfred A. Knopf, copyright renewed 1961, 1962 by Dashiell Hammett.

Library of Congress Cataloging in Publication Data

Gregory, Sinda, 1947–
    Private investigations.

    Bibliography: p.
    Includes index.
    1. Hammett, Dashiell, 1894–1961—Criticism and interpretation.   2. Detective and mystery stories, American—History and criticism.   I. Title.
PS3515.A4347Z68   1985   813'.52   84-1389
ISBN 0-8093-1165-8

For Larry McCaffery

Contents

—⫫—

Foreword

Francis M. Nevins, Jr.

— ᗢ —

Of the making of books on Dashiell Hammett there seems to be no end. In less than five years publishers have issued three full-length biographies, two critical studies (including this one), and a bibliographic volume, not to mention periodical articles and academic dissertations. What can account for this outpouring of interest?

I suspect that Hammett attracts biographers because, more than most of his literary generation and certainly more than his fellow mystery writers, he fitted Walt Whitman's description of the American character and continent. He was vast, he contained multitudes. He was born in obscurity, made himself rich and famous, endured war and prison, died penniless and despised. At the same or different times he was a puritan and a womanizing drunk, a Marxist and a millionaire, a serious novelist and a best-selling commercial writer, an intimate of the elect and a friend of the oppressed. His life makes a story as rich as his fiction.

Why has that fiction attracted so many commentators? Certainly one reason is that Hammett took the genre of detective fiction and, by adding pace and bite and action and cynicism and all sorts of other new elements, Americanized it permanently. Along with less well known colleagues of the so-called Black Mask school, Hammett did to the whodunit what Copernicus did to Ptolemaic astronomy. Or, more precisely, and paraphrasing Marx's

comment about his own relation to Hegel, we might say that
Hammett found the genre standing on its head and set it on its
feet. Traditional detective fiction prior to Hammett was over-
whelmingly British and cerebral in orientation, with brilliant
amateurs in the mold of Sherlock Holmes using the power of pure
reason to penetrate to the truth of the most cunning criminal
plots. At its best, for example in early Ellery Queen, the formal
detective novel was a magnificent webwork of bizarre clues, convoluted story lines, deductive ingenuity, and intellectual excitement. Hammett had no objection to this kind of novel and, as
Sinda Gregory shows, used its elements again and again in his
own major work. But what he found missing from earlier formal
masterpieces was any sense of what the world outside the printed
page was like, and this he set out to integrate into the detective
genre. In Hammett's world investigators are professionals, not
amateurs; working because it is their job, not for the joy of solving a puzzle; cooperating with the police, not showing them up
as buffoons. Hammett's criminals too are usually professionals,
not civilized chess adversaries but, with a few notable exceptions,
nasty, brutish, and short on brains. But despite these shifts in sensibility, Hammett did not reject the formalists' image of the detective as Rational Man *par excellence*, and at times even his most
hard-bitten series character, the Continental Op, sounds a bit like
Hercule Poirot or Ellery Queen.

His truly radical revolution took place on the level of philosophy. The premise of formal deductive fiction is that all the dark-
ness is amenable to the light of reason, that in almost every respect all's right with the world. The murder of Sir George in the
library of his ancestral manor is a momentary aberration, but once
the detective exposes the culprit and organizes the clues into a
rationally harmonious mosaic, the world is restored, as W. H. Auden put it, to the innocence of Eden before the Fall. This crypto-
religious outlook is what Hammett threw out of the genre. His
world is harsh, cruel, and guilt-ridden. Pain and death are in the
atmosphere like oxygen. The whole system is corrupt beyond re-
demption. Solving one or a few murders is like putting a Band-
Aid on a cancer. Things are out of control. The beam can crush
anyone at any moment. We live only while blind chance spares
us. The only recourse is to live in internal exile, holding to a pri-

vate code of honor, trusting no one, loving no one, and such a life does not help either.

Today, thanks to the French, we have a word for this view of the world. Sinda Gregory never uses it but she shows conclusively how apt it is for describing Hammett's outlook. The word of course is *noir*. The world of Hammett is an incomprehensible place in which no one can really know another, a place of political and social corruption and personal alienation and existential despair. Such a world is incompatible with traditional detective fiction, but, for Hammett and later writers like Raymond Chandler and James M. Cain and Cornell Woolrich and also for the directors of *film noir*, it became the locus of a new and peculiarly American mystery tradition.

After *The Thin Man* (1934) Hammett for all practical purposes stopped writing. Perhaps, as some have argued, he had nothing more to say as a creative person and knew it. Perhaps, having committed himself to Marxism, he wanted to write detective fiction that would embody and defend his cause as G. K. Chesterton's Father Brown tales embodied and defended Roman Catholicism but could not figure a way to do it. In any event, what preoccupied Hammett from then on was the quest to help make a revolution in the external world that would be as radical as the revolution he had already made, all but single-handed, in the world of mystery fiction. Hammett the Marxist failed as profoundly as Hammett the writer succeeded.

He was vast. He contained multitudes.

Preface

—— ᔓᔕ ——

One might suppose that I came to this study of Dashiell Hammett's novels through an early interest in detective fiction, but such is not the case. As a youngster I read a great deal, but never mysteries; my sole exposure to the genre was through television in the late 1950s and early 60s, which seized on the popularity of the private eye and produced countless shows featuring detectives, crimes and solutions. But the mystery as seen on television was no mystery at all: there was a broad visual outline (the trench coat, a dangling cigarette, the disembodied arm striking the hero from the shadows); but the heart of detective fiction—the design of its puzzle, the intricacies of its clues, the coherency of its narrative—was largely absent.

Then in Professor Nina Baym's course, Best Selling Fiction 1860–1940, at the University of Illinois, I read *The Maltese Falcon*. Caught up by the aesthetics of Hammett's vision, I immediately read the other four novels. I was hooked, first by the vividness and cutting precision of his prose and by the intriguing complexity of his detective "heroes" and then, as I began considering the conventions of the genre, by the skillful structure of his fiction. Thus it was Hammett who brought me to detective fiction; it was after my discovery of him that I began to read and appreciate the field and, certainly, it was after my encounters with his fiction that I began to think through the implications of the form and to perceive the potential that the metaphors and structures inherent in the genre offer. Although detective fiction, like any genre writing, operates within prescribed conventions that define the nature of the work (and thus the scope of its vision), it is a powerful pattern: we search for meaning and for culpability in our most complex metaphysical and scientific investigations. Indeed, human consciousness constantly confronts the central crime of our lives: Why must we die? Who or what is going to kill us? What is the motive? And this pressing, desperate inquiry into the nature of chaos and personal vulnerability has primal origins which reverberate back to the preverbal terrors of the night when we lay as infants in the dark, acutely aware of crimes against the self, squalling for the comfort of the known.

Not only did Hammett's writing make me reconsider detective fiction, it also made me reevaluate my notions of what literature *is*. Like many people trained formally as a reader and interpreter of books, I had developed rather rigid ideas of what does and does not constitute "serious" literature. Certain forms, by virtue of their packaging, promotion, and eventual popularity, were relegated to the category of popular fiction, and thus were of no inherent interest to the serious student of literature. This situation is encouraged in part by universities and partly by the technology of publishing (specifically the paperback revolution) which has made a much greater number of books available—books that, for purposes of marketing and distribution, are categorized at every level of production, from editing to their placement on shelves in book stores. Although this categorization process may be inevitable and useful for certain practical purposes, it can also mislead, distort, and obscure. A novel of merit, whether it be science fiction by Philip K. Dick or Ursula LeGuin, a western by William Eastlake or Larry McMurtry, or a sports novel by Don DeLillo or Robert Coover, has its own integrity and its own life, within and without its genre. This is certainly the case with the novels of Dashiell Hammett, works that not only redefined and revitalized the established field of detective fiction, but also created a new and particularly American form of artistic expression.

PRIVATE
INVESTIGATIONS

1

Dashiell Hammett and the Hard-Boiled Detective Genre

—⌣—

*He knew then that men died at haphazard like that, and
lived only while blind chance spared them.*
　　　　　　　　—from The Maltese Falcon

When Dashiell Hammett died on January 10, 1961, at the age of
sixty-seven, he had not published an original short story or novel
for twenty-seven years. Other than an uncompleted autobiographical novel, he never wrote anything outside a genre traditionally labeled as popular entertainment, and he is said to have
considered his own writing unimportant. Yet despite his limited
output and his apparent low estimate of it, Hammett is considered America's master detective writer. More than that, however,
he was a creator of a distinct body of fiction that is unique in its
vitality, its language, and its vivid and singular vision. Raymond
Chandler said of Hammett that he "wrote scenes that seemed
never to have been written before,"[1] and Hammett's five novels,
all produced within a five-year period, are remarkable in their ability
to infuse the action on the page with such intensity that the fiction is complete in itself and points not only to the outer world
but also inward to the world of fiction and to the consciousness
that created it. He worked within the prescribed boundaries of a
highly stylized form of popular fiction and devised original, entertaining stories that were extremely popular with the pulp magazines' audience, but he also constructed serious fictions that were

1

thematically, structurally, and technically complex. At the same time that Hammett was helping establish the pattern for the quintessential private eye—a pattern which persists with only minor changes in the popular detective fiction of today—he was also manipulating that pattern, sometimes undercutting its formulas and sometimes deepening it with a complex irony that called into question the basic tenets of the genre.

Samuel Dashiell Hammett was born on May 27, 1894, in Saint Mary's County, Maryland. Although the Hammetts had been in the area for over a hundred years and had been involved in both business and farming, the family had never established itself financially; instead, depending on the skill, temperament, and luck of each generation, there were rises and falls of prosperity. According to Richard Layman's biography, Hammett's father had grandiose notions of wealth and success, but he proved to be as unsuccessful a businessman as he was a father and husband.[2] He moved his wife and family from one failing enterprise to another, and Dashiell, at thirteen, left school in a futile attempt to help his father salvage the latest venture. After that failed, Hammett began a series of widely varied jobs: a messenger for the Baltimore and Ohio Railroad, a stevedore, an office boy for a stockbroker, a nail-machine operator in a box factory, and a yardman. Although his father viewed these frequent job changes as proof of his son's shiftlessness (a charge he was to use against Hammett for years), biographical sources suggest that he left these jobs mainly out of boredom. Hammett lacked the education or the financial backing necessary for a good job and the temperament necessary for the mindless tasks of menial labor, but in 1915, he found an answer to his quandary when he responded to an advertisement in a Baltimore newspaper and became an operative for the Pinkerton Detective Agency.

Working as a detective was an ideal profession for a young man with few prospects who was eager for stimulation and adventure and, perhaps most of all, eager to prove his manhood. At twenty-one, he was tall but extremely thin and still living at home despite the strain between his father and himself. The Pinkerton job offered travel all over the United States and the opportunity to meet an assortment of men and women from various walks of life and social stations—and from both sides of the law. He worked on cases that ranged from the absurd to the mundane—he was once assigned to find a man who had stolen a Ferris wheel; he spent three months in a hospital trying to gain information from a patient who shared his room; he once shadowed a man who became lost and asked him for directions—experiences which must have helped develop his sense of irony and his appreciation for the absolute variety and inexplicability of human behavior. The job offered excitement, danger, and mental stimulation; his attitude toward the detective profession is perhaps most clearly expressed in a 1925 short story, "The Gutting of Couffignal," that features his first major hero, the Continental Op.

> "Now I'm a detective because I happen to like the work. It pays a fair salary, but I could find other jobs that would pay more. . . . I like being a detective, like the work. And liking work makes you want to do it as well as you can. Otherwise there'd be no sense to it. . . . I don't know anything else, don't enjoy anything else, don't want to know or enjoy anything else. You can't weigh that against any sum of money. Money is good stuff. I haven't anything against it. But in the past eighteen years I've been getting my fun out of chasing crooks and tackling puzzles, my satisfaction out of catching crooks and solving riddles. It's the only kind of sport I know anything about, and I can't imagine a pleasanter future than twenty-some years more of it."[3]

Hammett's employment as a detective for Pinkerton was perhaps the seminal experience of his life, but not merely because it provided "real" material that he was able to use to authenticate his stories. Certainly, his past vocation gave greater credence to his fiction; both Hammett and his publishers often reminded their readers that here was a writer of detective fiction who knew what he was writing about from firsthand observation. The experience, however, gave him more than plots and characters for his fiction: it provided him with a way of seeing the world and of defining himself in it. When Hammett first joined the Baltimore office, he was educated in the trade by the assistant manager, James Wright. Wright taught him the skills necessary for surveillance and investigation, but more importantly, he instilled in Hammett a philosophy that went beyond the Pinkerton office.[4] In some ways it was a simple code of behavior that enabled the operative to submerge his own personality—with all its vulnerabilities and emotions—

into a controlled persona that was better suited for investigative work. This adoption of a mask, of a way of seeming, was no doubt of particular benefit to a young man like Hammett who was throughout his life a reclusive and private person. He and his father had never gotten along, and his brother and he were not close—his most important ties were to his mother and his sister.[5] What Wright and the detective business offered him then was a model of manhood that was compatible with his own personality. To be a detective meant one was encouraged to be objective, anonymous, and apart. He had found a job that in a sense validated his own need for distance and made a virtue of keeping one's own counsel.

Hammett's career was interrupted by World War I when he enlisted in the Ambulance Corps in 1918 and spent a year stationed near Baltimore. During this time, a bout of influenza activated tuberculosis (a disease he probably inherited from his mother); after the war he tried to return to work, but he was too ill. Living at home became more and more difficult because of his father, and finally in May 1920, he moved to the West Coast where he once again tried to take up his profession in the Spokane office of Pinkerton. His health, however, was still too fragile for the demands of almost any job—he was thin, weak, and breathless and faint after any physical exertion—and he was hospitalized in Spokane and San Diego from November 1920 to May 1921. When he was released he married Josephine Dolan, a nurse he had met while a patient, and tried once more to take up the detective business—this time in San Francisco—but he worked for only six months. In December 1921, he quit his job; between the disruptions of the war and his sickness, he had worked four and one-half years.

This account of continuing poor health, of one breakdown and hospital stay after another, seems clear evidence that Hammett was physically incapable of remaining a detective. He was unable to walk the distances often necessary when tailing a subject, unable to work the long hours a case might require, and unable to defend himself in violent confrontations. Yet Hammett never alluded to his physical condition when discussing his resignation, never acknowledged that a lack of physical strength made an active life impossible. Instead he gave other reasons for leaving Pinkerton. William F. Nolan quotes Hammett as saying: "I was beginning to sour on being a detective. . . . The excitement was no longer there, and losing a trip to Australia put the cap on it for me."[6] The Australian trip was a case in which the agency had been hired to find two hundred thousand dollars in gold that had been stolen from a ship during its crossing to California. The gold was hidden somewhere on board, and if it were not found before the return trip to Australia, Hammett was to have sailed back with the ship. According to Hammett he found the gold only hours before the ship was to depart, lost a trip to a country he was eager to visit, and resigned from Pinkerton's. "I was furious with myself. . . . Why couldn't I have discovered the gold one day out to sea? I'd lost my trip. I'd also lost my desire to remain with Pinkerton."[7]

This account made a colorful and dramatic story—one which, in the guise of confessing to a foolish honesty, underlined the integrity of its teller—but Hammett privately gave Lillian Hellman another, more serious reason for his quitting Pinkerton's. In the account told her by Hammett, he was offered five thousand dollars by an officer in the Anaconda Copper Company to kill labor union leader Frank Little. Hammett knew he had been hired as a strikebreaker, but when a job which put him in the role of a company man also asked him to be an assassin, he refused.

> He seldom talked about the past unless I asked questions, but through the years he was to repeat that bribe offer so many times that I came to believe, knowing him now, that it was a kind of key to his life. He had given a man the right to think he would murder, and the fact that Frank Little was lynched with three other men in what was known as the Everett Massacre must have been, for Hammett, an abiding horror.[8] I think I can date Hammett's belief that he was living in a corrupt society from Little's murder.[9]

Thus, while evidence suggests Hammett was forced to leave the detective business because of poor health, he himself perceived a different "truth" in the situation: he came to see the profession that he had embraced so eagerly as a young man as an amoral force to be purchased by anyone or any group with enough money. What Hammett's experience as a detective seems to have given him, then, was an intimate contact with pervasive criminality

that he carried into his fiction and a genuine abhorrence of un-
bridled capitalistic power that he carried into his personal life.

Sometime during his career as a detective, Hammett became
interested in writing, and after he left Pinkerton, he tried to find
a career that would allow him to write while at the same time to
support his family. He attended Munson's Business College in San
Francisco for one and one-half years and took writing and stenog-
raphy classes to train himself as a reporter. Also during this period he was teaching himself to write fiction: his first two published stories—signed under a pseudonym, Peter Collinson, and
appearing in the December 1922 issues of *Brief Stories* and *Black
Mask*—were in the style of a new brand of detective fiction whose
beginnings paralleled Hammett's own career. Despite these early
successes in finding a publisher, it was a difficult time; he spent
all but about four hours each day in bed—time he passed by
studying, reading, and writing.[10] During these hours of reflection,
he decided that newspaper work did not interest him as much as
advertising, and he began writing freelance copy for various San
Francisco businesses. In addition to this work, he continued to
publish fiction, including his first Continental Op story, "Arson
Plus," which appeared in the October 1, 1923, issue of *Black Mask*.
Although he published thirty-four more stories between then and
March 1926, at that time he left his fiction and took a full-time
job writing newspaper advertising copy for a San Francisco jew-
eler, Albert S. Samuels (the person to whom *The Dain Curse* is
dedicated)—a decision that may have been partly owing to his
wife's second pregnancy. He worked there for only five months;
his tuberculosis had worsened to the point of severe hemorrhag-
ing. Samuels found him one day in his office, unconscious in a
pool of blood.

By this time, Hammett must have seen this recurrent pattern
of physical breakdown as his future. He was forced to turn to his
father and ask for financial help—a gesture, given their relationship, that must have pained and humiliated him. His relations
with his wife were also strained; she thought he had become too
different from the man she had nursed and then married.[11] How
these personal problems and economic pressures appeared to
Hammett, we can only guess, but that time must have been a
period of crisis for him, a period in which it would have been easy

for him to have given up and become the invalid his wife, father, and doctors considered him to be. Instead, Hammett focused his energies on writing. He moved into a small apartment, essentially ending his marriage, and began doing freelance advertising—probably most of it accomplished from his bed. In October, six months after a total collapse, he published an article in *Western Advertising*; in January, he began reviewing mystery novels for the *Saturday Review of Literature*; in February, May, and June, his short stories appeared in *Black Mask*; by the end of the year, he had finished the first half of *Red Harvest*. Thus within a few months of being classified by army doctors as totally disabled, Hammett had reestablished an independent life for himself. He was beginning to make a living at his writing and, more importantly, beginning a period of creativity that would produce five novels and dozens of short stories over the next seven years. This burst of energy, by Lillian Hellman's account, came from a man convinced he was dying. In her introduction to *The Big Knockover*, she describes Hammett's decision to turn to writing. "Since he thought he had a limited amount of time to live, he decided to spend it on something he wanted to do." [12]

And what Hammett wanted to do was create fiction. From 1927 to 1934 he wrote fifty-two short stories which were published in various pulp magazines. Among these stories were four—"The Cleansing of Poisonville," "Crime Wanted—Male or Female," "Dynamite," and "The 19th Murder"—which were published in the November 1927–February 1928 issues of *Black Mask*. Each was a complete story in itself, but Hammett revised them, and in 1929, they were published together as his first novel, *Red Harvest*. His next three novels followed in quick succession. *The Dain Curse*, published in 1929, was also originally four self-contained stories that had been published in *Black Mask* as "Black Lives" (November 1928), "The Hollow Temple" (December 1928), "Black Honeymoon" (January 1929), and "Black Riddle" (February 1929). His third novel, *The Maltese Falcon*, was first published as a five-part serial in *Black Mask* (September 1929–January 1930) and later as a novel in 1930. *The Glass Key*, his fourth novel, appeared in *Black Mask* in 1930 as four novelettes ("The Glass Key" in March, "The Cyclone Shot" in April, "Dagger Point" in May, and "The Shattered Key" in June) and was published as a novel in 1931. [13]

Hammett's last novel, *The Thin Man* (the only work not to appear in short form in *Black Mask*), appeared in 1934. After a remarkably productive period from 1928 to 1934 in which he wrote five novels and numerous short stories, nothing more appeared from Hammett until 1961 when a fifty-page section of a never-completed novel, *Tulip*, was published after his death.

Although Hammett's career as a writer only lasted approximately ten years, the popularity of his work continued. He lived in Hollywood as one of its most famous popular writers—sixteen movies were made from his work (*The Maltese Falcon* was produced three times; *The Thin Man* led to a series of films using the original characters; *The Glass Key* had two versions; *Red Harvest* had one). He was employed for several years as a screenwriter, but he produced only one script for which he received screenplay credit—an adaptation of Lillian Hellman's *Watch on the Rhine* in 1943. During the forties and fifties, three weekly radio series—"The Adventures of Sam Spade," "The Thin Man," and "The Fat Man"—were based on his characters; in the midfifties, Nick and Nora Charles became the basis for a television series. In 1978, there was a made-for-television movie of *The Dain Curse*; in 1982, Francis Ford Coppola produced a movie based on Joe Gores's novel, *Hammett*, in which Hammett appears as himself in a fictionalized account of his life and his writing methods.

Back in 1930, however, before he became transformed by history and the public into one of his own characters, Hammett met twenty-four-year-old Lillian Hellman, a then unknown playwright who had come to Hollywood to find work as a screenwriter. According to Hellman, she first met Hammett when he was on the fifth night of a long drunk. This period may have been the peak of his creativity and popularity, but it was also a time of heavy drinking and partying when Hammett alternated between days of intense work and nights in the company of Ben Hecht and a succession of women. This was the Hollywood of extravagance, decadence, rising stars, and surreal parties—Hammett was to write that "the town was loud with wild hearts and the poetry of success."[14] Hammett's literary career was to end for all practical purposes with the 1934 publication of *The Thin Man*, but Hellman's career began that same year with the success of her first Broadway play, *The Children's Hour*. Hammett had been a great influence in her first play, and he was to continue to play an important role in Hellman's career until his death.

As Hammett's literary output waned, during his Hollywood period, his interest in politics began to take up more and more of his energies. As evidenced by his five novels, Hammett was deeply critical of the American political system, and by the midthirties he was involved with many other writers and intellectuals of his day in supporting left-wing and antifascist causes.[15] Hammett was a Marxist, and there is evidence to suggest he joined the Communist party sometime during this period. Lillian Hellman says in *Scoundrel Time* that she is "fairly sure" Hammett joined the party in 1937 or 1938.[16] His involvement with the Communists did not preclude an active and fervent patriotism. Despite his age and poor health, he enlisted in the army shortly after World War II broke out, and at the age of forty-eight, he began a three-year tour of duty in the Aleutian Islands, where he was in charge of the base newspaper. While there, he developed emphysema, and his health deteriorated even more. After his release and return to civilian life, he resumed heavy drinking; his problems with alcohol and emphysema, combined with the damage done to his lungs by tuberculosis, led to a breakdown in 1948. Convinced by his doctor that drinking would destroy him completely, he abruptly stopped; his health improved, but he was never to be fully well.

Following the war, Hammett continued his support of left-wing causes. His involvement in the Communist party reached a climax in 1951. Hammett had been connected with the Civil Rights Congress for several years, and when four Communist members were brought to trial charged with conspiracy against the government, he acted on a committee that posted their bond. When the four failed to appear in court, the judge ordered Hammett to reveal the names of those who had contributed to the bond fund. According to Hellman's account, Hammett himself did not know the names of any contributors, but he felt so strongly that the court had no right to force the names to be revealed that he refused to base his defense on lack of knowledge. In *An Unfinished Woman*, Hellman describes the evening before Hammett was to appear in court.

The night before he was to appear in court, I said, "Why don't you say that you don't know the names?"

"No," he said, "I can't say that."

"Why?"

"I don't know why. I guess it has something to do with keeping my word, but I don't want to talk about that. Nothing much will happen, although I think we'll go to jail for a while, but you're not to worry because"—and then suddenly I couldn't understand him because the voice had dropped and the words were coming in a most untypical nervous rush. I said I couldn't hear him, and he raised his voice and dropped his head. "I hate this damn kind of talk, but maybe I better tell you that if it were more than jail, if it were my life, I would give it for what I think democracy is, and I don't let cops or judges tell me what I think democracy is."[17]

The next day, Hammett was found guilty of contempt, and on July 10, 1951, he began a six-month term in federal prison. When he was released, he was sick and was to remain sick for the rest of his life; his work was blacklisted, and the remainder of his fortune was garnisheed by the government for alleged income tax infractions.

For the next ten years, Hammett continued to be as politically active as possible, given his poor health and lack of income. He taught classes at the Jefferson School of Social Science and worked with several groups involved in leftist issues. In March 1953, he was called to testify before a Senate subcommittee headed by Joseph McCarthy, a committee investigating "subversive" literature found in State Department libraries overseas,[18] and in February 1955, he was called before a New York State legislative committee investigating charitable agencies suspected of Communist sympathies. Despite repeated attempts over the years to get back to writing, Hammett produced nothing except for fifty pages of an unfinished novel—the new writing career he wanted to pursue outside detective fiction never materialized. The last four years of his life were spent in almost total seclusion with Lillian Hellman—years passed as so much of his life had been, in studying and reading, especially in the areas of natural science, mathematics, and physics. He died of lung cancer and, as befitted a patriot and a veteran, was buried at Arlington National Cemetery.

Although Hammett's career coincided with the development of

the hard-boiled school of detective fiction, he is not the "father" of the genre. Other writers were also contributing to this new form, and while many were talentless hacks, some were able, literate craftsmen. Many of the best writers were associated with *Black Mask*, a pulp magazine begun in 1920 by H. L. Mencken and George Jean Nathan. Under a series of editors, including George W. Sutton, Jr. (1922–24), Phil Cody (1924–26), and Joseph T. Shaw (1926–36), *Black Mask* cultivated and then became the most prestigious journal featuring a new genre of detective fiction. Sutton was the first to publish the work of Dashiell Hammett; Shaw, in particular, set out to promote the new fiction and expand its audience and, in doing so, helped to articulate what these new stories should be. According to Shaw in his introduction to *The Hard-Boiled Omnibus*, a collection of early *Black Mask* stories, there was a well-defined editorial policy that went beyond the usual considerations of profit; it encouraged what Shaw felt to be a literary form in the making that differed from previous detective fiction. This new style sought to emphasize "character and the problems inherent in human behavior and crime solution"[19] and indirectly encouraged a freer, more colloquial and natural language. Hammett was not working alone in this new form; Shaw lists other writers like Raymond Chandler, Raoul Whitfield, George Harmon Coxe, Roger Torrey, Forrest Rosaire, Paul Cain, and Lester Dent as other practitioners.[20] A more comprehensive catalogue would also include Carroll John Daly, one of the earliest contributors to the genre, as well as J. J. Des Ormeaux, Norbert Davis, Frederick Nebel, and Erle Stanley Gardner. Of all these writers, however, none did more than Hammett to formulate the conventions of the hard-boiled genre. Together with the rest of the *Black Mask* writers, he helped create a new mythological hero who has become a fixture in the American psyche—the tough, cynical private detective staring gloomily across a cluttered desk in a run-down office building.

Though this relatively new type of fiction seemed as contemporary as bootleg whiskey and bobbed hair, it had its roots in the classical detective tradition that officially began in 1841 with Poe's "Murders in the Rue Morgue." Although works squarely in this classical tradition continued to sell well in England and America, the hard-boiled school that emerged after World War I had a radically different sensibility with a more timely popular appeal. The new form seemed to reflect the anxieties and violence of the times; the harsh, pained voice of these stories was appropriate for a post-war world that had been shocked into new perspectives. While Hemingway wrote *The Sun Also Rises* and Eliot wrote *The Waste Land*—and thus captured the imagination of intellectual America—people like Carroll John Daly and Raoul Whitfield produced stories that also told of a wasteland, and they sold them for a dime in drugstores, bus depots, and corner newsstands. These writers were drawn to the pulp magazine for various reasons: the market was large, fluid, and profitable for an established author; it could provide the means of living for many while they worked on other writing outside the genre; it gave writers of limited talent and imagination a formula that could be duplicated time and again and continue to pay.

Hammett's own reason or reasons for entering a field of writing that seemed artistically limited can only be speculated upon. It would be easy to see his decision to write detective fiction as the result of circumstances: his experience in the field coupled with the popularity of the subject. Yet such a view fails to account for two important paradoxes. First of all, at the same time that his books are almost universally acclaimed as the best of American detective fiction, they are also among the best examples of the antidetective novel. As Hammett maintained the outward form and pattern of the hard-boiled story, he also infused it with irony, paradox, parody, and humor so that, like the Maltese falcon, all is not as it seems. Thus, the black-and-white appeal of the detective story—a detective who pursues, a villain who eludes, a mystery created by evil and dissipated by good—is present in Hammett's fiction with disquieting contradictions that keep the reader slightly off balance. Reading a Hammett novel is like trying to put a lid on a box that is too large. You can jam it down by cheating a bit at the corners, but it will never really fit. And for a form whose most common metaphor is a jigsaw puzzle that must be assembled, each clue settling into place with a satisfying little "click," this sort of poor fit seems inconceivable.

The second paradox is the contradiction between Hammett's own philosophy and that of the genre. It is difficult to imagine a literary form more antithetical to his own beliefs. Traditionally the classical detective story—a product of nineteenth century empiricism—had stressed the superiority of reason and the inevitable domination of clear-thinking law over the chaos of lawlessness. A subsequent discussion of the differences between the classical and the hard-boiled story will show that the latter form did not accept this blanket certainty that reason will always win out, but both kinds of popular detective fiction can be interpreted at their most basic levels as allegories about the individual's search for meaning and structure. This search presupposes that reason can ferret out and discern order and, more importantly, that such an order exists in the first place. Hammett's fiction denies these fundamental assumptions. In his novels reason, just because it presumes an external order to life, will always fail in the end to explain fully human conduct and emotions. For Hammett the power of mystery is absolute because human consciousness is absolutely mysterious.[21]

Although these paradoxes may seem irreconcilable with the accepted standards of the detective story, Hammett uses them to create tensions that reverberate on several levels. Throughout his novels, Hammett does something few popular writers have ever been able to do as skillfully: he takes advantage of those very conventions usually assumed to be detrimental to true art. He uses the formulaic nature of the detective story like a tuning fork. Relying on the fact that readers come to his books expecting them to be part of the collective consciousness of detective fiction, Hammett plays on the dissonances in the readers' minds between what they think they should be reading and what is actually there. Perhaps the most significant example of this playing is found in the Hammett detective. In most hard-boiled stories, the detective is tough, violent, and uncompromising, but the reader always knows that beneath it all the detective is honest, virtuous, and heroic. Hammett's detectives seem, on a superficial reading, to be perfect embodiments of these qualities and were, in fact, responsible to a large degree for the proliferation of these conventions. Yet, there is also a real indictment of these characters in Hammett's fiction. At the same time that his detectives fulfill the role of the hero as popular fiction demands, they are, on another level, ambiguous, complex figures whose heroic qualities are highly suspect. They exhibit all the external trappings of the typical hard-

boiled hero from loyalty to one's job and client right down to their
refusal to "play the sap" for others; but Hammett injects their
heroism with coldness, callousness, and nihilism. Thus, even while
he helped to define this particular twentieth century brand of
heroism, Hammett also questioned its values.

Not only did Hammett make the detective a more complex figure than did his fellow writers, he also manipulated his plots so
that, while they seemed like other detective stories, their inner
structure was a framework for even more ambiguity and irony.
Unlike most detective fiction, the structure of his books was not
merely a vehicle for colorful characters (as tends to be the case in
the usual hard-boiled story), nor was it used to present an abstract
problem in logic (as is often the case in the classical style developed by Poe). Often Hammett's structures are self-parodic, as in
Red Harvest, where the clutter of corpses reaches ludicrous pro-
portions, or in *The Dain Curse*, where the excessive convolutions
of plot become almost a caricature of mystery fiction. Suspense,
so much a part of most detective stories, is often purposefully
unexploited by Hammett, or as in the case of the temple scene in
The Dain Curse, the suspense is made so ornate that the detective
story becomes a gothic thriller. Although carefully constructed
to make logical sense, his plots have a disconcerting way of undermining what seem to be the major points of the books. For
example, *The Maltese Falcon* is a novel in which the fundamental motivation is the detective's determination to avenge his partner's death and to recover a valuable treasure. Yet at the end we
discover that the identity of the killer was known all along by the
detective—the mystery we assumed was the focus of the book
never really existed—while the treasure that caused all the violence turns out to be a fake. Hammett's plots, then, and the overall structure of his novels satisfy genre conventions by answering
the questions that must, by definition of the form, be raised (who
is the murderer? how was it done? how was the solution found?)
while at the same time they nullify through irony and paradox
the validity of those answers.

Hammett was certainly fully aware of the formulas of this genre.
He reviewed seventy-three detective novels in the *Saturday Review of Literature* and the *New York Evening Post*.[22] In these re-
views, a clear picture comes through of what Hammett expected

in a good detective story: conciseness of plot with no unnecessary clutter in action or character, logical clues, and a plausible mystery. Typical of his criticism was a review of Christopher Bush's novel *The Death of Cosmo Revere*. A brief extract from that article illustrates what Hammett felt to be important for the success of a mystery.

> Another involved, cleverly plotted tale of murder, forgery and other crimes in rural England. . . . The book's weaknesses are several unnecessarily tiresome stretches where nothing happens, the dullness of the two detectives—it is almost impossible to tell them apart—and a lack of clarity or vividness in the telling.[23]

While this no-nonsense approach to detective fiction might seem to contradict my claim that Hammett's work is of greater complexity than the rest of the genre, it merely points out one of the reasons why his fiction was so successful as hard-boiled entertainment. Hammett was a careful craftsman whose recognition and application of standard conventions enabled him to write detective stories that epitomized the form. Not only did he contribute to the development of these conventions, he also made use of those conventions already established by contemporary writers whose work he was familiar with.

Thus, Hammett's fiction was successful on two levels. On the casual reading typically expected for popular fiction, the novels are absorbing and powerful; on a closer, more careful reading of the sort generally reserved for literature, the novels offer a richness of language and vision that is expected of true art. But before proceeding to an examination of the art in Hammett's work, it is useful at this point to define the hard-boiled genre, and to do so properly, it is necessary to understand the tradition from which it grew—the classical detective story.

Generally acknowledged to have begun with Poe's "Murders in the Rue Morgue," the classical detective story is predominantly a puzzle-oriented story which stresses careful plotting and even more careful attention to its own rules. It is a gentleman's form with a strict sense of fair play and decorum. The bond between reader and writer is based on friendly competition with a very strong ethical element: we may be fooled by the author but we can never

be lied to. R. A. Knox, in his "Ten Commandments of Detection,"
states the case for the detective story as sporting event and stresses
the necessity of staying within the confines of the rules.

> And now, what are the rules governing the art of the detective story?
> Let us remember in the first place that these are rules; and you cannot
> afford to overlook them, because the detective story is a game. People
> try to write poetry without rhyme and novels without plots and prose
> without meaning and so on; they may be right or they may be wrong,
> but such liberties must not be taken in the field of which we are speak-
> ing. For every detective story is a game played between the author and
> the reader; the author has scored if he can reach the last chapter with-
> out letting the reader see how the crime was committed, although he
> has given him hints all through which ought theoretically to have let
> him work it out for himself. And there will be no triumph in doing
> that if the author has broken the rules.[24]

The specific rules have been articulated by many fans and critics
of detective fiction, almost always in numbered outline form. G. K.
Chesterton, in "How to Write a Detective Story," gives his own
five basic principles that are similar to most of the other lists. In
my later discussion it will become clear that hard-boiled fiction
can almost be defined by its violations of these principles.

1. The aim of the story is to illuminate, not obscure. "The story is
   written for the moment when the reader does understand, not merely
   for the many preliminary moments when he does not understand."
2. ". . . the soul of detective fiction is not complexity but simplicity. . . . The writer is there to explain the mystery; but he ought not
   to be needed to explain the explanation."
3. ". . . the fact or figure explaining everything should be a familiar
   fact or figure."
4. "Since the reader is aware that an author is behind the puzzle, he is
   bound to rules of both common sense and artistic consistency.
   Characters should be present whose presence fill an artistic need to
   complete the story."
5. ". . . a tale has to be founded on truth." The detective story should
   not be a pure mathematical abstraction.[25]

Along with this strict belief in a set of gentlemanly rules, the
classical detective writer believes also in the ultimate triumph of

reason. A. E. Murch's definition of the detective story as "a tale in which the primary interest lies in the methodical discovery, by rational means, of the exact circumstances of a mysterious event or a series of events"[26] emphasizes the most significant element of the form: rationality. Although many of the most popular stories in this classical form can be seen on close examination to be neither particularly reasonable nor rational, they successfully sustain the illusion that reason has solved the crime. Indeed, every solution must come *solely* through the application of the detective's intellect; thus, one of the form's strictest prohibitions is that chance or luck must play no significant part in the solving of the crime. The solution is there, the author promises the reader, if only you are rational and intelligent enough to see through the puzzle. The detective's specialized knowledge (like Sherlock Holmes's expertise in tobacco ash) that enables him to interpret clues more logically is not luck but the enhancement of reason through education. The denouement of every classical detective story asserts that, once more, the good person's capacity for ratiocination and for placing the world in order is stronger than the bad one's capacity to disrupt. The "civilized" side of humans— their sense of property, communal rules, law, reason—is thus stronger than their baser instincts—their breaking of contracts, theft, murder, chaos—and the reader sleeps easier knowing that no mystery, no question, no vacuum is beyond the ken of the detective's analytical mind.

This belief in the power of reason is correlated with the classical detective's belief in essential order. The emphasis on rules and the necessity for an ordered, logical approach to the crime suggest an abhorrence of disorderly behavior and a need to eliminate ambiguity. Fundamental to this type of detective fiction is the shared understanding between author and reader that the crime is an individual aberration and is not symptomatic of a whole society. In *Mortal Consequences* Julian Symons suggests that "what crime literature offered to its readers for half a century from 1890 onward was a reassuring world in which those who tried to disturb the established order were always discovered and punished."[27] This fiction served to "assert the static nature of society"[28] and assured its readers that if evil existed it would always be overcome by good. As W. H. Auden views this fiction, the world of the classical detective story is in a state of grace. "The fantasy, then, which the detective story addict indulges is the fantasy of being restored to the Garden of Eden, to a state of innocence, where he may know love as love and not law."[29]

This view of crime—as the manifestation of loss of control in a poorly socialized individual—is in keeping with traditional themes in British literature. The criminal provides only a temporary element of uncertainty and doubt in a basically sound, reasonable, law-abiding, and fulfilling society. The detective—one of society's staunchest supporters—restores order; the prevailing temper of society wins again. John G. Cawelti, in *Adventure, Mystery, and Romance*, summarizes this view as follows: "evil is an abnormal disruption of an essentially benevolent social order caused by a specific set of criminal motives."[30] Thus, the detective's zeal to punish the wicked is rarely a personal vendetta; instead, he represents the absolute sanctity of society. The duty he feels is not merely to keep the wrongdoer from prospering but also to reveal both the moral and the intellectual superiority of the existing order.

These three primary characteristics of the classical detective story—strict sense of rules and sporting behavior, emphasis on the supremacy of reason, and belief in the existing social order— were clearly appealing to popular audiences in England and the United States prior to World War I. And American mystery writers like Mary Roberts Rinehart, S. S. Van Dine (Philo Vance), Earl Derr Biggers (Charlie Chan), and Frederic Dannay and Manfred B. Lee (Ellery Queen) continued the classical tradition after the war. But as changing values disrupted intellectual, artistic, and social life in the 1920s and produced a new kind of serious American literature, the hard-boiled school of detective fiction emerged as an alternative to the classical style. The tidy puzzle, the carefully drawn lines between good and evil, and the finality of both the mystery and the solution seemed no more appropriate to many detective story writers than did drawing room drama to Sinclair Lewis and Sherwood Anderson.

In the climate of changing attitudes, intensified by the stock market crash (which occurred the same year that *Red Harvest* was published), the classical detective working for the system may have seemed like a company man to the popular audience of pulp fiction. The hard-boiled story offered as an alternative an individual who worked outside the system for the good of the average person. This new form turned around almost all the classical conventions and defied most of the established rules. There was no longer an emphasis on fair play and good sportsmanship between reader and author and no friendly competition—the writer of the hard-boiled style was not interested in a contest of wits with his reader. Instead he emphasized characterization and a lively story rather than plot. His lack of interest in the novel-as-riddle is shown by the basic arbitrariness of the solution. It does not really matter *who* killed Roger Ackroyd in the hard-boiled work of fiction; often after reading a novel and learning the "solution," the reader still has no idea how it was reached, nor is there much of an inclination, as there is with many classical detective stories, to backtrack through the book to see how the solution was interwoven in the text. Unlike the classical detective writer who plants specific clues throughout the story to alert the reader to the villain's identity, the hard-boiled writer devises a solution that is based more on emotional effectiveness than on the logical working out of clues. In most of the novels, clues *do* exist and a reader can use them to formulate a likely solution, but the clues usually lack the exactness found in a novel by Sayers or by Christie.[31]

The rules that classical detective writers like Chesterton formulated can be almost completely rewritten to fit the hard-boiled story.

1. The aim of the story is not towards illumination at the end. The fact that one person out of several equally unsavory suspects is guilty of a particular crime does not obviate or clarify the past. In extreme examples like Spillane and Chandler, it is obvious that the story is, in fact, written "for the many preliminary moments" when the reader does not understand; in Spillane, the solution is often so transparent for any alert reader who has read more than one Mike Hammer novel that a denouement is unnecessary; in Chandler, the solution is so convoluted and difficult to follow that the reader never fully understands what has been happening.
2. The soul of hard-boiled detective fiction is very often complexity rather than simplicity. The world of corruption and evil is complex and pervasive. There is never any respite from this world and rarely is there a character whose innocence is above suspicion.

3. The guilty party may be as familiar as the detective's client or as obscure as the chauffeur's landlady. In most novels, it would be physically impossible to fit all the suspects into the parlor at the end.
4. The assignment of guilt is rarely based on common sense beyond the most lenient of applications of this term. More importantly, the artistic consistency of the story does not hinge on who did it.
5. Like the traditional detective story, "a tale has to be founded on truth," but what the hard-boiled writer sees as truth may be—and often is—entirely different from what the classical writer sees.

What stands out from this adaptation of Chesterton's principles is hard-boiled fiction's lack of rules and its open-ended form. Since there is no single answer in the hard-boiled story and no single criminal, the competition between writer and reader, so much a part of classical detective fiction, is meaningless. John G. Cawelti sees this difference in attitudes as indicative of the two forms. "While the classical detective's investigation typically passes over a variety of possible suspects until it lights at last on the least likely person, his hard-boiled counterpart becomes emotionally involved in a complex process of changing implications."[32] These "changing implications" make a strict adherence to rules impossible. Likewise the very nature of hard-boiled fiction makes the issue irrelevant: why should the detective follow the rules if everyone else is cheating?

Just as the hard-boiled detective disregards the rules, he also disavows the classical detective's faith in reason. Although he is not stupid, his primary talents are not mental, and he rarely demonstrates the analytical powers of a Hercule Poirot or a Sherlock Holmes. He finally figures out the crime by forcing his way through a problem whose boundaries are constantly shifting. The pattern is one of ever-increasing complexity; the simple murder at the beginning of the story is wholly absorbed by the end into a larger scheme with unsettling implications about the nature of our world. The detective learns much more than the identity of the murderer. His knowledge is not so much a product of reason as it is the result of the detective's personal involvement with the case. In the classical detective story, reason is possible because the crime has a sort of stasis built into it—its clues, its procedures, its perpetrators tend to be fixed and irrevocable. The detective usually can deal with the problem objectively and dispassionately without fear that the essence of the crime will suddenly change. Crime in hard-boiled fiction, on the other hand, is organic—it grows and spreads, and since the puzzle is not governed by reason, its solution cannot be either.

Ratiocination is not a major factor in this type of fiction for another important reason: the detective's intrusion into the events alters and affects those events in a way that is fundamentally different from the classical detective's effect on a situation. In hard-boiled fiction, the representative of reason, the detective, becomes unreasonable, governed by emotion rather than by logic. *He* causes things to happen, to transmute, by every attempt of his to reason things out. In the following dialogue from *Red Harvest*, Dinah Brand comments on the Op's plan to "stir things up" in Personville in order to see what would happen:

> "So that's the way you scientific detectives work. My God! for a fat, middle-aged, hard-boiled pig-headed guy you've got the vaguest way of doing things I ever heard of."
>
> "Plans are all right sometimes," I said. "And sometimes just stirring things up is all right—if you're tough enough to survive, and keep your eyes open so you'll see what you want when it comes to the top."[33]

While the hard-boiled detective may begin as an objective observer, he soon becomes personally involved, and with that involvement, the power of reason diminishes. The detective himself becomes a part of the puzzle. He is forced at the end to question not only other people's motives but his own as well. John G. Cawelti sees this involvement as inevitable. "The hard-boiled detective sets out to investigate a crime but invariably finds that he must go beyond the solution to some kind of personal choice of action."[34] An obvious example of this can be found in *The Maltese Falcon*. At the end of this Hammett novel, the reader does not ask, "what is the truth of the mystery?" but rather, "what kind of man is Sam Spade?" The character of the detective is a greater puzzle than the falcon itself.

Not only is reason inadequate because of the shifting nature of the crime and the increasing subjectivity of the detective, but reason is also not important in this fiction because of a fundamental belief that our world is not a particularly reasonable place. The use of reason to attack a problem implies that the events of the world are ordered and logical and that the crime is a temporary aberration of the social order. In hard-boiled fiction, however, the criminal act is the norm: police take pay-offs, men of power and respect use hired guns, the bellhop will send up a woman for five dollars. In an environment where corruption and crime are everywhere, the detective's goal is not to light up the whole world but rather to illuminate one squalid corner of it and to try to survive the consequences—there is rarely any sense at the end of these novels that order has been restored. The detective in the classical tradition emerges whole at the end of his experiences; his values have been confirmed, his reliance on reason wins out, and his belief in the power of social order is unshaken. The hard-boiled detective, however, is changed. The world is uglier than he had expected; the corpse he finds at the beginning of the case is only slightly worse off than the dozens of frightened, unhappy victims who populate the city, terrorized by the mob, by corrupt law officials, and by individual viciousness. The detective's skull has been relandscaped, his limbs have been nicked, and often he has found the love of his life and lost her again, either to jail or to the trajectory of a wild bullet. Instead of order being restored, the world is shown to be more insane than ever.

In addition to these deviations from the classical detective story in rules, reason, and world view, hard-boiled fiction differs from the traditional genre in setting, in language, and in an ethical code that replaces a prewar sense of objective propriety with a postwar relativism. Raymond Chandler said of Hammett that he "took murder out of the Venetian vase and dropped it into the alley."[35] Hard-boiled fiction did that and more: it established itself as an urban genre whose big city atmosphere pervades the work until the city itself becomes almost a character. The extremes of squalor and elegance, the claustrophobic oppression of the people, cars, and buildings, the excitement of the motion, the unreality of lights and lifestyles that blur day and night provide the stimuli for the frantic pace of most hard-boiled fiction. The leisurely weekend murder on a country estate often lacks the intensity of this urban setting—an intensity that pervades the story with the anxious sense that potential violence is a part of every moment, of every scene. Chicago and New York were, of course, perfect locations for the hard-boiled stories because of their history of corruption and crime and their reputation for toughness and grit. Yet California, and especially Los Angeles, has produced the most vivid sense of place in the hard-boiled genre. Whether or not it was ever the Eden that people remember, what is important in the use of California as a setting is the sense of loss, of corruption like a worm in a rose that permeates the hard-boiled fiction set there.

But whether Los Angeles or San Francisco or Chicago or New York is the locale, the presence of the city is always felt. It is a perfect physical counterpart to the chaos, the lack of communal feeling, and the loneliness that seem endemic in the private eye's world. John G. Cawelti calls this city landscape a "wasteland," a "man-made desert or cavern of lost humanity,"[36] in which the detective-hero finds himself in a futile quest to seek and destroy the source of corruption. Any success against the pervasive immorality can only be temporary; the cynicism towards politicians is too strong to allow any hope for a final solution. As one private eye puts it: "There ain't nothing in governments unless you're a politician. And as I said before, I ain't a crook."[37] The way of corruption is the way of the world, and only romantic idealists like hard-boiled detectives would work to change it. Yet this determination to bring the city to its knees, to clean it up and make it decent, has within it an obvious contradiction: the private eye identifies himself with the decadent city and not with the middle-class civility that its purification would bring. Although he finds himself continually fighting the overwhelming strength of the city, he has no desire to live anywhere else. His criticism and his attempts to change it go side by side with his often lyrical, passionate celebration of its vitality, and his own identity is best defined when he is in combat with the city.

Just as hard-boiled fiction sought to make crime more realistic by setting it on city streets, it also tried to bring the language of these stories closer to the speech of ordinary people. James Cain states the case for this return to realistic language in his preface to *Three of a Kind*. "I merely try to write as the characters would write, and I never forget that the average man, from the fields, the streets, the bars, the offices, and even the gutters of this country has acquired a vividness of speech that goes beyond anything I could invent, and that if I stick to this heritage, this *logos* of the

American countryside, I shall maintain a maximum of effectiveness with very little effort."[38] This emphasis on natural-sounding language was partially a result of larger literary movements of the day and partially owing to the influence of Joseph T. Shaw, who urged his writers to create stories that echoed the modern voice. Shaw wanted the language to be clear and believable and "written with objectivity, economy, restraint."[39] Suspicious of the high-flown, eloquent rhetoric (the rhetoric frequently found in the classical detective story) that had been used to gloss over war, depression, and unemployment, people responded to the tough, contained voice of hard-boiled fiction. Although this voice rarely sounds like the speech of everyday citizens, the language can be vigorous, dynamic, and entertaining. At its worst, this attempt to mimic the language of real people sounds foolish and self-conscious, but at its best, it is remarkable in its style, its rhythm, and its ability to convey personality. In *Mortal Consequences*, Julian Symons points out the difference between the traditional and the hard-boiled style. "The Great Detective's language was affected or colorless; that of the hard-boiled dick was pungent as cigar smoke or garlic."[40] Whether they were writing about a mobster turned nightclub owner or a shoe-shine boy, the hard-boiled writers tried to create dialogue that did more than just advance the telling of the story. The classical detective work emphasized story—the intricate plot and the puzzle were the central considerations—but hard-boiled writers wanted the language, as well as the action, to *be* the story. According to Raymond Chandler, "The ideal mystery was one you would read if the end was missing."[41]

The two main characteristics of this new attempt at more realistic language were slang and metaphor. Philo Vance and even Sherlock Holmes used slang, as did other classical detectives, but it was usually a single phrase or a self-conscious bit of informality in an otherwise noncolloquial style. In hard-boiled fiction, however, slang became pervasive. There was esoteric jargon of the streets ("Make the sneak and keep cover till noon, and his frame-up will be a wash-out" [*Red Harvest*, p. 51]), new uses for old words ("She looked up, smiled, tucked her nail tools in a peeling plastic handbag and hipped it in my direction"[42]), and contractions that echoed the short cuts of speech people often use ("I ought to have beat it, but some' dy'd come out on the balcony"[43]).

Whether or not this slang ever succeeded in conveying the tone and rhythms of everyday language, it did help free the genre from the poised, predictable prose that often characterized the classical detective story.

Like slang, the use of metaphor was an attempt to revitalize the language of the genre. It might seem inconsistent for a style that prides itself on terse, laconic narratives to use figures of speech extensively, but metaphor served a variety of functions. The hard-boiled detective is often a wiseacre, a man verbally on top of things even if he is lost in every other way. He may be confused by the case, sapped frequently from behind by a variety of objects, and constantly betrayed by those around him, but he has the quickest wit in the group, and the apt metaphor at just the right moment demonstrates this. These figures of speech often involve women, guns, or the sounds bodies make under varying punishments. Whatever their source, these metaphors serve to show the detective's relationship to other folk heroes, from Davy Crockett to Muhammad Ali, who show their superiority by their wit and verbal quickness as well as by their talent. Often these metaphors are purely clichés—the woman as cat, the city as monster, the mob as a cancerous growth—and sometimes they work, as with "pain gave Sail's mouth the shape a rubber band takes when it lies loose on a desk."[44] The best metaphors are Raymond Chandler's, for they are as unpredictable as they are appropriate: a voice "as cool as boarding house soup," a smell "as overpowering as boiled alcohol under a blanket," or hair "as artificial as a night club lobby."[45]

Although the differences between hard-boiled and classical detective fiction in terms of language and setting are the most obvious, the differences in character between the two kinds of detectives are perhaps more fundamental to understanding the genres. Russel Nye summarizes the external, sociological differences: the classical detective, often an amateur from the upper classes, works within the system to solve a case involving the country club set while the hard-boiled private eye, working outside and at times in conflict with the system, is involved in a world of violence in which no class is immune.[46] But the internal difference between the two is even more profound: the hard-boiled detective is basically a moralist with a strong ethical code that has little to do

with a social definition of ethics. The private eye has a rigid notion of right and wrong, but *he* draws the distinction, not the law
or the community. His actions and decisions depend upon this
inner code. How can a man allow his conscience to be dictated to
by a society at best vicious and corrupt and at worst random and
meaningless? Thus, the central conflict in this fiction is not, as
in the classical detective story, between criminal and society but
between the private eye and society. He pursues the killer because
pursuit is written into his code, not to restore order to the world.
He looks for answers for himself, not for others, and his pride lies
in his refusal to compromise himself—even when that is what
both law and common sense demand. As John G. Cawelti observes, "The figure whose honor is at stake in the hard-boiled
story is not some palpitating female but the detective himself."[47]
John Paterson, an admirer of Hammett and Chandler, sees in this
insistence on personal honor above society's the primary appeal
of the private eye: "He is the symbol of the isolated individual
who, in the sense that he has been estranged from the community
rather than banished from it, is an exile. He speaks for men who
have lost faith in the values of their society."[48]

Existing in a world bereft of social and moral certitudes, the
hard-boiled detective is a figure of isolation, a figure always on the
edge of communion. He has no family, no real friends, and his
ties to his past are minimal—as he prefers. Like the Western hero,
Raymond Chandler's Marlowe has disdain for the shopkeepers and
farmers of the world.

> I would have stayed in the town where I was born and worked in the
> hardware store and married the boss's daughter and had five kids and
> read them the funny paper on Sunday morning and smacked their heads
> when they got out of line and squabbled with the wife about how much
> spending money they were to get and what programs they could have
> on the radio or TV set. I might even have got rich—small-town rich,
> an eight room house, two cars in the garage, chicken every Sunday and
> the *Reader's Digest* on the living room table, the wife with a cast iron
> permanent and me with a brain like a sack of Portland cement.[49]

In theory, the hard-boiled detective is a democratic proletarian
who comes from plain stock. His tastes run to steak, potatoes,
and bourbon, and he is often openly anti-intellectual. In practice,

however, he often scorns the mundane and powerless existence of the ordinary man at the same time that he fights to protect him. John G. Cawelti sees this disdain for the average citizen as a sort of adolescent revolt. "His way of life [the sleazy office, the crummy apartment] may look like a failure, but actually it is a form of rebellion, a rejection of the ordinary concepts of success and respectability."[50] Yet this is probably too easy an explanation.

The hard-boiled detective, because of the conventions of the genre, is a man fated to be betrayed. When he becomes close to people and invests in friendship or love, the outcome is usually disastrous. He is a lone figure—a man who, if he becomes tied down, loses his identity. He cannot get the woman at the end; he cannot become domesticated or socialized; he cannot reject his maverick ways for bedroom slippers and a pipe. A typical ending, therefore, is one in which both the solution to the mystery and the danger of socialization are resolved in one stroke: the woman is the villain or his client (often an elderly man representing the father/family figure) is guilty. The hard-boiled private detective, very much an idealized figure, is almost too pure to live in this world. His individuality refuses to be compromised; his ethics and sense of behavior are dictated by his own conscience, not by a corrupt and hypocritical society. His aloneness, therefore, is a result of his virtue. He is isolated because few people share his strict morality.

This role as stern moralist might seem incongruous for a character who, in some versions, feels no compunction about ignoring the law and who often kills with little or no sense of guilt. Clearly his is an ambivalent role: as a detective he represents the law, but his methods can be as criminal and violent as the wrongdoer he is tracking. The fact is that many hard-boiled writers have produced poorly written novels with melodramatic vicious rebels as their "heroes"; it is a genre susceptible to sensational exploitation of human misery and a glorification of violence. The hard-boiled detective can be and often is a pathological killer who rationalizes his violence by claims to a higher authority than mere law. But the genre has also produced books by authors like Raymond Chandler and Ross Macdonald who are earnest in their efforts to articulate what is wrong with society and to demonstrate why outrage and even violence can sometimes be sane responses.

Yet more relevant to this study than the debate over the socio-logical and ethical implications of hard-boiled detective fiction[51] is the genre's susceptibility to simplification and one-dimensionality. Precisely because the genre *is* popular fiction, the conventions of the form almost always take precedence over the language and vision of the work. But such is not the case with Dashiell Hammett—his use of the detective format is unique. Although his novels portray violence graphically, it is violence mitigated by its appropriateness to the work and its lack of ro-manticization. In her eulogy at Hammett's funeral, Lillian Hell-man said, "Dash wrote about violence, but he had contempt for it, and thus he had contempt for heroics."[52] His novels are not the morally didactic works that are eager to affirm the glory and re-wards of brave, honest, and good acts, as is common with many forms of popular fiction including the hard-boiled story. Ham-mett uses the hard-boiled form not to sensationalize violence nor to preach, but because its particular pattern suited his artistic in-tentions. What makes his works special is this very tension that arises between maintaining and transmuting the form. Hammett uses the detective story in its recognizable form, but he infuses it with a heightened sensibility and complexity so that it becomes art as well as entertainment.

In the next five chapters, each devoted to one of his five novels, I will examine the interplay between form and content in Ham-mett's works. Each chapter will begin with an analysis of form: setting, plot, point of view, pacing, language, and methods of character development will all be discussed in terms of the indi-vidual novel being considered and its place in Hammett's work as a whole. Each novel will be placed within the context of hard-boiled fiction's conventions as well as discussed from the stand-point of how it deviates from these conventions. After this anal-ysis of the principal formal features of the novels, I will examine the way these features contribute to the development of Ham-mett's main thematic interests—the nature of personal relation-ships, the limits of reason, the concept of order, and various meta-fictional issues.

2

Red Harvest: The Detective as Cipher

— ⇀⇀⇀ —

*"Don't kid yourselves that there's any law in Poisonville ex-
cept what you make for yourself."*
—the Op, in Red Harvest

Dashiell Hammett's first novel, *Red Harvest*, was published appropriately enough in 1929, when an economic and social ca-
tastrophe was beginning in America. *Red Harvest* is, in part, a
distillation of that nightmare. Just as the stockmarket crash
compromised the validity of the American dream, this novel examines the failure of both the community and the individual to
maintain justice, order, and human rights; on one level *Red Harvest* is an exposure of the discrepancy between how our political,
moral, and family systems are supposed to work and how, in fact,
they *do* work. Yet Hammett's novel is more than a political or
social tract, although its exposure of the corruption at the center
of the American political and social scene is more penetrating
and relentless in its own way than that of any other American
novel of the period, including *The Great Gatsby*. *Red Harvest*
deals with gangsters and gang warfare and features a hard-boiled
detective called in to investigate a murder, but Hammett uses
these familiar elements to explore sophisticated themes rarely
found in pulp magazines and popular fiction. As in all his novels,
Hammett deals here with the notion that we create our sense of
order and reality; in particular, *Red Harvest* examines the way
people build versions of reality based on personal obsessions—
whether they be Dinah Brand's obsession with money, the Op's

obsession with job, or Elihu Willsson's obsession for power—and then proceed to lead their lives as if these versions were adequate to deal with the world as it is. Personville, a microcosm for America and for a larger world, is a city built of such obsessions and reality-models; the breakdown of its citizens and, ultimately, of the Op is for Hammett indicative of what happens when people govern their lives by principles they feel they control, only to be, in the end, overwhelmed by the very system they themselves developed.[1]

Red Harvest is the story of Personville, "an ugly city of forty thousand people, set in an ugly notch between two ugly mountains" (p. 4). The book's opening lines immediately establish its principal focus—the Op and his encounter with Personville—and demonstrate Hammett's brilliant rendering of colloquialisms throughout the novel.

> I first heard Personville called Poisonville by a red-haired mucker named Hickey Dewey in the Big Ship in Butte. He also called his shirt a shoit. I didn't think anything of what he had done to the city's name. Later I heard men who could manage their r's give it the same pronunciation. I still didn't see anything in it but the meaningless sort of humor that used to make richardsnary the thieves' word for dictionary. A few years later I went to Personville and learned better. (P. 3)

That Personville's name (suggesting people, humanity) has been changed to "Poisonville" (a source of death) by people familiar with its history is the first of many indications of the city's deterioration and decline. Personville is a western mining city whose industry is the primary source of the citizens' livelihood, but through the years, even as the industry has supported the city's economy, the mines have made the environment oppressive and unpleasant.

> The city wasn't pretty. Most of its builders had gone in for gaudiness. Maybe they had been successful at first. Since then the smelters whose brick stacks stuck up tall against a gloomy mountain to the south had yellow-smoked everything into uniform dinginess. The result was an ugly city of forty thousand people, set in an ugly notch between two ugly mountains that had been all dirtied up by mining. Spread over

this was a grimy sky that looked as if it had come out of the smelters' stacks. (Pp. 3–4)

There is far more wrong in Personville, of course, than its dinginess, grime, and faded gaudiness: the town's ugliness is merely an exterior sign of the overwhelming inner corruption and decay in those who live there. An important paradox seems to work throughout the book: from both an economic and personal standpoint, what sustains Personville and gives it identity is precisely what makes it such a hellhole. Its pollution, in both a physical and spiritual sense, is even more dramatic because of its geographical position; by placing the city in the West, Hammett suggests a sort of ultimate corruption: the West—the promised land whose expanse offers freedom, escape, and the realization of America's promise of opportunity and unlimited possibility—has become as "dirtied up" as the rest of the country.[2]

Although the town's setting in the West is significant, Hammett also makes the city a more general symbol for America. The very name "Personville" is an early indication that Hammett intends to use his setting in a purposefully mythic manner. And despite Hammett's use of various western clichés in the plot itself (which will be examined in more detail subsequently), something deliberately regionless and anonymous about the town and its inhabitants gives the reader a sense that Hammett means Personville to be *anywhere* in the United States that has been poisoned by greed, lust for power, and ruthlessness.[3] A catalog of Personville's street names, for example, reveals a curious conglomeration void of all reference to the town's locality or special features: Forest, Painter, Union, King, Laurel, Broadway, Hurricane, Green, Porter—these could be the streets of any city in America.

This sense of Hammett telescoping the geography of several American locations to create his own mythic setting is heightened by the anomaly of having crooks in a small western city behaving and talking exactly as if they were in Chicago: thus, *Red Harvest* is filled with the same speeding black sedans, spraying bullets, fixed prize fights, and big city politics that Americans would associate with the Midwest and East. Indeed, when carefully considered, Hammett's setting here is not realistic at all but is an amalgamation of urban and western elements yoked together for his own narrative purposes. How else to explain the presence in Personville—a town of forty thousand which is condescendingly referred to by one of its citizens as being "out here in the bushes" (p. 67)—of trolley cars, chauffeur-driven limousines, taxis, women dressed in furs for a night on the town, and a roadhouse called the Silver Arrow which is described as "a very electric-lighted imitation castle" (p. 124)? The characters inhabiting Personville are a similarly peculiar combination; when a crowd gathers in front of city hall to peer at the murdered body of Donald Willsson, it is said to consist of "men from mines and smelters still in their working clothes, gaudy boys from pool rooms and dance halls, sleek men with slick pale faces, men with the dull look of respectable husbands, a few just as respectable and dull women, and some ladies of the night" (p. 6). Even more revealing about Hammett's intent to combine western and urban elements is his creation of a rich and diverse series of names for Personville's crooked politicians and underworld figures. Such names as "Old" Elihu Willsson, Reno Starkey, Whisper Thaler, Lew Yard, Pete the Finn, Kid Cooper, Dinah Brand, Ike Bush, Blackie Whalen, Put Collings, Dutch Jake Wahl, Yakima Shorty, Peak Murray, and Kid McLeod are a blend of western and eastern influences, just as Personville is itself.

This combination of Wild West and urban elements is important to the plot as well as to the specific way that Hammett develops Personville as a setting. When the novel opens, the city is being terrorized by a group of gangsters who had been called in earlier by Elihu Willsson, the town's most powerful citizen, in order to break up attempts at unionization. Following their violent and bloody victory over the striking workers, these thugs refused to relinquish power to the man who hired them; instead, they stay on in official and unofficial positions and run the city as a legitimized crime syndicate. Called in by Willsson's son, newly returned from Europe and ignorant of his father's complicity in the corruption, the Continental Op finds himself investigating the murder of his client—the young reformer has been killed even before the Op meets him. The detective remains, however, hired by the elder Mr. Willsson to find his son's murderer, rid the town of the gangsters, and return the power to himself. Though the Op uncovers the identity of the killer early in the book, he has become so quickly immersed in the turbulence of the gang war that when Elihu attempts to get him off the case, he refuses to leave. He remains in Personville until most of the principal characters in the novel are dead—Dinah Brand, the mercenary vamp whom everyone, including the Op, is attracted to; Dan Rolff, the "lunger" who lives with Dinah; Whisper Thaler, the handsome racketeer; Pete Noonan, the crooked police chief; and more than twenty other victims.

Thus summarized, *Red Harvest* seems to follow the classic "horse opera" pattern of many western novels and movies: a powerful but mysterious stranger (the Op) rides into a western town, called there to establish law and order by the town's biggest rancher (Elihu). The cast of characters is completed by the presence of Noonan as the "hired gun" brought in as marshall; Dan Rolff as the barfly; Whisper Thaler, Reno Starkey, Pete the Finn, and Lew Yard as the outlaws; and Dinah Brand as the saloon girl. What follows is a predictable series of bloody confrontations between various factions, with people hurrying from place to place in cars rather than on horses. Yet there are important differences. Unlike the typical Western pattern, for example, there is no climactic showdown, where matters are resolved cleanly (if violently), in a clearly defined area—guns at noon on Main Street. In *Red Harvest* and in most hard-boiled fiction, the orderly, ritualistic confrontation is replaced by chaotic and often frantic battles that take place anywhere and anytime and against forces which may be unknown and unseen.[4]

Just as the novel differs from the pattern of the Western in these fundamental ways, *Red Harvest* differs as well from the typical hard-boiled story in terms of how it presents action. For instance, Hammett includes the violence and frantic action typical of the genre, but he makes very different use of their *effect*. He uses the genre's high mortality rate to help sustain the novel's action but exaggerates this to such a degree (over thirty people die, including nearly every main character except the Op) that the device becomes almost parodically extreme until, at the end, we are numb. On the other hand, and more crucially, Hammett defeats our expectations by being almost delicate about the bloodletting; most of the important murders do not happen "on stage" where the reader can see them but are reported later on (for example, Elihu's

killing of the intruder, Dinah's death, the death of Donald Willsson, and the shooting of Reno Starkey at the end). Despite the
accumulation of corpses, there are remarkably few actual details
about the deaths, and when they are provided, they are oddly devoid of brutality in presentation. Sometimes death arrives so
quickly and is passed over with such little emphasis that the actual death is made to seem no more significant than any other
gesture.

> Stepping over wreckage, the bootlegger came slowly down the steps
> to the sidewalk.
> Reno called him a lousy fish-eater and shot him four times in the
> face and body.
> Pete went down. A man behind me laughed.
> Reno hurled the remaining bomb through the doorway. (P. 182)

At other times, Hammett describes a murder so obliquely that
the reader is more puzzled than horrified. This is true, for example, with the indirect way Ike Bush's death is revealed—"Ike
Bush took his arm out of the referee's hand and pitched down on
top of Kid Cooper. A black knife handle stuck out of the nape of
Bush's neck" (p. 73)—and also with the death scene of one of
Noonan's hired detectives.

> The gray-mustached detective who had sat beside me in the car car-
> ried a red ax. We stepped on the porch.
> Noise and fire came out under a window sill.
> The gray-mustached detective fell down, hiding the ax under his
> corpse.
> The rest of us ran away. (P. 113)

Both of these death scenes, of course, are brutal, but as in all of
Hammett's fiction, the brutality arises out of our response to the
unfolding events, not from the language itself. As will be seen
when we examine Hammett's use of language and point of view,
the controlled, objective narration of these scenes suggests certain things about the Op's personality. But another effect of this
language is to drain most of the emotion from the prose—prose
which aims to report carefully but not to arouse suspense or "gut-
level" reactions of horror or disgust. Of course, as Hemingway

had also demonstrated, the use of deadpan prose can produce the opposite of this "cold" effect when the *reader* supplies the sense of shock, sentimentality, or horror by responding to the dynamics of the scene. But Hammett's reliance on this kind of prose largely eliminates the traditional mystery writer's build-up of drama and suspense. For instance, when the Op solves the novel's first important murder—that of Donald Willsson—and confronts the murderer with his crime, there is no attempt at a suspenseful buildup—indeed, quite the opposite is true, since neither the language nor the logic of the scene prepares the reader for what will follow.

> At ten I dressed, went up to the First National Bank, found young Albury, and asked him to certify Willsson's check for me. He kept me waiting a while. I suppose he phoned the old man's residence to find out if the check was on the up-and-up. Finally he brought it back to me, properly scribbled on.
>
> I sponged an envelope, put the old man's letter and check in it, addressed it to the Agency in San Francisco, stuck a stamp on it, and went out and dropped it in the mail-box on the corner.
>
> Then I returned to the bank and said to the boy:
>
> "Now tell me why you killed him." (P. 53)

Despite their neutral tone, such scenes are powerfully immediate, perhaps because they have not been infected with the usual (and hence expected) emotionally charged language. Hammett was anxious in all his fiction to achieve this immediacy by translating events into language as directly as possible; this is the key to the rapid tempo of his fiction, as his comments on the art of novel writing indicate.

> The contemporary novelist's job is to take pieces of life and arrange them on paper, and the more direct their passage from street to paper the more lifelike they should turn out.
>
> The contemporary novel, it seems to me, needs tempo—not to cram into each page as many things as possible—but to make what is set down *truly contemporary*, to give the impression of things happening *here and now*, to force upon the reader a feeling of *immediacy*. . . . He must know how things happen—not how they are remembered in later years—and he must write them down that way.[5]

Hammett's ability to create this "direct . . . passage from street to paper" and "to give the impression of things happening *here and now*" is evident in all his works, but nowhere was his prose under surer control than in *Red Harvest*. Even in a scene of extreme complexity of action, his prose remains in rigid control; chaos may be all around the Op, such as during the Whiskeytown shoot-out near the end of the novel, but the reporting of events could not be clearer.

> Men crawled all over me, opening the valise, helping themselves to the contents, bombs made of short sections of two-inch pipe, packed in sawdust in the bag. Bullets bit chunks out of the car's curtains.
>
> Reno reached back for one of the bombs, hopped out to the sidewalk, paid no attention to a streak of blood that suddenly appeared in the middle of his left cheek, and heaved his piece of stuffed pipe at the brick building's door.
>
> A sheet of flame was followed by deafening noise. Hunks of things pelted us while we tried to keep from being knocked over by the concussion. There was no door to keep anybody out of the red brick building.
>
> A man ran forward, swung his arm, let a pipeful of hell go through the doorway. The shutters came off the downstairs windows, fire and glass flying behind them. (P. 180)

Hammett's mode of pacing and plot structure differ from that found in the typical detective story in other important ways, as well. Careful plotting is not usually a primary consideration in hard-boiled detective fiction, and although most of its stories attempt to create a bona fide puzzle which is resolved after a careful build-up of suspense and mystery, the plots themselves are often weak or illogical. Sometimes these flaws in the plot are conscious, stylistic decisions, as in Raymond Chandler's dizzying, convoluted novels, but more frequently the weak plots are simply the result of carelessness. In contrast, Hammett's plots are constructed with the precision usually identified with the classical detective story. His handling of plot, however, is often different from either the classical or hard-boiled style: in both *Red Harvest* and *The Dain Curse*, the mysteries and murders are explained throughout the course of the book, rather than in the traditional last-chapter denouement. Part of the reason for this "solve-as-you-go" method can be explained by the fact that both novels appeared as four separate novellas in *Black Mask* before they were published as novels. Obviously, then, the need to have the parts self-contained so that the individual stories made sense was a factor in the structure of the novels. Their episodic nature, however, cannot be solely due to serialization, for as William F. Nolan notes in his casebook on Hammett, "Comparing the magazine segments against the book, one finds, as with all of Hammett's major novels from *Black Mask*, a reworking process that covers the entire story, page by page."[6] With such careful reworking, it would have been relatively easy for Hammett to have restructured the two novels, leaving the solution to the crimes unrevealed until the end, but in both cases, the results would have been very different. What Hammett tried to do in the two Op novels was to use structure and plot not merely to advance the story line and provide the detective with a framework for his heroics but as a significant element in the art and theme of his works as well. Just as significantly, by downplaying the suspense and puzzle-solving aspects common to most detective fiction, Hammett openly indicates that he is more interested in the Op's character and reactions to events than he is in providing the reader with suspense and the prolonged excitement of wondering about the identity of the villain.

As will be established in my discussion of the Op's character, he is quickly drawn into the expanding circle of violence in Personville and eventually becomes himself an agent of this violence. Although the reader may feel there is some justification for his actions, the Op is made to appear as guilty and morally reprehensible as the rest of the gangsters in the novel. Thus the usual assignment of guilt and innocence—the most fundamental part of most detective fiction—is secondary to a more complex, ambiguous consideration of the character of the detective. Emphasis on character is common in hard-boiled fiction, but this emphasis is usually developed at the expense of a logical, coherent plot. In *Red Harvest*, however, the plot is carefully constructed with subtle, yet findable, clues planted throughout the narrative (for example, the fact that the lights are off when the Op awakens at Dinah's house, the false assumption about the dying man's words). But as readers, we are not really tempted to play a guessing game; as the corpses pile up and the double crosses become more convoluted, the sheer bulk of the plot has a way of canceling itself out of the reader's interest. Indeed, in *Red Harvest* Hammett seems to be parodying the hard-boiled mystery's propensity for creating multiple murders by introducing such an extravagant number of victims that the usual question of *"Who* is going to die?" is less relevant than *"When* will he or she die?" Not only does this exaggerated number of murders tend to make the violence less rather than more intense, it also has the effect of dissipating the suspense that usually comes when the detective establishes the innocence or guilt of all the parties involved. In the final scene in which the Op discovers who killed Dinah Brand and who was responsible for the last round of murder in Personville, the revelation of the killer's identity has little dramatic impact. This partially results from the episodic nature of the novel that keeps the dramatic tension from building to the end. Three times earlier in the novel there have been explanations for the main murders: in chapter 7 we learn who killed Donald Willsson; in chapter 14 we learn who killed the brother of the police chief, Jim Noonan; and in chapter 19 the Op explains the motives and guilt behind the gang war. By the end of the book there can be little real suspense because almost everyone involved in the case is dead.

Thus the classic question—"Who done it?"—is a moot one here, for in *Red Harvest* almost everyone "done it." We learn that Reno Starkey was responsible for Dinah Brand's murder, but by this time there has been so much cheating, lying, and violence on the part of every character in the novel that Reno seems no more guilty or despicable than anyone else. This lack of emphasis on the identity of the killer is demonstrated in the composition of the last scene. The Op enters a warehouse where he believes he will find the body of Whisper Thaler and where (we probably suspect) he believes he will discover the answer to Dinah's death. He has started searching the building when he hears voices coming from another room.

I had counted nine steps when a voice spoke clearly above us. It said:

"Sure, I killed the bitch."

A gun said something, the same thing four times, roaring like a 16-inch rifle under the iron roof.

The first voice said: "All right." (P. 155)

What is intriguing about this exchange is the calculated ambiguity in the identity of the voices; we hear the actual confession before we learn the identity of the killer. Instead of building to a straightforward climax, Hammett drags out the revelation of the killer's identity until the suspense has been all but eliminated; there is finally—a full page later—an oblique remark of Reno's that clarifies the mystery. "How the hell did you figure you didn't croak her?" (p. 196). It is a scene that has no suggestion of antagonism between the Op and Reno; it is also deliberately evasive about making the point with which nearly every other hard-boiled novel concludes: that the violence and brutality of the detective have been vindicated by his unmasking a criminal even more violent and brutal than himself.

> He stopped, pretending interest in the shape the red puddle was taking. I knew pain had stopped him, but I knew he would go on talking as soon as he got himself in hand. He meant to die as he had lived, inside the same tough shell. Talking could be torture, but he wouldn't stop on that account, not while anybody was there to see him. He was Reno Starkey who could take anything the world had without batting an eye, and he would play it out that way to the end. . . . A tired looking ambulance crew—Poisonville gave them plenty of work—brought a litter into the room, ending Reno's tale. I was glad of it. I had all the information I wanted, and sitting there listening to and watching him talk himself to death wasn't pleasant. (Pp. 197–98)

With this absence of ill feeling, the Op's description of Reno's death hardly supplies the sense of victory we expect at the end of hard-boiled detective fiction. By similar sorts of skillful manipulations of the elements common to all hard-boiled fiction, Hammett creates in *Red Harvest* a novel whose structure and tone, whose *process* of unfolding on the page, subtly underscores the themes he wishes to develop and allows him to focus our attention on the Op.

It should be remembered that the Continental Op has a "history" that extends beyond the confines of *Red Harvest*: he made his first appearance in a story in *Black Mask* in October 1923 and his last in the same magazine in November 1931.[7] Throughout this lengthy series the Op remains unnamed. Unlike the other famous detective series—Sherlock Holmes, Philo Vance, Father Brown, Nero Wolfe/Archie Goodwin—that have given the public a full character sketch with a history (so full, as in the case of Holmes and Wolfe, that book-length "biographies" have been published on them), the Op series as a whole produces little more insight into his background, private life, or physical appearance than any individual story. This lack of reference to his history or personal characteristics is of considerable importance, for it points up one of the major differences between Hammett and other detective writers: unlike the creators of nearly all other well-known detective fiction, Hammett did not construct his works primarily as an ongoing framing device for isolating and developing a heroic personality.[8] Indeed, not only is the Op given almost no identifying personal eccentricities, he is not even given a name. In these omissions, Hammett is making a calculated, artistic decision, although in a letter to the editor of *Black Mask*, he shrugged off the issue by saying, "I didn't deliberately keep him nameless, but he got through 'Arson Plus' and 'Slippery Fingers' without needing a name, so I suppose I may as well let him run along that way."[9] This claim to such a casual approach to writing is suspect, for it contradicts the evident complexity and control of Hammett's finished products.[10] Although the reason for the Op's namelessness may have begun, perhaps, as Hammett suggests in this letter, the decision to carry it through the entire series seems more likely to have stemmed from two sources: a common tradition in popular fiction of using epithets and nicknames and the equally common tradition in literature of using names in an abstract, symbolic manner. The Op's name, however, is certainly colorless when compared to similar epithets in popular fiction, and it lacks symbolic reference. What the name does accomplish is to suggest a subtle quality of mystery inherent in his character—a mystery which becomes the central puzzle which readers must unravel as they proceed.[11]

Just as the lack of a name makes the Op's character less distinct, the lack of personal background and physical description contributes to his anonymity. There are a few references to the Op's physical appearance in *Red Harvest*, but they are almost always obliquely presented and tell us little more about him than age, height, and weight. For example, we deduce his age when he tells us that he is "about the same age" as Elihu's secretary (p. 15), who, three pages earlier, was said to be forty years old. The other details we are given sketch a picture of a bland, unimposing figure—he is about five feet six or seven inches tall (p. 14) and weighs 190 pounds (p. 15). Beyond these physical facts Hammett provides no personal background that could contribute to an heroic image. Certainly Dinah's description of him being "fat and middle-aged" (p. 79) contrasts sharply with the usual picture we have of hard-boiled detectives (including Hammett's own Sam Spade) who are typically tall, strong, and ruggedly handsome.

The anonymity and mystery which surround the Op's character raise a crucial issue in *Red Harvest*: what purpose does the first person mode of narration serve Hammett here and in *The Dain Curse*? Clearly Hammett does not use the first person point of view in these two novels for the same reasons that most writers do in their fiction (such as to provide immediate psychological insight into character motivation or to help us to identify with the narrator). Although the Op reports the action in *Red Harvest* as a direct observer, he does so in the largely neutral monotone we have earlier discussed. He also rarely offers the sort of judgments, explanations, and insights we expect from first person narrators. Ironically for a genre devoted to uncovering solutions and deciphering mysteries, the Op presents his tale without any direct commentary and analysis that could clarify the action and assist us in following his own reasoning.

Thus, despite the presence of a few carefully inserted clues throughout the book, the reader is almost surely taken by surprise at each of the Op's revelations of culpability; any insights into the Op's personal reactions to events or into his psychological makeup result from the *reader's* conclusions and the *reader's* ability to put the unexplained pieces of the Op's psyche together. Even a description of his dreams (pp. 149–51) is presented in a straightforward, unanalytical manner, with the Op offering no explanation or justification for including them at all, despite their obvious psychological significance. As with Hemingway's hard-boiled prose which pares away emotionally charged language and allows the choice of details and the dynamics of setting and plot to carry the significance of the scene, the Op's narration requires a great deal of reader participation to make sense out of what is happening. The fact that the Op provides so many specific details about the case—street names, hotel names, physical descriptions and names of nearly all major and minor participants—seems to give the book a heightened reality, but without any interpretation from him, this sheer bulk of facts actually works against our ability to understand and draw connections in the novel. We are so overwhelmed by specifics that it is difficult to separate the significant from the trivial or to gain an overview of what is going on.[12]

The justification for this objective hard-boiled prose lies partly, as we have already seen, in Hammett's desire to develop a style which would be both vivid and immediate. In his insistence on "facts" rather than speculation or supposition and in his refusal to use emotional or interpretive language when describing a scene, he sought to avoid the kind of sentimentalism that Hemingway's prose was occasionally unable to avoid. But this style is also justified as an appropriate extension of the Op's value system as well, for he prides himself on his ability to respond to situations directly, without subjectivity or foolish emotionalism. What the Op emphasizes in his handling of the Personville case is action, not plans or interpretation; as he tells Dinah when being criticized for operating in such a "vague" manner: "Plans are all right sometimes. And sometimes just stirring things up is all right—if you're tough enough to survive, and keep your eyes open so you'll see what you want when it comes to the top" (p. 79). In an earlier scene, Elihu even commends the Op for his straightforward manner of speech; when Elihu begins to goad him on with rough romanticism and studied, tough-guy eloquence, the Op angrily deromanticizes and deflates the conversation, while giving a clear indication of his own attitude about the relationship between words and action.

"You're a great talker," he said. "I know that. A two-fisted, you-be-damned man with your words. But have you got anything else? Have you got the guts to match your gall? Or is it just the language you've got?"

There was no use in trying to get along with the old boy. I scowled and reminded him:

"Didn't I tell you not to bother me unless you wanted to talk sense for a change?"

"You did, my lad." There was a foolish sort of triumph in his voice. "And I'll talk you your sense. I want a man to clean this pig-sty of a

Poisonville for me, to smoke out the rats, little and big. It's a man's job. Are you a man?"

"What's the use of getting poetic about it?" I growled. "If you've got a fairly honest piece of work to be done in my line, and you want to pay a decent price, maybe I'll take it on. But a lot of foolishness about smoking rats and pig-pens doesn't mean anything to me." (P. 39)

Disdainful of "poetic" language, the Op usually makes sure that his own voice remains objective, technically correct, and devoid of much imagery. This frequently allows Hammett to create a sharp contrast between the Op's neutral, "proper" language and the wonderfully varied and esoteric voices of the lowlife figures he so often encounters. Hammett's ability to render this colorful argot may well be his fiction's greatest single triumph (perhaps only Céline can rival him), and he obviously enjoys creating set pieces such as the following, where the Op confronts McSwain. The Op opens the scene by using the esoteric language McSwain is familiar with, but once he gets what he wants, he quickly stops "the merry-go-round" and reverts back to his own lingo.

[The Op] "You never did anything but let people gyp you. You don't have to go up against him, McSwain. Give me the dope, and I'll make the play—if it's any good."

He thought that over, licking his lips, letting the toothpick fall down to stick on his coat front. . . . He took my hand excitedly and demanded:

"Honest to God?"

"Honest to God."

"His real moniker is Al Kennedy. He was in on the Keystone Trust knock-over in Philly two years ago, when Scissors Haggerty's mob croaked two messengers. Al didn't do the killing, but he was in on the caper. He used to scrap around Philly. The rest of them got copped, but he made the sneak. That's why he's sticking out here in the bushes. That's why he won't never let them put his mug in the papers or on any cards. That's why he's a pork-and-beaner when he's as good as the best. See? This Ike Bush is Al Kennedy that the Philly bulls want for the Keystone trick. See? He was in on the—"

"I see. I see." I stopped the merry-go-round. "The next thing is to get to see him. How do we do that?" (P. 67)

If the Op often finds himself isolated from those around him—an isolation resulting from his refusal to "open up" to others, from his allegiance to his job, even from his language—it is an interesting paradox that the Op is *not* a loner like the traditional private eye. Unlike almost all of the hard-boiled detectives who work from a small one-man office and who pride themselves on their independence (Philip Marlowe, Mike Hammer, Race Williams), the Op is part of an organization. Thus he is not a renegade maverick at odds with the police and as likely to be manhandled by cops as by criminals. The Continental Detective Agency is, in fact, a business that approaches crime and violence with no moralistic or evangelical zeal. The Op's anonymity is reinforced by his position in such an agency.[13] Unlike S. S. Van Dine's Philo Vance, Miss Marple, Father Brown, and other classical detectives who work on cases as dilettantes for the thrill and interest of the game or the hard-boiled detectives who are motivated by money and then by passion, the Op's approach is mainly professional. When, as in the case of *Red Harvest*, he steps out of that role, it is with the knowledge that his boss, the Old Man (whose name is also never given), will give him "merry hell." Because he works within an organizational structure that has established policies and procedures, the Op is never really free of answering to others for his actions in a case.

There is another important sense in which the Op's separation from others is of a different nature from that of fictional private detectives who were his contemporaries or who were to follow him. The hard-boiled detective, like his western counterpart, the cowboy, is traditionally a man who is an outsider, but often this loneliness is itself used to heighten the heroic dimensions of the character being portrayed. Raymond Chandler's Philip Marlowe presents an eloquent description of this solitary life in a scene from *The Little Sister*.

I put the duster away folded with the dust in it, leaned back and just sat, not smoking, not even thinking. I was a blank man. I had no face, no meaning, no personality, hardly a name. I didn't want to eat. I didn't even want a drink. I was the page from yesterday's calendar crumpled at the bottom of the waste basket.

So I pulled the phone towards me and dialed Mavis Weld's number. It rang and rang and rang. Nine times. That's a lot of ringing, Marlowe. I guess there's nobody home. Nobody home to you. I hung up. Who

would you like to call now? You got a friend somewhere that might
like to hear your voice? No. Nobody.

Let the telephone ring, please. Let there be somebody to call up and
plug me into the human race again. Even a cop. Even a Maglashan.
Nobody has to like me. I just want to get off this frozen star.[14]

Even Carroll John Daly's crudely drawn Race Williams, who explains, "I always play a lone hand,"[15] uses this isolation as proof
of his superiority. For the Op, however, isolation and loneliness
are not romantic, heroic conditions of one who chooses to separate himself from the corrupting influences of society in order to
preserve his honor; instead, he sees his separation as a natural
part of his job. To fulfill the demands of his job most efficiently,
he remains outside the case, seemingly untouched by the passions of those he must investigate. As a professional investigator,
he feels himself free from the sorts of personal demands and commitments that private eyes like Marlowe and Lew Archer find impossible to ignore; his responsibility is to job, not people—a position which has important moral ramifications, as we shall see.

The importance of the Op's close identification with his agency
("When I say *me*, I mean the Continental Agency" [p. 41])[16] can
be better understood by a brief examination of the conventions of
the lone-wolf tradition in detective fiction. The typical hard-boiled
private eye—a composite of popular detectives, including, of course,
the Op himself—is a man who is disdainful and suspicious of
most commonly held notions about God, country, and home. He
believes that politicians are crooked, that women are dangerous,
that the average citizen is a spineless bore, that cops are corrupt;
further, he is cynical towards all institutions: justice is inadequate or blind, marriage is for suckers, universities are for pan-
sies. The degree of cynicism present in given works varies, of
course, from author to author. Writers like J. J. Des Ormeaux and
Jonathan Latimer, for example, usually project a kind of wry, good-
natured disillusionment into their works; on the other hand, certain writers like Paul Cain leave the reader with an impression of
bleak fatalism. Thus in Cain's *Fast One*, detective Gerry Kells
dies after having been shot three times, stabbed in the back with
an ice pick, and severely injured in a car crash; the book concludes with Kells dragging himself from the wrecked car to a tem-

porary shelter and Cain commenting laconically, "There, after a little while, life went away from him."[17] But however deep-running the authors' cynicism seems to be, it is always mitigated for their detective figures—perhaps by the love of a woman, the loyalty to a friend, or, if nothing else, the sense of personal integrity. The classic example of this kind of "mitigated cynicism" can be found in Raymond Chandler's Philip Marlowe, who prides himself on hard-nosed cynicism while seeing himself as a knight errant in an evil land. The cynicism of the typical hard-boiled detective, then, is often a cover for romanticism and sentimentality. The same Race Williams who claims to feel "the satisfaction of one who has completed a good day's work"[18] after killing a man also tells us, "If there's one thing I always feel I've got time for, that is to look at a little child—especially a sleeping one."[19]

On the surface, the Op seems very much like his fellow detectives; he appears to share their cynical view of the world that is the basis for the wry, ironic tone found so often in hard-boiled fiction. In fact, the Op's detached and cool voice was interpreted by other detective writers of the time as the standard tone of the genre. Yet there is an essential difference between the Op's cynicism and that of his contemporaries. Most detectives of the genre maintain their cynicism as a matter of style but not of personal commitment; their cool aloofness and quick, sarcastic wit set them apart and make them feel superior to clients, cops, and criminals. But the cynicism that seems to permeate their books is often a cover for high ideals and a strict morality that would be unappealing if presented directly. Given the social and cultural revolution that took place after World War I, the clean-cut hero who espoused loyalty to all the standard virtues may have seemed foolish to some readers. But give this idealistic hero a rough, tough veneer, a new vocabulary that excludes all words that might be deemed sissified, and a new sensibility based on the absence of sensibility, and the result is a detective like Mal Ourney in Raoul Whitfield's *Green Ice* (published one year after *Red Harvest*).[20] In this novel Mal serves a two-year sentence for manslaughter in order to protect a former girlfriend who was drinking and driving a car that killed two pedestrians; because it was *his* whiskey she was drinking, Mal claims to have been driving the car and pleads guilty to the charge. If this gesture is not enough to compromise the cynical exterior of the most hard-nosed hero, Mal decides while in jail to crusade against the big names of crime who recruit innocent men and women into their operations. As he explains it: "I was out of the Big House—my bankers had better than seventy-five thousand dollars in safe spots, and I had a job to do. . . . I was after the breeders of crime."[21] Whatever hard-boiled stance he maintains through the book, his toughness and cynicism are finally secondary to his loyalty to a friend, his love for a woman, and his zealous attempt to make the world better.

But while many hard-boiled detectives often have such idealistic visions of themselves and their work, the Op is a pragmatic professional with a professional's disdain for histrionics. In short, the cynicism that is largely a matter of style with other hard-boiled detectives is an integral part of the Op's character. His philosophy is simple: do not believe in *anything* except doing your job as efficiently as possible. When Dinah Brand, the "loose" woman of *Red Harvest*, begins to sense this, the Op tells us: "She put her face close to mine, and her eyes looked as if they had found something horrible in mine. 'Oh, you're rotten,' she said. 'You don't give a damn what happens to me. You're using me as you use the others—that dynamite you wanted. I trusted you'" (p. 123). In a similar scene toward the end of *The Dain Curse*, Gabrielle Leggett, the Op's client, echoes Dinah Brand's indictment when she calls the Op "A monster. A nice one, an especially nice one to have around when you're in trouble, but a monster just the same, without any human foolishness like love in him."[22] Instead of traditional beliefs, emotions, and values the Op has his job, and although this emphasis on one's job and on performing well in that job is often compared to the Hemingway code, Hammett's attitude about the Op's "code" is much more ambiguous than Hemingway's.[23] Hemingway clearly seems to see the code of his characters as a dignified, meaningful alternative to two unacceptable courses of action: either a man pretends that society is sane and continues to lead his life according to its tenets or he gives up and fritters away his life. Thus we are obviously meant to view Jake Barnes in *The Sun Also Rises* and Harry Morgan in *To Have and Have Not* as tragic heroes in the same way that Raoul Whitfield, Carroll John Daly, and other creators of tough-guy detectives mean to have us view their heroes. However, Hammett's

attitude towards the Op and his job-related set of personal guidelines is much more complicated than the usual equations we can
make between writer and detective in detective fiction. Unlike
the creators of most hard-boiled fiction Hammett intends for us
to appraise his detective's credibility, weighing both what he says
and what he does, instead of accepting unquestioningly his narrative authority. Hammett draws what seems to be on one level a
definitive portrait of a hard-boiled detective, but a sharp dramatic
irony at work in his fiction qualifies this portrait: Hammett is
not presenting the Op as the brave, simple hero whose code of
conduct endows him with a superior sensibility and virtue. Instead Hammett is interested in examining the *consequences* of
the Op's beliefs; in the process, he creates a character whose motives, actions, and values are as complex and ambiguous as the
world in which he operates. In short, while the Op may initially
seem to be the quintessential hard-boiled detective, it is also clear
that Hammett is suspicious of the philosophy that goes with that
role. Although Hammett was one of the creators of the hard-boiled
detective, his two Op books also criticize and undercut that character; while the rest of the hard-boiled writers—Hemingway among
them—were eager to present their characters as heroic men pit-
ted against an amoral world, Hammett did not believe such a hero
could exist because heroics were irrelevant in such a world. The
Op is neither a hero nor a villain. His choice to be what he is—
detached, hardened, emotionless—enables him to function more
or less efficiently. Yet Hammett is also very much aware of the
dangers, both for the individual and for the community, of such a
position. Sometimes, as Hammett shows in *Red Harvest*, qualities such as moral neutrality and allegiance to one's job may lead
to destructive consequences; indeed, once the Op loses his emotional detachment in the case, we see him become an active participant in the corruption and violence he has ostensibly set out
to eliminate.

The Op's role in the "red harvest" of death in the novel's title
is crucial. He begins his involvement in the case with the kind of
professional interest that carries with it a professional curiosity.
When he leaves the home of his client, having observed some suspicious actions on the part of Willsson's wife, he remarks simply,
"I went away wondering why the green toe of her left slipper was

dark and damp with something that could have been blood" (p. 6), and he goes about the business of collecting clues with efficiency and skill. The Op emphasizes this no-nonsense approach; in the scene in which he is hired by the old man to investigate Donald's death, he clarifies his position in the case and the extent to which he is willing to reestablish the old man's power. Appropriately enough, the word "job" appears four times in the paragraph—a strong indication to the old man that the Op's involvement in Personville is purely a business arrangement. "I'm not playing politics for you. I'm not hiring out to help you kick them back in line—with the job being called off then. If you want the job done you'll plank down enough money to pay for a complete job. Any that's left over will be returned to you. But you're going to get a complete job or nothing. That's the way it'll have to be. Take it or leave it" (p. 41). Several pages later, the Op uses a similarly objectified description of his investigation. "I spent most of the afternoon writing my three days' reports on the Donald Willsson *operation*. Then I sat around, burned Fatimas, and thought about the Elihu Willsson *operation* until dinner time" (p. 60, italics mine).

This insistence on professionalism and on the contractual, businesslike aspects of being a detective changes rapidly in the course of the novel. What precipitates the shift in the Op's attitude is simple, straightforward, and consistent with the pattern of betrayal and revenge so common in hard-boiled fiction: Pete Noonan, the Personville police chief, and his deputies surround the hideout of Whisper Thaler, a local racketeer also suspected of murder. When the Op offers to enter the building in an effort to talk with Thaler, he is double-crossed—Noonan's forces open fire on him from the rear. The Op escapes this ambush, but the result is an abrupt departure from his earlier businesslike involvement in the case. In this scene, he explains his change in attitude to Whisper and Dinah:

> "I don't like the way Personville's been treating me. I've got my chance now, and I'm going to even up. I take it you're back in the club again, all brothers together, let bygones be bygones. You want to be let alone. There was a time when I wanted to be let alone. If I had been, maybe I'd be riding back to San Francisco. But I wasn't. Especially I wasn't let

alone by that fat Noonan. He's had two tries at my scalp in two days. That's plenty. Now it's my turn to run him ragged, and that's exactly what I'm going to do. Poisonville is ripe for the harvest. It's a job I like, and I'm going to do it." (Pp. 62–63)

Obviously the dimensions of the "job" have been altered. The detached professional has become an involved participant; from this point on, all of the deaths in Personville result, either directly or indirectly, from the Op's manipulations and interventions.

When the Op turns the business that brought him to Personville into a personal vendetta, we witness a shift in attitude characteristic of many hard-boiled detectives. While they may enter a case for money (as Mike Hammer once tells his secretary, "Whenever there's a murder, there's money, chick"),[24] other motives often supervene: revenge, honor, and, finally, personal justice. A business arrangement becomes a struggle against the forces of evil and injustice. This transformation can be presented in the comic strip rhetoric of *The Shadow* ("He must get back to his own room at all costs—yet he must, prodded by his sense of duty as an American citizen give some signal")[25] or in the more literary style of Philip Marlowe. However skillfully or unskillfully this process is described, the shift from a hardened, cynical mercenary to a crusading, idealistic champion of the common person is one of the form's oldest traditions (it is fully evident, for instance, in the early 1920s works of Carroll John Daly). The hard-boiled private detective has an integrity and personal honor which may be camouflaged by a show of toughness and cynicism, but ultimately these qualities are revealed in a moral outrage against the corruption of the world. The case, then, becomes a crusade. But in *Red Harvest* the Op rejects his professionalism not to become the white knight who will liberate the countryside from evil and corruption but to get even. He may solve the mysteries and act out the heroic tough-guy role we expect of him, but in the process he brings greater and greater violence to the city. Thus the simple assurances of the pattern have been overlaid by Hammett's more complex purposes.

As a detective, the Op has, of course, the right to manipulate people and to lie to them in the course of his investigation. In the first chapter, he refuses to explain his presence even to the wife of his client, Donald Willsson.

She returned to her digging with: "I suppose all mining towns are like this. Are you engaged in mining?"

"Not just now."

She looked at the clock on the mantel and said:

"It's inconsiderate of Donald to bring you out here and then keep you waiting, at this time of night, long after business hours."

I said that was all right.

"Though perhaps it isn't a business matter," she suggested.

I didn't say anything. . . .

"I'm really not ordinarily so much of a busybody as you probably think," she said gaily. "But you're so excessively secretive that I can't help being curious. You aren't a bootlegger, are you? Donald changes them so often."

I let her get whatever she could out of a grin. (P. 5)

Later, when questioning Bill Quint, the labor leader of Personville, the Op lies about his identity and even gives him a fake business card. That these lies and manipulations may be wrong or immoral is never an issue with the Op, for he pursues any strategy as long as it brings him closer to the only goal he seems to have: the proper performance of his job. In the course of one's job, a consideration of morality is irrelevant. As he remarks to a fellow detective, "It's right enough for the Agency to have rules and regulations, but when you're out on a job, you've got to do it the best way you can" (p. 109). The job, then, must be done and done well, with whatever methods necessary. Morality is never a factor, since the means will always be justified by the ends. This moral neutrality may be useful to the Op in handling his cases efficiently, but the consequences become disastrous when he loses his emotional detachment from the Personville case and his involvement becomes self-centered; after being double-crossed, he begins to care intensely about the case, but not about the consequences (death, in most instances) for the people involved. In violation of his personal code (one does one's job as efficiently and emotionlessly as possible), the Op begins to use his role in Personville as a means of seeking personal vindication. Before long, he even admits to Dinah that he is deriving a personal sense of satisfaction from his death-dealing manipulations.

"I could have gone to him [Elihu] this afternoon and showed him that I had them ruined. He'd have listened to reason. He'd have come over to my side, have given me the support I needed to swing the play legally. I could have done that. But it's easier to have them killed off, easier and surer, and now that I'm feeling this way, more satisfying. I don't know how I'm going to come out with the Agency. The Old Man will boil me in oil if he ever finds out what I've been doing. . . .

"Look. I sat at Willsson's table tonight and played them like you'd play trout, and got just as much fun out of it. I looked at Noonan and knew he hadn't a chance in a thousand in living another day because of what I'd done to him, and I laughed, and felt warm and happy inside. That's not me. I've got hard skin all over what's left of my soul, and after twenty years of messing around with crime I can look at any sort of murder without seeing anything in it but my bread and butter, the day's work. But this getting a rear out of planning deaths is not natural to me. It's what this place has done to me." (P. 145)

As this passage vividly suggests, the dangers implicit in applying the Op's code of moral neutrality (accomplish your job by whatever means at your disposal) to a personal situation are far-reaching. The "something horrible" that Dinah sees in the Op's eyes is precisely this neutrality, for it creates a vacuum where no person is responsible for another, and because he bears no responsibility, he has no interest in the outcome of his actions—even if it is death.

Enraged by the double cross of the police chief, Pete Noonan, the Op's participation in the red harvest enters a new phase that is a logical extension of his previous tactics. Just as he lied without any moral qualms, he is now capable of even more radical manipulations which are similarly unaffected by morality. In order to stir up some kind of action after he has decided to open "Poisonville up from Adam's apple to ankle" (p. 59), the Op blackmails a young fighter, Ike Bush, who is scheduled to throw a fight which has been fixed by the mob. Ike wins the fight, forced to double-cross his backers by the Op's threat, but as he stands in the center of the ring, his arms raised in victory by the referee, Ike is murdered by a knife thrown from the balcony. The Op makes no comment about his own reaction to this turn of events, offers no apology, and certainly gives no indication that Ike's death has meant anything to him. He merely reports that "when they turned him over the point of the knife was sticking out in front" (p. 75); this neutral remark is his only reference to a man whose death he has caused. Although this murder is just one of many that could be attributed to the Op's method of operation, Ike's murder seems more damning simply because he is an innocent of sorts, a man who died because he was a pawn in the Op's game. In a similar manner, the Op "juggled death and destruction" (p. 144) throughout the novel with scarcely a glimmer of emotional reaction.

But by far the most dramatic instance of the Op's detachment from other people's deaths occurs when he wakes up on the morning following his drunken confessional evening with Dinah to find his hand holding an ice pick which is buried in Dinah's breast. He reports his actions in this scene with complete objectivity; his descriptions are clear, factual, and specific, right down to the observation that Dinah has a run in her right stocking.

I opened my eyes in the dull light of morning sun filtering through drawn blinds.

I was lying face down on the dining room floor, my head resting on my left forearm. My right arm was stretched straight out. My right hand held the round blue and white handle of Dinah Brand's ice pick. The pick's six inch needle-sharp blade was buried in Dinah Brand's left breast.

She was lying on her back, dead. Her long muscular legs were stretched out toward the kitchen door. There was a run down the front of her right stocking.

Slowly, gently, as if afraid of awakening her, I let go the ice pick, drew up my arm, and got up.

My eyes burned. My throat and mouth were hot, woolly. I went into the kitchen, found a bottle of gin, tilted it to my mouth, and kept it there until I had to breathe. The kitchen clock said seven-forty-one.

With the gin in me I returned to the dining room, switched on the lights, and looked at the dead girl.

Not much blood was in sight: a spot the size of a silver dollar around the hole the ice pick made in her blue silk dress. There was a bruise on her right cheek, just under the cheek bone. Another bruise, finger-made, was on her right wrist. Her hands were empty. I moved her enough to see that nothing was under her. . . . In the dining room again, I knelt beside the dead girl and used my handkerchief to wipe the ice pick handle clean of any prints my fingers had left on it. I did the same to glasses, bottles, light buttons, and the pieces of furniture I had touched, or was likely to have touched.

Then I washed my hands, examined my clothes for blood, made sure I was leaving none of my property behind, and went to the front door.

I opened it, wiped the inner knob, closed it behind me, wiped the outer knob, and went away. (Pp. 151–52)

Although it could be argued that this distancing is an attempt by the Op to hold the real pain inside (as is often the case with Hemingway's characters), it seems much more likely that the Op's lack of apparent emotion in this scene is genuine. He literally washes his hands free of responsibility. He is able to tidy up, stepping over her body, not because he is suppressing his pain, but because there is in fact so little pain.

This failure of the Op to feel sadness or loss is central to Hammett's attitude towards the Op and his code. The Op's moral neutrality, developed as an extension of his notion of job, is finally condemned more strongly by Hammett than the Op's active participation in the case. The Op violates his code when he begins to enjoy the killing, but for Hammett this departure from code is of secondary consideration. Although the Op seems most disturbed by his failure to live up to his code, clearly what Hammett finds more dangerous is the code itself, which allows men to subordinate moral responsibility to an allegiance to an abstract, self-devised system.

Of course, the theory behind the job code is appealing: by creating a framework which the Op can use to determine his actions, the code cuts through disturbing ambiguities in the situations the Op must confront. Does the fact that Elihu Willsson is a ruthless tyrant, who rules by autocratic, anti–labor-union power and oppression, influence the Op's decision to return Personville to him? No, Elihu is the Agency client—he has paid for their loyalty. Is the Op responsible for the deaths of twenty-five people? No, he was merely doing his job. Should the murder of Dinah Brand, with whom the Op shared a goodly amount of companionship and alcohol, upset him? No, she was an extension of the quarry whom he had been paid to track down. The Op depends on the strictness of his code to rationalize his actions and emotionless responses to situations; by obeying rules and regulations, he is freed from the moral responsibilities and ethical choices that inevitably arise with any complex dilemma. There is a satisfying simplicity in his work—find a client, solve a crime, leave the client—that has its attractive qualities. And while this system may exclude love and fellowship, it also keeps him free of guilt, loneliness, and despair.

Yet as we observe the Op coldly arranging people's deaths, impassively observing the pain, corruption, and destruction that run rampant in Personville, and utterly refusing to acknowledge his own responsibility in these events, we are surely meant by Hammett to question such a code of behavior. Hammett criticizes the Op's code for its ends-justify-the-means premise and its refusal to consider human morality or man's responsibility to others. He also has a pragmatic objection to such a system: given the pervasiveness of corruption that exists in the modern world (as exemplified in Personville) and given the power of this corruption to infect others, it becomes unreasonable to expect *any* personal system to remain unaffected.

Indeed, probably the most obvious thematic elements in *Red Harvest* are its criticisms of the debased social and political climate existing in America during the 1920s. As a representation of these rotten conditions, Personville is a city whose corruption is so pervasive that it stands as a powerful indictment of big city politics and capitalism. Its most powerful citizen, Elihu Willsson, is almost a caricature of a robber baron. In his version of the town's history, reported by the Op, Willsson views the city as belonging to him by right. "The substance of it was that he had built Personville brick by brick with his own hands and he was going to keep it or wipe it off the side of the hill. Nobody could threaten him in his own city, no matter who they were. He had let them alone, but when they started telling him, Elihu Willsson, what he had to do and what he couldn't do, he would show them who was who" (p. 40). From the outset of the novel, then, the city is shown to be "owned" by a single, power-hungry individual. The notions of democracy and a shared citizen involvement in the community have never existed in Personville, and Willsson has managed to insure that they never develop by gaining a monopolistic control over the city's economy and its political machinery. The Op's summary of this process is also a summary, in miniature, of what happened in many American communities during the latter part of the nineteenth century and early part of the twentieth century.

For forty years old Elihu Willsson—father of the man who had been killed this night—had owned Personville, heart, soul, skin, and guts. He was president and majority stockholder of the Personville Mining Corporation, ditto of the First National Bank, owner of the *Morning*

Herald and *Evening Herald*, the city's only newspapers, and at least part owner of nearly every other enterprise of any importance. Along with these pieces of property he owned a United States senator, a couple of representatives, the governor, the mayor, and most of the state legislature. Elihu Willsson was Personville, and he was almost the whole state. (P. 8)

Before the novel opens, Willsson's control was challenged by the IWW's efforts to organize labor in his mines; what followed was the kind of bloody confrontation between labor and management that America in the twenties was reading about almost daily in the newspapers. "The strike lasted eight months. Both sides bled plenty. The wobblies had to do their own bleeding. Old Elihu hired gunmen, strike-breakers, national guardsmen and even parts of the regular army, to do his. When the last skull had been cracked, the last rib kicked in, organized labor in Personville was a used firecracker" (p. 9). But in his struggle to keep personal control of the city, Willsson underestimated the power of the hired gunmen to whom he had turned for help. The atmosphere of lawlessness and violence which had always marked Personville made it easy for mobsters to take over the city and run it in a farcical imitation of government, without a single suggestion that the people are being served. Corruption in Personville's political operation is total, from the governor who is owned by Elihu to the local politicians who build a city hall as a money-making project, right down to the police who steal money and jewelry from a dead woman. Even the liberal reformer, Donald Willsson, bought his liquor from bootleggers.

In this grim and grotesque vision of the American city, the individual has little chance of remaining untouched, for Personville is the collective nightmare of all citizens—it is what America has made of itself, born, in part, out of our traditional celebration of the self-made individual. In this regard, names like Rockefeller, Ford, Carnegie, and Hearst come to mind; so do the James Brothers, Al Capone, and Hammett's fictional Elihu Willsson. This critique of American urban politics—evident, as well, in Hammett's later novel, *The Glass Key*—is an important, if rather obvious, aspect of the novel, for it suggests the larger implications that Hammett wished to establish in the detective novel format. As a

perceptive reviewer of *Red Harvest* observed, Hammett's use of
Personville goes far beyond the usual hard-boiled strategy of using
setting as a convenient source of violence and bizarre occurrences.

> The mere fact that an author of obvious intelligence can write such a
> tale and persuade an American publisher to print it throws a valuable
> light on American conditions. If there is anywhere on the North
> American continent a town even remotely like Personville, then it is
> a sociological phenomenon which we must take into our reckoning,
> and I cannot believe that Mr. Hammett has made up Personville purely
> out of his desire to have a background for sensational happenings.[26]

Like some sort of monster in a Hollywood horror film, Personville exudes a poison that can contaminate anyone who comes in
contact with it—even the Op, whose code would seem to make
him immune from such influences. When Dinah asks the Op why
he has brought an ice pick with him from the kitchen, he reveals
the extent to which he has been poisoned by his dealings with
the city.

> "To show you how my mind's running. A couple of days ago, if I thought
> about it at all, it was as a good tool to pry off chunks of ice." I ran a
> finger down to its half-foot of round steel blade to the needle point.
> "Not a bad thing to pin a man to his clothes with. That's the way I'm
> begging on the level. I can't even see a mechanical cigar lighter with-
> out thinking of filling one with nitroglycerine for somembody you don't
> like. There's a piece of copper wire lying in the gutter in front of your
> house—thin, soft, and just long enough to go around a neck with two
> ends to hold on. I had one hell of a time to keep from picking it up and
> stuffing it in my pocket, just in case—"
> "You're crazy."
> "I know it. That's what I've been telling you. I'm going blood simple."
> (Pp. 145–46)

Such, then, is the corrupting influence of Personville that the Op—
despite his code and despite being an indirect representative of
law as an operative of the Continental Agency—becomes as lawless as the gangsters and crooked politicians. As an experienced
detective, the Op has become accustomed to violence, but Personville has managed to break down his code's dictum to remain

emotionally detached; as he tells Dinah: "I've arranged a killing or two in my time, when they were necessary. But this is the first time I've ever got the fever. It's this damned burg. You can't go straight here. . . . Poisonville is right. It's poisoned me" (pp. 142, 145).

Personville's "poison" has affected other members of the community as well. The corruption in the town's political system has also affected virtually every social and personal aspect of the citizens' lives; the morality that is missing in Personville's institutions of justice and law is absent as well in the personal relationships of those who live there. Perhaps the most striking evidence of the kind of personal corruption afflicting Personville is the way in which love becomes a destructive force. Loving others makes one vulnerable. Dinah Brand, for example, is able to establish power and to take advantage of all the men who love her: she uses Bill Quint to gain inside information about the labor force; she sells out Whisper Thaler to his enemies; she physically abuses Dan Rolff, her consumptive friend who lives with her; she exploits the young bank clerk, Robert Albury, until he runs out of money; she saves the love letters sent to her by Elihu Willsson for potential blackmail. For those people who love others, that love either forces them into acts of violence or leaves them emotionally devastated: Helen Albury is driven "crazy as a bedbug" (p. 171) when her brother is killed; Robert Albury kills the younger Willsson out of jealousy of Dinah; McSwain kills Pete Noonan's brother because he seduced his wife and then abandoned her (she later drives a car in front of a train); Noonan's intense love for his dead brother is one of the major causes for the town's red harvest. This list of such miseries could be expanded, for every single instance of love— either love between father and son, between friends, between husband and wife, or between lovers—ends in abuse, betrayal, and violence. Personal relationships, then, are as twisted and perverse in Personville as are its politics and are just as likely to be dictated by struggles for power and money. Friends remain friends only as long as the relationships are profitable; personal loyalty is a commodity always for sale.

What is missing, then, in the citizens of Personville is the same thing that is missing in the Op: a sense of personal morality and integrity which, while based on right and wrong, still recognizes the need for flexibility in a complex world. Like the Op, the people of Personville have devised systems that *seem* to give them control and definition, and like him, they feel that their systems make them impervious to the dangers and complexities of Personville. These systems, or personal codes, are attempts to order their world through schemes that seem to provide principles to govern action in any situation. Dinah, for instance, believes in money—money not merely as a way of accumulating possessions but as a means of control, of keeping things even, and of making certain you get back as much as you give. As she tells the Op during an argument over what he owes her for information: "It's not so much the money. It's the principle of the thing. If a girl's got something that's worth something to somebody, she's a boob if she doesn't collect" (p. 33). Her obsession with money is therefore not so much based on greed as it is a system to protect herself in a world that wants to screw her, sexually, emotionally, and economically. The simplicity of the system is attractive, for it quantifies her relationships with people and with Personville. Her personal world is sloppy and haphazard; there is constant reference to her ill-fitting expensive clothes, her ripped stockings, a tear in the shoulder of a new dress. Her manners are defiantly crude. "'I was raised in a convent,' she told me. 'I won the good behavior prize every year I was there. I thought little girls who put extra spoons of sugar in their chocolate went to hell for gluttony. I didn't even know there was such a thing as profanity until I was eighteen. The first time I heard any I damned near fainted.' She spit on the rug in front of her, tilted her chair back, put her crossed feet on my bed, and asked: 'What do you think of that?'" (p. 119). But this sloppiness and vulgarity is somehow redeemed for her by money—with it she has control and independence. She gives the Op information about her former boyfriend, Whisper Thaler, and expects to be repaid, but for her, the money signifies that she has won. As she explains to the Op: "He's got no right to talk to me that way. He doesn't own me. Maybe he thinks he does, but I'll show him different" (p. 76). Yet the end result of this system is disastrous. Besides making her "utterly filthy" (p. 76), as Dan Rolff calls her,[27] it simply does not operate efficiently. Despite her physical strength and gutsiness, she, too, is a victim of the red harvest, for she overestimates her system's capacity to control the world around her and protect her from its viciousness.

The bases of the other systems in the novel are likewise shown to be "utterly filthy" and inadequate. Elihu Willsson's obsession with power eventually betrays him, for he is unable to control events in Personville as absolutely as he desires. Pete Noonan's ruthlessness is finally stymied when he finds his code—one based on the belief that he is stronger and capable of greater violence than anyone else—breaking down, leaving him "green around the gills" (p. 143). Even Myrtle Jennison, a girlfriend of Dinah, learns that a system based on good looks, youth, and vitality is ultimately useless in a world where disease can reduce you to "a horrible swollen body in a coarse white nightgown" (p. 86). All such systems at work in Personville are thus shown to be unsatisfactory, for they are naïvely ignorant of the power, danger, and utter corruption of the world, as represented in Personville. In an effort to survive, each character constructs a simplistic system based on expediency rather than one which recognizes the need for flexibility and, even more importantly, human morality.

Such scrutiny of system making may seem out of place in a hard-boiled novel, but Hammett's concerns as a writer extend beyond the bounds of the genre. In Personville Hammett creates a vivid, furious world of violence and peoples it with killers, liars, and thieves, yet the issues he raises are not limited to those of a typical gangster novel. Hammett is concerned with how people should live, and if ethics and Personville seem incompatible, it should be noted that it is precisely in an atmosphere like Personville—where violence and chaos pervade the social and political fabric—that one's system can best be challenged and tested. There is an anomaly in weaving into *Red Harvest* an ethical inquiry into system making, but it is an anomaly that invests the novel with a fascinating complexity. *Red Harvest* is one of the most compelling works of hard-boiled fiction because the action is exciting, the plot intriguing, and the characters vivid, yet the literary success of the novel lies in Hammett's ability to imbue the conventions of the genre with an exhilarating and reverberating intensity of language and style.

3

The Dain Curse: The Epistemology of the Detective Story

— ⤳ —

"That's the kind of story it is. I warned you there was no sense to it."
                              —*the Op, in* The Dain Curse

Although the Continental Op appears again as the main character and narrator of Dashiell Hammett's second novel, *The Dain Curse* (1929), there are surprisingly few similarities in Hammett's first two novels. The tough, corrupt atmosphere of Personville with its gangsters, bootleg whiskey, colorful language, and crooked politicians is replaced in *The Dain Curse* by a shifting series of settings and ambiences that range from urbane, continental intrigue to small-town melodrama. Murder and violence are still very much present, but the book's highly stylized action and self-conscious artifice invest its unfolding with a playful quality that was lacking in *Red Harvest*. In his second novel, Hammett uses the elements of various mystery genres—the classical mystery story, the gothic thriller, the small-town potboiler—to build a work which directly explores the fiction-making process. Indeed, on one level the novel is an exercise book in "types" of mystery fiction. Yet despite its qualities of artifice and fancifulness, *The Dain Curse* is not a "light" novel. Hammett may play with the form and style of the detective novel, but his intent is not primarily parodic; rather, *The Dain Curse* is a novel about how we impose a fictional sense of order in our lives and in our literature. As he willfully emphasizes the artifice of his own writing, he also suggests that what we see, what we believe, and what we think is what we have created ourselves.

Not only does the tone of *The Dain Curse* differ from Hammett's first novel, but the Op is presented in a significantly different manner. He is physically the same, of course—"a middle-aged fat man" (p. 112) who remains unnamed—but his personal code, a major issue in *Red Harvest*, receives little attention in *The Dain Curse*.[1] In addition, the Op has changed from instigator to interpreter; that is, whereas in *Red Harvest* the Op actively participates in the murders and mayhem, in *The Dain Curse* his presence usually makes no difference in the unfolding of the sequence of violence. The Op struggles throughout the novel to illuminate and interpret the bizarre events surrounding his client, yet, at the same time, he emphasizes that any order is likely to be suspect and that even the most probable solution is only one rendering of the "reality" of the case. The role of the Op, therefore, becomes complex and ambiguous in a different manner than appeared previously: though Hammett allows him to act out a series of "character roles" that could be seen as a survey of detective types, the Op himself constantly undercuts these roles by frequently suggesting that he is well aware that these roles are, in fact, only *imitations*, for he is very uncertain whether or not the detective—or anyone—can ever uncover any final solutions to life's mysteries. Stepping out of his detective roles occasionally, he analyzes the elements in the case with his novelist friend, Owen Fitzstephan (who turns out to be the murderer himself), and debates the very issues which are the basis of detective fiction; these discussions generate a self-reflexive, metafictional thrust to the novel and, in a large sense, allow Hammett to develop a sophisticated inquiry into the basis of how we arrive at what we know.[2]

Whereas Hammett uses the plot in *Red Harvest* primarily to focus our attention on the Op, he employs the complex configurations of events in *The Dain Curse* for more abstract purposes—largely, to develop his metafictional and epistemological concerns and to illustrate the difficulties of arriving at Truth. The plot structure of this book does resemble *Red Harvest* in that both reveal the answers to puzzles before the final conclusion, rather than waiting for the end of the book as in most detective stories.

Yet, while in the first book the answers to the mysteries at least remained stable, in *The Dain Curse* these answers are constantly shifting. Hammett divides and labels his second book into three parts—"The Dains," "The Temple," and "Quesada." Each part ends its section with a solution which, in turn, changes the answer to the preceding puzzle. To illustrate this process, we might imagine children playing with a small set of Lincoln logs. With rather limited material, they build a simple cabin using all of the pieces at their disposal; later they are given additional material and begin to restructure the cabin, using the larger quantity of logs, until the cabin is now a ranch house, complete with fence. Now they are given a final set of materials, and in order to use all of the pieces, they are forced to start once again, restructuring and yet still using past materials, as well as the new ones. The final result is a complex system of buildings and corrals—all of which are built out of the same basic material with which they began. This method of using ever-increasing amounts of material is central to *The Dain Curse*'s development. Because of this approach, plot plays a more central role here than in *Red Harvest* since its structure actually illustrates the central theme in an isomorphic manner: from the structure of the plot we learn that we can only make sense of things from what we know—and what we know will always be limited.

Like most novels of this form, however, *The Dain Curse* begins with an apparently simple crime: the Op answers a routine call to investigate the theft of a few small diamonds from the home of Edgar Leggett, a mysterious yet locally respectable scientist who works out of a laboratory in his own residence. In the process of "Part One: The Dains," the Op discovers that this theft is only a minor incident in a case that involves multiple murders and spans twenty-five years and three continents. As the Byzantine history of the case is gradually revealed during the course of the Op's investigation, we learn that Leggett, a young Frenchman studying art in Paris, was trapped into matrimony by Lily Dain, the impoverished daughter of a British naval officer; shortly after their marriage, she had a child, Gabrielle. Alice, the sister of Lily, was intensely jealous of the marriage and wanted Leggett for herself—not out of love for Leggett but because she and Lily "were true sisters, inseparable, hating one another poisonously" (p. 56).

To acquire Leggett, she planned the murder of her sister. The details of the murder are left in doubt, but she purposefully involved her niece, Gabrielle, by training her to play a game with guns. Alice's claim that Gabrielle actually shot her mother is later questioned by the Op, but Leggett was convinced by it at the time and took the blame for the murder in order to protect his daughter. He was tried, sentenced to Devil's Island, escaped from there to South America, and, after a further series of murders and intrigues, managed to settle in the United States without being detected. Years later, Alice and Gabrielle found him there, living in San Francisco, and Alice married him. Within a few years, however, men appear who know the history of the family, including the violent period Leggett spent in South America, and they attempt to blackmail Alice Dain. She pays one of the men in the diamonds that were reported stolen and thus begins the whole chain of events that lead to the Op's involvement in the case. At the end of this section, following a climactic scene in which the details of this history are brought out, Alice is killed, but not before she pronounces the "curse" of the Dains to her niece. "'You're her daughter,' she cried, 'and you're cursed with the same black soul and rotten blood that she and I and all the Dains have had; and you're cursed with your mother's blood on your hands in babyhood; and with the twisted mind and the need for drugs that are my gifts to you; and your life will be black as your mother's and mine were black; and the lives of those you touch will be black as Maurice's was black'" (p. 58).

The setting of this first section is an interesting contrast to the other two parts of the novel and to *Red Harvest*, as well. The action takes place in San Francisco, but the city itself is not important to the plot's development; unlike the poisonous, corrupting urban monster that was depicted in Hammett's first novel, San Francisco is neutral and unobtrusive. References to streets and locales carry no thematic or symbolic weight. In his next two novels—*The Maltese Falcon* and *The Glass Key*—the notion of urban decay and corruption will once more serve to emphasize setting, but here the city is simply not a factor in the book's development. Indeed, the more significant aspect of setting in this section is the Leggett home. As is so frequently the case in classical detective fiction, the most dramatic moments of action in

The Dain Curse—many of the crimes, the confrontation with the villain, the revelation of "truth"—all take place in a single, secluded residence. The Leggett house would be appropriate in a classical detective story for obvious reasons: it is tastefully wealthy, with antique oriental rugs, handcrafted walnut furniture, and valuable Japanese prints. There is a sitting room with brocaded chairs, a study, and a laboratory on the second floor—exactly the sort of setting found so often in works by G. K. Chesterton, Agatha Christie, and many other classical detective writers.

In addition to the physical setting, other elements add to this classical detective atmosphere. The history behind the Leggett/ Dain family has a distinct quality of old-world decadence that we rarely find in a hard-boiled novel—the subtly incestuous love triangle in Paris, fratricide, the escape from Devil's Island. There is even a servant to be suspected and a wide-eyed fiancé (a male ingénue figure named Eric Collinson) who is said to be "young, blonde, tall, broad, sunburned, and dressy, with the good-looking unintelligent face of one who would know everything about polo, or shooting, or flying, or something of that sort" (p. 13). The description of Leggett by Fitzstephan is, in itself, highly suggestive of the Sherlock Holmes/Auguste Dupin type of classical detective. "There's something obscure in him, something dark and inviting. He is, for instance, physically ascetic—neither smoking or drinking, eating meagerly, sleeping, I'm told, only three or four hours a night—but mentally, or spiritually, sensual—does that mean anything to you?—to the point of decadence. You used to think I had an abnormal appetite for the fantastic. You should know him" (p. 20).

In this atmosphere so like that of the classical detective story, the Op remains essentially the hard-nosed private eye, responding, for example, to Collinson's sarcastic comment about the dangers he has put Gabrielle through ("I hope you're satisfied with the way your work got done") with the terse reply, "It got done" (p. 60). But in the climatic scene of part 1, the Op quickly assumes the role of the classical detective. Here all the prime suspects are gathered in the study (a traditional setting for murder and denouement in classical detective stories), clustered around the body of Leggett which lies slumped over his desk. This scene clearly imitates the tone and construction of a classical work as the Op recognizes, through logically analyzing clues, that the note assumed to be a suicide message is, instead, a letter the man intended to leave behind after his escape. In the exchanges between the Op and the other people in the study, there is even a prolonging of suspense, which is very uncharacteristic of Hammett's usual style.

> "Did he leave any messages besides the one I read?"
> "None that's been found," O'Gar said. "Why?"
> "Any that you know of, Mrs. Leggett?" I asked.
> She shook her head.
> "Why?" O'Gar asked again.
> "He didn't commit suicide," I said. "He was murdered."
> Gabrielle Leggett screamed shrilly and sprung out of her chair, pointing a sharp-nailed white finger at Mrs. Leggett. (P. 52)

During this scene, the Op is highly conscious of the effect of his presence on the suspect, and like any good actor, he adjusts the tone of his voice to match his role.

> I filled my lungs and went on, not exactly bellowing, but getting plenty of noise out. (P. 53)
> I didn't give her a chance to answer any of these questions but sailed ahead, turning my voice loose. (P. 54)
> "You," I thundered, my voice in fine form by now. (P. 54)

When the conventional moment arrives when the Op must make his formal accusation (in this case, of Alice Dain Leggett), he slips into the role of the supremely confident, all-knowing private detective, complete with rhetorical flourishes. "'He shielded you. He had always shielded you. *You*,' I thundered, my voice in fine form by now, 'killed your sister Lily, his first wife, and let him take the fall for you. *You* went to London with him after that. Would you have gone with your sister's murderer if you had been innocent? *You* had him traced here, and *you* came here after him, and *you* married him. *You* were the one who decided he had married the wrong sister, and *you* killed her'" (pp. 54–55). There is a considerable amount of humor and irony in the Op's posturing in this role, but there is also a more subtle irony at work that assumes greater significance as the novel progresses: despite his authoritative, persuasive tone and his carefully analyzed explanation of motive and method, the Op's solution here is wrong, and as we discover somewhat later, the Op is well aware of the fact that his explanation may be incorrect (as he tells Fitzstephan his view of the case, the Op admits, "One guess at the truth is about as good as another" [p. 62]). But only the Op and, of course, the murderer realize that his explanation is insufficient and that he is merely playing a role in his dramatic confrontation scene; like the characters in any classical story (and its readers), all the other people involved in the case accept the Op's constructed theory because it seems to obey the rules of logic and casuality and because, more simply, his "fiction" provides a satisfactory system which explains away the mystery. In this scene the Op, like the classical detective, *seems* to define the "reality" of the Leggett case, and because the reality he creates out of the events appears logical, he is convincing. We are also given, however, the Op's later conversation with Fitzstephan in which he admits that other explanations would also fit the facts.

The second section of *The Dain Curse*, "The Temple," offers a distinctly different ambience and a distinctly different role for the Op. Although the temple of the chapter's title is located in San Francisco,[3] almost everything about the setting is highly reminiscent of a gothic thriller.[4] Inside the temple where Hammett focuses most of the chapter's action, there is a strange exotic cult that claims to be a reincarnation of a Gallic church, dating from the period of King Arthur. Members of this cult, the Temple of the Holy Grail, experience bizarre, religious "visions" and worship at a marble altar of "brilliant white, crystal, and silver" (p. 80) in the cult's main chamber—a surreal, inner courtyard whose walls, rising six stories to an open roof, are completely white and smooth except for a single door. The leaders of the cult, Aaronia and Joseph Haldorn, are a strikingly dramatic couple, and as described by the Op, their dark inscrutability and otherworldly appearance seem perfectly in keeping with the gothic atmosphere of their temple.

I saw her eyes [Aaronia Haldorn's] first. They were enormous, almost black, warm, and heavily fringed with almost black lashes. They were the only live, human, real things in her face. There was warmth and there was beauty in her oval, olive-skinned face, but, except for the eyes, it was warmth and beauty that didn't seem to have anything to do with reality. It was as if her face were not a face, but a mask that she had worn until it had almost become a face. Even her mouth, which was a mouth to talk about, looked not so much like flesh as like a too perfect imitation of flesh, softer and redder and maybe warmer than genuine flesh, but not genuine flesh. Above this face, or mask, uncut black hair was tied close to her head, parted in the middle, and drawn across temples and upper ears to end in a knot on the nape of her neck. Her neck was long, strong, slender; her body tall, fully fleshed, supple; her clothes dark and silky, part of her body. (P. 39)

Joseph Haldorn was tall, built like a statue, and wore a black silk robe. His hair was thick, long, white, and glossy. His thick beard, trimmed round, was white and glossy. . . . His face, healthily pink, was without line or wrinkle. It was a tranquil face, especially the clear brown eyes, somehow making you feel at peace with the world. (P. 72)

When the second section opens, Gabrielle Leggett has gone to the temple to recover from the emotional stress caused by having witnessed the death of her parents. Hired by the family lawyer, who is suspicious of the Haldorns, the Op moves into a room across the hall from Gabrielle. During the Op's first night there, events prove the lawyer's fears to be well-founded: Joseph Haldorn has gone mad, and as part of his insanity, he has become obsessed with Gabrielle. In the Op's struggles to protect his client, he faces dangers that a hero in a gothic melodrama might encounter. For example, he meets a monstrous "ghost" with whom he struggles and barely subdues. "Not more than three feet away, there in the black room, a pale bright thing like a body, but not like flesh, stood writhing before me" (p. 87). Next, while groping his way through a labyrinth of darkened rooms and halls, the Op discovers the body of Gabrielle's doctor lying on the steps of the altar as if he had been made a sacrificial victim. When the Op finds Gabrielle, she appears like a sensationalized Lady Macbeth.

Gabrielle Leggett came around a corner just ahead of us. She was barefooted. Her only clothing was a yellow silk nightgown that was splashed with dark stains. In both hands, held out in front of her as she walked, she carried a large dagger, almost a sword. It was red and wet. Her hands and bare arms were red and wet. There was a dab of blood on one of her cheeks. Her eyes were clear, bright, and calm. Her small forehead was smooth, her mouth and chin firmly set. (P. 79)

Such parodic excesses also invest the scene in which the Op must fight with mad Joseph, who, believing himself to be God, is able to struggle with supernatural strength.

I yelled, "Stop," at him. He wouldn't stop. I was afraid. I fired. The bullet hit his cheek. I saw the hole it made. No muscle twitched in his face; not even his eyes blinked. He walked deliberately, not hurrying, towards me.

I worked the automatic's trigger, pumping six more bullets into his face and body. I saw them go in. And he came on steadily, showing in no way that he was conscious of them. His eyes and face were stern, but not angry. When he was close to me the knife in his hand went up high above his head. That's no way to fight with a knife; but he wasn't fighting; he was bringing retribution to me, and he paid as little atten-tion to my attempts to stop him as a parent does to those of a small child he's punishing.

I was fighting. When the knife, shining over our heads, started down I went in under it, bending my right forearm against his knife-arm, driving the dagger in my left hand at his throat. I drove the heavy blade into his throat, until the hilt's cross stopped it. Then I was through. (P. 95)

When the gory violence and melodramatic action are over, the Op has successfully fulfilled part of his role as gothic hero: he has rescued the helpless heroine and destroyed the "supernatural" op-ponent. But the hero in a gothic melodrama is also expected to separate appearances from reality in the story and, ultimately, to vanquish the supernatural by bringing order and reason to the mysterious events. Just as he did in the first section, however, Hammett makes it impossible for the Op to fulfill his role by subtly undermining the Op's ability to see beneath the surface of things and to dissipate the final mystery. The motif, then, of de-lusion and false appearances runs throughout the section, includ-ing the discussions between the Op and Fitzstephan, which act as a kind of self-referential, running commentary on the Op's role in the case. For instance, the outward appearance of the temple's building certainly provides no clues about what it contains: the exotic Temple of the Holy Grail (which itself turns out to be a phony fraud scheme) is located in "a six-story yellow brick apartment building" (p. 37). Similarly, the external appearance of Joseph Haldorn belies his madness and violence and provides the Op with a very mistaken sense of comfort and serenity.

> It was a tranquil face, especially the clear brown eyes, somehow making you feel at peace with the world. The same soothing quality was in his baritone voice:
> He said: "We are happy to have you here."
> The words were merely polite, meaningless, yet, as he said them, I actually believed that for some reason he was happy. Now I understood Gabrielle Leggett's desire to come to this place. I said that I, too, was happy to be there, and while I was saying it I actually thought I was. (Pp. 72–73)

Throughout this section the Op is repeatedly misled in this manner, for external signs are consistently ambiguous or deceiving. Indeed, on several occasions the Op is unable to distinguish illusion from reality. When he confronts the ghost in Minnie Hershey's room, his struggles enact, in miniature, his relationship to the shifting, deceptive elements of the Dain case.

> It was tall, yet not so tall as it seemed. . . . Its feet—it had feet, but I don't know what their shape was. They had no shape, just as the thing's legs and torso, arms and hands, head and face, had no shape, no fixed form. . . . No feature or member ever stopped twisting, quivering, writhing long enough for its average outline, its proper shape, to be seen. . . . I knew then that I was off-balance from breathing the dead-flower stuff, but I couldn't—though I tried to—tell myself that I did not see this thing. It was there. It was there within reach of my hand if I leaned forward, shivering, writhing, between me and the door. I didn't believe in the supernatural—but what of that? The thing was there. It was there and it was not, I knew, a trick of luminous paint, a man with a sheet over him. (Pp. 87–88)

Like the ghost confronting the Op, nothing in the Dain case will stop "twisting, quivering, writhing long enough for its average outline, its proper shape, to be seen," and the Op's efforts to determine the shape are made all the more difficult because he can trust none of his senses. Thus the Op's ability to *see*, to understand, and to bring things into focus is constantly thwarted, as in the following scene:

I was half-way between the second and the first floors when I saw something move below—or, rather, saw the movement of something without actually seeing it. It moved from the direction of the street-door towards the interior of the house. I was looking towards the elevator at the time as I walked down the stairs. The banister shut off my view of the street-door. What I saw was a flash of movement across half a dozen of the spaces between the banister's uprights. By the time I had brought my eyes into focus there, there was nothing to see. I thought I had seen a face, but that's what anybody would have thought in my position, and all I had actually seen was the movement of something pale. (P. 77)

By the end of part 2, the Op does manage to rescue Gabrielle and to explain some of the mystery surrounding the peculiar elements in the case (he discovers that the ghost was only a technological gimmick and that Gabrielle had been tricked into believing she had murdered Riese), but even at the section's conclusion, while he explains the meaning of the events to Fitzstephan, the Op acknowledges his inability to provide any *final* answers. After he suggests to Fitzstephan that Joseph Haldorn had tried to murder his wife, the Op replies to Fitzstephan's incredulity by saying:

"Yeah, but what difference does that make? It might as well have been anybody else for all the sense it makes. I hope you're not trying to keep this nonsense straight in your mind. You know damned well this didn't happen."
"Then what," he asked, looking puzzled, "did happen?"
"I don't know. I don't think anybody knows. I'm telling you what I saw plus the part of what Aaronia Haldorn told me which fits in with what I saw. To fit in with what I saw, most of it must have happened pretty nearly as I've told you. If you want to believe it did, all right. I don't. I'd rather believe I saw things that weren't there." (P. 103)

Coming as these remarks do after the conventional "solution" has been supplied and all the loose ends tied together, the Op's admission undercuts our expectations: the detective is supposed to reassure us through confident claims to accuracy and not, as the Op does here, to suggest the arbitrary basis of final truths. Although an explanation has been provided which fits the facts, the real mystery remains intact since, as the Op suggests, there are many other theories which would serve as well.

In the third section of *The Dain Curse* there is another change of setting and of detective story "types." According to the Op's description, Quesada, where much of the action in this setting occurs, is a typical coastal small town. "Quesada was a one-hotel town pasted on the rocky side of a young mountain that sloped into the Pacific Ocean some eighty miles from San Francisco. Quesada's beach was much too hard and jagged for bathing, so Quesada had never got much summer-resort money. For a while it had been a hustling rum-running port, but that racket was dead now: bootleggers had learned there was more profit and less worry in handling domestic hootch than imported. Quesada had gone back to sleep" (p. 110). Thus the continental atmosphere of the first section and the gothic atmosphere of the second are here replaced by a rural ambience that provides the Op with a new role: the romantic, protective hero. Quesada is the sort of community where a person has not "a chance in the world of getting anything to eat . . . before seven o'clock" (p. 111), where it is difficult to find your way "unless you knew the country" (p. 111), and where the law enforcement officers have common, folksy names like Dick Cotton and Ben Rolly. When the Op is looking for Rolly (the deputy sheriff), he encounters a citizenry which is "countrified" both in language and in custom, despite its proximity to San Francisco.

> I went back to Quesada . . . and asked the clerk—a dapper boy, this one—who was responsible for law and order there.
> "The marshall's Dick Cotton," he told me; "but he went up to the city last night. Ben Rolly's deputy sheriff. You can likely find him over at his old man's office."
> "Where's that?"
> "Next door to the garage."

I found it, a one-story red brick building with wide glass windows labeled *J. King Rolly, Real Estate, Mortgages, Loans, Stocks and Bonds, Insurance, Notes, Employment Agency, Notary Public, Moving and Storage*, and a lot more that I've forgotten.

Two men were inside, sitting with their feet on a battered desk behind a battered counter. One man was a man of fifty and with hair, eyes, and skin of indefinite, washed-out shades—an amiable, aimless-looking man in shabby clothes. The other was twenty years younger and in twenty years would look just like him.

"I'm hunting," I said, "for the deputy sheriff."

"Me," the younger man said, easing his feet from desk to floor. He didn't get up. Instead, he put a foot out, hooked a chair by its rounds, pulled it from the wall, and returned his feet to the desk-top. "Set down. This is Pa," wiggling a thumb at the other man. "You don't have to mind him." (P. 115)

Hammett creates several other scenes which also illustrate country etiquette and vividly contrast city and country ways. A scene such as the following seems drawn right out of a comedy of manners:

"Howdy, Mary," Rolly greeted her. "Why ain't you over to the Carters'?"

"I'm sick, Mr. Rolly." She spoke without accent. "Chills—so I just stayed home today."

"Tch, tch, tch. That's too bad. Have you had the doc?"

She said she hadn't. Rolly said she ought to. She said she didn't need him: she had chills often. Rolly said that might be so, but that was all the more reason for having him: it was best to play safe and have things like that looked after. She said yes but doctors took so much money, and it was bad enough being sick without having to pay for it. He said in the long run it was likely to cost folks more not having a doctor than having him. I had begun to think they were going to keep it up all day when Rolly finally brought the talk around to the Carters again, asking the woman about her work there. (P. 122)

Appropriately enough, this change in setting also signals a further transformation of the Op's role; having already adopted the roles of classical detective and gothic hero, he now seems to become the gentlemanly, romantic hero of a domestic melodrama. His new persona is a complex, multileveled blend of tough-guy, psychologist, homespun philosopher, and gentleman protector. He remains, of course, the sleuth who solves the mystery, but this effort appears largely subordinate to his personal ministrations to Gabrielle, whom he protects and cures of her morphine habit. Not only does he watch out for her physical well-being, the Op also generally reestablishes her sense of worth. Thus the Op functions as a kind of father figure who advises Gabrielle where to stay, hires a nurse to watch out for her, and even tells her when she should get under the bed covers (p. 157). Gabrielle places herself totally in his hands, and like the most old-fashioned of heroes, the Op takes care of her without any attempt to compromise her virtue. At one point, he even pretends to Gabrielle that his tough-guy professionalism is merely a disguise that masks a sentimental heart.

> "I'm twice your age, sister; an old man. I'm damned if I'll make a chump of myself by telling you why I did it [helped her], why it was neither revolting nor disgusting, why I'd do it again and be glad of the chance."
> She jumped out of her chair, her eyes round and dark, her mouth trembling.
> "You mean—?"
> "I don't mean anything that I'll admit," I said; "and if you're going to parade around with that robe hanging open you're going to get yourself some bronchitis. You ex-hop heads have to be careful about catching cold." (P. 199)

Despite the Op's ability to project himself into these various roles, Gabrielle Leggett eventually sees through his masks and indicates that she understands the nature of his multileveled persona. In a revealing scene which follows the one in which the Op implies that he might love her, Gabrielle confronts him with his deception. "You sat there this noon and deliberately tried to make me think you were in love with me. . . . I honestly believed you all afternoon—and it *did* help. I believed you until you came in just now, and then I saw—. . . A monster. A nice one, an especially nice one to have around when you're in trouble, but a monster just the same, without any human foolishness like love in him" (p. 204). Although, as we have seen, this issue of the Op's absolute allegiance to his job at the expense of human involvement recedes in importance in *The Dain Curse*, it occasionally does resurface in scenes such as this one. Certainly here, as in *Red Harvest*, the Op's professionalism seems genuine enough; in trying to solve the Dain case as efficiently as possible, his help-fulness and seeming concern towards Gabrielle are perfectly in keeping with that end. Her accusation that he is a "monster" and her earlier observation that "there's no personal relationship with you. It's professional with you—your work" (p. 168) indicate that she finally sees him for what he is.

In addition to providing such insight into the Op's character, Gabrielle Leggett helps unify the widely varying sections of the novel. While the nature of the Op's role changes in each of the three sections, her character remains constant: she is the stereo-typical female victim. Whether she is the heroine of a classical story, a gothic thriller, or a country romance, she is passive and helpless to the point of catatonia, unable to control or interpret anything that happens around her, and constantly needing men to rescue her from other men. Indeed, the whole saga of Gabrielle Leggett is so outrageous and excessive that it could be read as a darkly humorous parody of the trials and tribulations genre of popular fiction and films. At the age of five she is involved in the murder of her mother (perhaps even having pulled the trigger her-self and certainly having witnessed it), and thereafter she is raised by her mad, murderous aunt. As an adult, she witnesses the mur-ders of several people (her father is murdered as well as her step-mother, her husband, and her doctor); she is kidnapped; she at-tempts suicide; she is molested by every family member mentioned in the book; and she is also addicted to morphine, mentally un-stable, and sexually frigid. As the Op sums things up, "All the calamities known to man have been piled up on you" (p. 167).

The villain of the case likewise ends his career in a manner so excessive that it is more whimsical and parodic than realistic. Unlike the typical murderer in most hard-boiled fiction who is dispatched in a hail of bullets or who dies in a dramatic show-down with the detective or who is prosaically executed by the state, Fitzstephan meets with a truly extraordinary fate. Although he is almost literally blown in two, losing his right arm, right leg, and the right side of his face, he eventually recovers to explain his own involvement in the case to the Op. After being found insane at the trial, he is sent to a mental institution for a year and is then released into the custody of Joseph Haldorn's widow—a woman he himself once tried to murder—who whisks him away to an island off Puget Sound.

Although this final twist in the case—the murderer disappearing to a western isle with one of his intended victims—is bizarre, it is an appropriate end to *The Dain Curse*. Just as in *Red Harvest*, where personal relationships were twisted and corrupt, the traditional alliances of people—husband/wife, lovers, parent/child, friends—are characterized by strange, unaccountable, often destructive emotions. Most of the rules governing relationships have been broken down along with the traditional view that love unifies, heals, and makes life cohere. If the final assessment of relationships is less bleak here than in Hammett's first novel (at the novel's conclusion, Gabrielle has been taken in by her in-laws and seems happy with them), this is due more to tone than to content, for the samples we see of human relations here range from the distasteful and unethical attempts at seduction by the family lawyer to the pathetic infidelities of Mrs. Cotton. Many of these relationships start with and end in violence: one of the sisters murders another and then raises her niece only to have the power to force the girl's father to marry her; Joseph Haldorn tries to murder his wife because of his love for Gabrielle—and does so right before the eyes of his son; in Quesada a husband murders his wife because she has been unfaithful. In *The Dain Curse* relationships are so twisted and intensely passionate that people's behavior becomes virtually inexplicable by normal standards. For example, Alice Dain hates her sister so much that she skillfully plays the part of the loving aunt for years. "There was nothing her Aunt Alice wouldn't do for her dear niece; because her preferring me infuriated Lily, not that Lily herself loved the child so much, but that we were sisters; and whatever one wanted the other wanted, not to share, but exclusively" (p. 57). Even Aaronia Haldorn, who appears to be relatively sane, has an attachment for Fitzstephan that is irrational and mad; despite the fact that he has tried to kill her, she is willing to take him, a hopeless cripple, away after he is released from the mental institution. Fitzstephan is himself the clearest, most extreme example of these grotesque relationships. The primary impetus for much of the violence and horror in the novel is his alleged love for Gabrielle, a woman he views as his rightful property, "bought with the deaths he has caused" (p. 209). In developing these emotional excesses, wild extremes of passion and hatred, and unpredictable responses to events, Hammett is not only presenting a commentary on the precarious, unstable nature of human emotions and personality. Just as importantly, Hammett uses these unfathomable extremes to justify a manipulation of the plot elements, deepening the mystery and making it virtually impossible for us—or for the Op—to put the pieces of the case into a coherent whole. As we shall see, the labyrinthine nature of the plot is an important aspect of Hammett's self-conscious, metafictional intent in the novel.

Although the three sections of *The Dain Curse* are separate and closed installments with differences of excess in each, the overall effect of the plot is unified because each section reinforces Hammett's central intent in the novel—to explore the knowing process by an examination of the formal properties of fiction in general and of detective fiction in particular. Thus, each of the three sections can be viewed, on one level, as Hammett's effort to examine the way that different mystery genres operate, to see how they relate to one another and what their form implies. But Hammett does not just develop these "types" in a straightforward fashion, rather, his manipulations are so obviously excessive, often almost parodically so, that a playful self-consciousness is present in *The Dain Curse* that was utterly absent in *Red Harvest*. Certainly readers familiar with the genres Hammett was mimicking in the three sections would find his manipulations often amusing or at least technically interesting and would thus be distanced from the action of the book in a way uncharacteristic of most detective fiction. Indeed, the story is too fantastic for the issue of credibility or realism to ever really arise. By making the plot so outlandish and by providing a series of contradictory denouements, Hammett forces us to see the absurdity of one of the principal assumptions of the detective genre: that a single truth exists somewhere that accounts for mystery, whether it be the mystery of a crime or the mystery of why people feel and act as they do. Hammett's intent to examine how we arrive at such truths—truths which he reveals to be "fictions"—is evident not only in his manipulations of plot but also in the way he develops the key relationship between the Op and Fitzstephan, detective and murderer.

As we have seen, each section of *The Dain Curse* concludes

with the Op arriving at an explanation of what has happened and who the guilty parties are, based on the evidence at his disposal. Each denouement satisfies our expectations of the genre: puzzling clues are clarified, missing pieces supplied, guilt assigned, and loose ends worked into a coherent system. Each conventional conclusion, however, is undermined by the action of the next section which introduces matters that make the previous solution inadequate. What happens on the level of plot, of course, is that *new* puzzling events occur, evidently related to the earlier events; new clues and information are supplied which place previous action in a totally new light. Obviously, such a system of plot development undercuts the usual epistemological assumptions of detective fiction. As we saw in chapter 1, the detective's main duty, either in the classical or hard-boiled story, is to separate illusion from reality and to arrive eventually, by use of reason and logic, at a final answer which dispels the mystery in the case. In *The Dain Curse*, however, Hammett ironically creates a detective who believes that final solutions are merely fictional projections of our need to impose order on an inexplicable and fundamentally mysterious universe. The Op's views about his own personal role in interpreting these mysteries will be examined more fully when we turn to his relationship with Fitzstephan, but these attitudes suggest that, even on the level of the novel's action, he is not a trustworthy perceiver. It is not that he has some particular bias that distorts his perception; it is simply the partial nature of all perception. Again and again, the Op is placed in circumstances where he realizes that what he sees is likely to be deceptive. Certainly the woman who appeared on the Leggett porch at the beginning of the novel (Alice Leggett) whom the Op describes as "about my age, forty, with darkish blond hair, a pleasant plump face, and dimpled pink cheeks" with "a lavender-flowered white housedress" (p. 5) does not *look* like the vicious murderer of her sister and several others, just as the ghost the Op fights in the temple *looks* real enough at that time. With our senses so patently unreliable, our ability to reason inductively and to draw conclusions from our experiences becomes suspect. Indeed, the fact that our hold on reality is so tenuous and our methods of arriving at truth are so haphazard makes us cling to our illusions of order ever the more tightly. In one of the novel's key passages, the Op explains to Gabrielle his recognition of how unreliable our mechanisms for arriving at truth are.

> "Nobody thinks clearly, no matter what they pretend. Thinking's a dizzy business, a matter of catching as many of those foggy glimpses as you can and fitting them together the best way you can. That's why people hang on so tight to their beliefs and opinions; because, compared to the haphazard way in which they're arrived at, even the goofiest opinion seems wonderfully clear, sane, and self-evident. And if you let it get away from you, then you've got to dive back into that foggy muddle to wrangle yourself out another to take its place." (P. 166)

The Op ultimately fails at the "dizzy business" of fitting these "foggy glimpses" together perfectly. He is correct in identifying Owen Fitzstephan as the murderer and is able to deduce the course of his crimes,[5] but he overlooks the most portentous clue of all: Fitzstephan is a Dain and, as such, is susceptible to the "Dain Curse." When Owen tells him this fact, the detective—the man who supposedly has everything under control by the end of the story—can only respond, "I'll be damned" (p. 202). This detail of Owen's ancestry may have no bearing on the mechanics of the crimes themselves, and the Op is able to figure out Owen's guilt without this knowledge, but it is an added element that emphasizes Hammett's central point all the more strongly: that we can never know *enough*, either about others or ourselves, to comprehend life. As the Op puts it at one point, "Evidence of goofiness is easily found: the more you dig into yourself, the more you turn up" (p. 166), and because we cannot know enough, we should hesitate about making moral judgments, which is one reason why the Op avoids self-righteous denunciations of the chief villains in both *Red Harvest* and *The Dain Curse*. At the conclusion of the novel, Owen's insanity is viewed by the courts and public as the key to his crimes and the ultimate explanation for his behavior. But the Op is well aware that, while such designations as "insanity" conveniently label or categorize actions, they do not explain them. To call a man insane does not explain his behavior any more fully than to claim it results from a family curse. Throughout the novel, the Op rejects the validity of all systems that classify. For instance, when Fitzstephan tries to explain the fact that his friend Ralph Coleman "always had the most consistently logical and credible reasons for having done the most idiotic things" by labeling him "an advertising man," the Op disdainfully comments, "as if that explained it" (p. 100). Likewise, the Op tells Ben Rolly that he mistrusts the theory of the curse. "The trouble with it is it's worked out too well, too regularly. It's the first one I ever ran across that did." Rolly agrees with him but adds that in this kind of world anything is possible. "Still and all, you do hear of them working out. There's things that happen that make a fellow think there's things in the world—in life—that he don't know much about. . . . It's inscrutable" (p. 117). Certainly the Op is unwilling to use a label like insanity to dismiss the ambiguities of events because he fully realizes the inexplicable nature of nearly all people and events; as he tells Gabrielle, "anybody who started hunting for evidence of insanity in himself would certainly find plenty, because all but stupid minds were jumbled affairs" (p. 172). As will be seen, this skepticism of the ability of *any* humanly devised system, no matter how complex, to provide final solutions is also crucial for the metafictional concerns of *The Dain Curse*.

If the plot of *The Dain Curse*, with its successive, contradictory revelations, serves to undermine the usual authority of the detective-as-reasoner, so, too, do the debates between Fitzstephan and the Op develop these same epistemological notions. Introducing the series of conversations between the murderer and the detective in which both men analyze the meaning of the case and debate various issues concerning literature and reason is probably Hammett's most brilliant strategic success in the novel, for these discussions allow him to create a complex and playful ironic commentary on the action in the novel *and* on the fictional strategy he himself employs in its presentation. More specifically, these running conversations serve at least five interconnected functions in the novel: (1) they allow the Op to bring together all the clues before us and to announce his analysis of them; (2) they *further* the mystery (rather than clarifying it) since Fitzstephan constantly tries to confuse the issues and throw the Op off the track; (3) they generate a metafictional commentary on the assumptions underlying traditional fiction in general and detective fiction in particular; (4) they comment upon Hammett's own ap-

proach to detective writing; and (5) they focus the central epistemological issues of the book by demonstrating how closely related the concept of "fiction making" is for the novelist, for the
detective, and for the ordinary person.

When the name Owen Fitzstephan is casually introduced in
connection with the Leggett case (chapter 1), the Op recalls that
they had been "fairly chummy for a month or two" (p. 18) when
they had first met on a case in New York, and he decides to look
him up to obtain some inside information about the Leggett
household. The two key facts that we must always keep in mind
while trying to analyze Fitzstephan's role in the novel are that he
is a professional novelist and that he is the villain, the man responsible for most of the murders and therefore anxious to keep
the Op off the scent of his trail. Because Owen is the murderer,
we must always view his remarks with suspicion—and Hammett
has a considerable amount of fun in presenting Owen's comments in the context of an elaborate game of wits between these
two unlikely adversaries. But it is also no accident that Fitzstephan is given the profession of a novelist, for this allows Hammett to create an intricate interplay between Fitzstephan—a kind
of traditional novelist figure—and the Op—who becomes the
embodiment of the spokesman for Hammett's own theory of fiction writing.

When the Op first calls on Fitzstephan, we are told of the writer
that he is "a man who pretended to be lazier than he was, would
rather talk than do anything else, and had a lot of what seemed
to be accurate information and original ideas on any subject that
happened to come up, as long as it was a little out of the ordinary"
(p. 18). This description might well apply to many eccentric fictional detectives, from Dupin to Holmes to Philo Vance, and as it
turns out, Fitzstephan is eager to play amateur detective by "as-
sisting" the Op in unraveling the case. Throughout the novel the
two men spend considerable time together going over the case's
facts, analyzing new evidence, and developing potential solutions. On a very simple level, Owen plays a kind of straight man,
a conventional role often found in detective fiction: like that of
Watson in the Sherlock Holmes series, Fitzstephan's presence
provides an excuse for the Op to lay out the elements of the complicated case, explain his reasoning about the connection of the

clues, and discuss alternative solutions. Fitzstephan assists this process in the conventional manner by raising important issues, questioning the detective about unclear elements, and providing possible alternative answers. Naturally, however, the fact that Owen is the actual murderer makes all his remarks and observations highly ironic; he is anxious to assist the Op in creating an inductively developed premise or final solution, but only so long as it never implicates *him* in the case. Thus he not only deliberately obscures elements that are crucial to the case, but he also constantly reinforces the Op's conclusions when they are leading in the wrong direction.

Having the detective analyze the case with the murderer creates a series of amusing and dramatically effective incidents.[6] But there are also serious issues Hammett can present by using this approach. Not only does Fitzstephan play the role of murderer trying to disguise his involvement in the crimes, but he can also be shown to approach the entire case much as a *novelist* would—with a novelist's strong sense of proper narrative structure, the tendency to rely on psychological systems to explain character motivation, the delight in colorful, vivid details, and the desire for absolute answers that will produce a pleasing, aesthetic whole. Obviously, each of the "novelistic biases" is very useful to Fitzstephan, for if the Op were to try to solve the Dain case as if it were a case in a traditional novel, he would probably fail; life, Hammett always implies, simply does not supply the kind of ready answers that most novelists are so anxious to provide. Fitzstephan embodies exactly the kind of novelistic stance that Hammett personally despised and which he was reacting against in his own work. The Op, on the other hand, represents Hammett's disdain for theatrics and simplistic solutions and a distrust of easy psychological explanations for complex human behavior; like Hammett the Op is well aware that most fiction—and especially detective fiction (including the "fictional presentations" of newspaper reporting)[7]—is too quick to assume there are absolute answers and too ready to take what is colorful and aesthetically correct as true, hence missing life as it really is—dull, trivial, and often utterly ambiguous and inscrutable, even to the trained detective's eye. Thus as we watch the Op grappling with the bizarre complexities of the Dain case, we should gradually realize that neither he nor Hammett is going to be able to supply the kind of well-rounded whole that we expect in a novel; it is in this way that Hammett's personal and metafictional themes can be seen to subtly intersect and support each other.

From their first encounter onward, the contrast between the Op's pragmatic, cautious method of handling the Dain case and Fitzstephan's more flamboyant, "novelistic" approach is clearly evident. One of Owen's first remarks to the Op—"Don't try to be subtle with me, my son; that's not your style at all" (p. 20)— indicates his awareness of the Op's straightforward approach to detection (these remarks are also a good example of many similar passages where Hammett may be playfully calling attention to his own literary strategies). This approach distrusts any efforts to dramatize or embellish a case—efforts that are, however, crucial for a good novelist. When Fitzstephan demands a quick evaluation of "what Leggett's been up to" the Op explains one of the key differences between their respective ways of handling their "material." "We don't do it that way. . . . You're a storywriter. I can't trust you not to build up on what I tell you. I'll save mine till after you've spoken your piece, so yours won't be twisted to fit mine" (p. 20).[8] As the exchange continues and Owen displays his novelistic tendencies by creating a neatly detailed psychological profile (a profile as noted earlier that evokes the Holmes/Dupin figure), the Op is quick to undercut what he sees as fabrication.

> "He's [Leggett] always interested me. There's something obscure in him, something dark and inviting. He is, for instance, physically ascetic—neither smoking or drinking, eating meagerly, sleeping, I'm told, only three or four hours a night—but mentally, or spiritually, sensual—does that mean anything to you?—to the point of decadence. You used to think I had an abnormal appetite for the fantastic. You should know him. His friends—no, he hasn't any—his choice companions are those who have the most outlandish ideas to offer: Marquard and his insane figures that aren't figures; Denbar Curt and his algebraism; the Haldorns and their Holy Grail sect; crazy Laura Joines; Farnham—"
>
> "And you," I put in, "with explanations and descriptions that explain and describe nothing. I hope you don't think any of what you've said means anything to me." (P. 20)

In a scene such as this one, it is obvious where Hammett's sympathies lie. The essence of the difference between the Op and Fitzstephan is not that Owen is a creative thinker and the Op a hardnosed pragmatist; it is rather that Owen consistently demands a single system to produce a single answer, while the Op knows that such systems evolve from *aesthetic* attitudes and our desire for order and clarity and that they simply are not adequate in the real world. In one of their crucial confrontations, the Op arrives at Owen's house to find "the novelist in Fitzstephan . . . busy trying to find what he called Mrs. Leggett's psychological basis" (p. 60–61). The rest of their conversation is a good example of the complex interplay that is present in all their encounters.

"The killing of her sister is plain enough, knowing her character as we do now," he said, "and so are the killing of her husband, her attempt to ruin her niece's life when she was exposed, and even her determination to kill herself on the stairs rather than be caught. But the quiet years in between—where do they fit in?"

"It's Leggett's murder that doesn't fit in," I argued. "The rest is all one piece. . . . She was simply a woman who wanted what she wanted and was willing to go to any length to get it. Look how patiently, and for how many years, she hid her hatred from the girl. And her wants weren't even very extravagant. You won't find the key to her in any complicated derangements. She was simple as an animal, with an animal's simple ignorance of right and wrong, dislike for being thwarted, and spitefulness when trapped."

Fitzstephan drank beer and asked:

"You'd reduce the Dain curse, then, to a primitive strain in the blood?"

"To less than that, to words in an angry woman's mouth."

"It's fellows like you that take all the color out of life. . . . Doesn't Gabrielle being made the tool of her mother's murder convince you of the necessity—at least the poetic necessity—of the curse?"

"Not even if she *was* the tool, and that's something I wouldn't bet on. . . . Gabrielle had been brought up to believe her father the murderer—so we can believe that. . . . But, from that point on, one guess at the truth is about as good as another. . . ."

"You jump around so," Fitzstephan complained. . . . "Why don't you stick to your answer? . . ."

"That was good enough to say then," I admitted; "but not now, in cold blood, with more facts to fit in." (Pp. 61–62)

Owen's desire for a simple, straightforward explanation is obviously motivated by his desire to keep the Op away from the complex realities of the case, but his comments here are also perfectly in keeping with the aesthetic impulse of his art, which relies on causal explanations and character motivation that readers can easily follow. In virtually all novels, no matter how intricately developed, there must finally be a "solution" provided, whereby the reader can solve the mystery of the plot by having paid careful attention to the "clues" planted by the author.[9] Owen obviously would like the Op to believe that the world operates on this same principle; consequently, he is constantly deriding the Op's qualified explanations and his tiresome attention to trivial details as being aesthetically uninteresting. "You've got it all certainly as tangled and confused as possible," he tells the Op, to which the Op replies, "It'll get worse before it's better" (p. 32); later Owen disgustedly comments: "Aw, shut up. You're never satisfied until you've got two buts and an if attached to everything. . . . Always belittling. You need more beer to expand your soul" (p. 63); and, similarly, after the Op begins another recital of the alternative explanations: "Not now. Later, after you've finished the story, you can attach your ifs and buts to it, distorting and twisting it, making it as cloudy and confusing and generally hopeless as you like" (pp. 103–4). But perhaps his strongest indictment occurs when he tells the Op: "Nobody's mysteries ought to be as tiresome as you're making this one. . . . I like the Nick Carter school better" (p. 154)—a remark which, again, calls our attention to Hammett's own self-reflexive interests.

For his part, the Op largely dismisses Fitzstephan's charges as being naïve and too "literary." When Owen calls him about a puzzling phone call that he has received, the Op is quick to deride his tendency to storify events. "Spring the puzzle. Don't be too literary with me, building up to climaxes and the like. I'm too crude for that—it'd only give me a bellyache" (p. 131). "Crude" or not, the Op has his own method of proceeding in a case, a method which is unglamorous, painfully slow, and realistic about its limitations. Despite Dupin and Holmes, the detective does not catch criminals because he has a superior artistic imagination. Thus, when Fitzstephan asks whether or not the criminal in this case may be too wily for him and has outwitted him, the Op says:

"You've got a flighty mind. That's no good in this business. You don't catch murderers by amusing yourself with interesting thoughts. You've got to sit down to all the facts you can get and turn them over and over till they click" (p. 153). The Op echoes this summary of his own approach to his work in two other passages.

> I spent most of the afternoon putting my findings and guesses on paper and trying to fit them together in some sort of order. (P. 33)

> I piled up the facts I had, put some guesses on them, and took a jump from the top of the heap into space. (P. 190)

As all three passages pointedly suggest, the Op hardly views himself as the embodiment of reason who can put the pieces of reality's mystery back into a coherent whole. Quite the contrary, he views the operations of the mind with considerable distrust, fully aware of the arbitrary nature of putting the pieces into any particular formation that seems to work. "Nobody thinks clearly," he says and later adds that all beliefs and opinions are derived in a "haphazard way" (p. 166). With such a skeptical outlook, it is not surprising that he never claims to have discovered any final solutions; as is appropriate in a novel plotted to continually add new information, the Op's "solutions" are always presented as temporary, convenient guesses which somehow manage to account for the evidence.[10]

The end products of people's criminal actions, then, are definable (theft, rape, murder), but the *human reality* that underlies these actions (motivation, passion, emotion, personality) can never be fully understood or conveniently explained. The question asked by Fitzstephan, "What happened after that?"—the classic response of the listener to the storyteller—and the Op's answer, "Nothing. . . . That's the kind of story it is. I warned you there was no sense to it" (p. 105), reverberate far beyond Gabrielle Leggett and her troubles. For Dashiell Hammett the "truth" is always elusive and any pattern that claims total validity is merely "a matter of catching as many of those foggy glimpses as you can and fitting them together the best you can" (p. 166). The Op interrupts a traditional denouement to ask Fitzstephan, "You actually believe what I've told you so far?" and when the answer is yes, he continues: "What a childish mind you've got. . . . Let me tell you the story about the wolf that went to the little girl's grandmother's house and—" (p. 104). Because the world, as Hammett sees it, is irrational and random, we can best interpret it and live in it if we are aware of the dangers of absolutes—a theme he develops more fully in *The Maltese Falcon*.

4

Ambiguity in *The Maltese Falcon*

—— ᗡᗤ ——

"Everybody," Spade responded mildly, "has something to conceal."

—*from* The Maltese Falcon

In contrast to the large number of characters and the elaborate, convoluted plots of the two Op novels, Hammett's third work, *The Maltese Falcon* (1930), may seem a compact, intimate work. Yet it is arguably Hammett's densest, most complex novel in terms of character, themes, and technique. In *The Maltese Falcon* Hammett's emphasis on the character of the detective (something evident in *Red Harvest*) is integrated with an emphasis on plot and structure (as in *The Dain Curse*) so that this third work is a brilliantly unified novel whose imagery, character development, style, plot, and theme are closely interwoven. *The Maltese Falcon* is a novel about mystery—it is, in fact, a declaration of the omnipotence of mystery and of the failure of human effort (on the part of both the reader and the detective) to ever dispel it. Throughout the novel nothing is as it seems, and that is the only truth on which we can rely. If such a premise seems inappropriate in a work of detective fiction, it is precisely the tension created by Hammett's development of this incongruity that charges *The Maltese Falcon* with such a powerful, unsettling ambiguity. Indeed, not only does Hammett's detective, Sam Spade, fail to reestablish order and account for what happened, he himself is ultimately the most mysterious factor in the case. And at the novel's conclusion—when we expect to be assured and illuminated—we are left with an indecipherable mystery that has grown larger, more pervasive, and more impenetrable as the book has developed.

Compared to *The Dain Curse* and *Red Harvest*, *The Maltese Falcon* has a relatively simple plot. An international gang of thieves —headed by an obese "gentleman" named Casper Gutman[1]—has come to San Francisco looking for a statue whose history dates back to the Crusades. The statue—the Maltese falcon—has passed through the hands of kings, pirates, art dealers, and bandits until it is finally owned by a Russian general who lives in a suburb of Constantinople. Gutman traces the statue there, and when his attempts to buy the falcon fail, he hires three agents—Brigid O'Shaughnessy, Joel Cairo, and Floyd Thursby—to steal it. These agents double-cross Gutman and each other: Thursby and O'Shaughnessy join forces and give the falcon to a sea captain whose ship is bound for San Francisco, while they themselves flee on another boat. At this point Gutman and Cairo become partners again, and accompanied by Cairo's homosexual lover, Wilmer, they follow the pair to San Francisco. While Brigid and Thursby await the arrival of the ship carrying the Maltese falcon, their alliance ends, and Brigid devises a plan to keep Thursby out of the way until she has possession of the falcon for herself. She goes to the detective agency of Miles Archer and Samuel Spade and hires Archer to follow Thursby, hoping that her former partner will be so jittery that, when he sees he is being followed, he will try to kill the detective and be jailed. When her plan fails, she shoots Archer herself, planning to implicate Thursby; in the meantime, however, Thursby is killed by Wilmer, the young gunman who accompanies Cairo. At this point, Sam Spade takes on the case, and the rest of the action involves his investigation into the death of his partner and the uncovering of the various intrigues surrounding the mysterious falcon, Brigid, Gutman, and Cairo. When Captain Jacobi arrives with the Maltese falcon, he is also shot by Wilmer, but before he dies he manages to give the falcon to Spade. During a climactic night in Spade's apartment when the falcon is found to be a worthless copy, Spade reveals the solution to the murder of his partner and turns over the gang, Brigid included, to the police.

As this summary suggests, there are complexities and confusions in the case, but the mystery is of a very different nature from

that found in Hammett's first two novels. For one thing, the circle
of suspects is much smaller in this case; there are fewer characters and, so, fewer subplots. The statue itself provides a focus for
the action and a clear point of reference both in terms of the characters and the plot—the falcon can be seen, touched, and quan-
tified monetarily, unlike the more nebulous sources of mystery
in the two Op novels. And despite the shifting alliances the action of this novel is more straightforward and more traditional in
its unfolding—possibly due to the fact that this was the first of
Hammett's books which was written as a novel and not as a series
of combined shorter episodes. At any rate, there are simply fewer
things *happening* here to distract, confuse, or mislead. And what
does happen is less violent than in the previous works. All the
murders occur off the page, and only with the death of Captain
Jacobi, who has been shot and who makes his way to Spade's office before he dies, do we actually "see" the bloody results of the
murders. Instead, the action here is characterized more by fisticuffs than murder, and fisticuffs in very specific situations: Spade
is punched by a policeman (whom he cannot hit back without
getting into trouble); Spade hits Joel Cairo while holding him at
gunpoint; Wilmer kicks Spade in the temple as Spade, drugged by
Gutman, lies on the floor; Wilmer is punched by Spade as his
arms are held by Cairo and Gutman; Spade slaps the smaller and
physically weaker Joel Cairo, and when Cairo tries to defend himself, "Spade stopped him with both palms held out on long rigid
arms and against his face."[2] All these instances of brutality have
in common a violence that one is helpless to fight against; a real
defense is impossible.[3] As we shall see in a later discussion, this
inability to defend oneself, this powerlessness to affect circumstances, will complement one of the major themes of the book—
that men live "only while blind chance spared them" (p. 66).

The most striking change in *The Maltese Falcon*, however, is
the shift in point of view from the first-person narration of *Red
Harvest* and *The Dain Curse* to a restricted third-person presentation. From an aspect of plot, such a shift is obviously necessary:
during the climactic scene when Spade explains to Brigid why he
must turn her in, it is clear that he has known all along that it
was she who shot his partner, Miles Archer.

"Miles hadn't many brains, but, Christ! he had too many years' experience as a detective to be caught like that by the man he was shadowing. Up a blind alley with his gun tucked away on his hip and his overcoat buttoned? Not a chance. He was as dumb as any man ought to be, but he wasn't quite that dumb. The only two ways out of the alley could be watched from the edge of Bush Street over the tunnel. You'd told us Thursby was a bad actor. He couldn't have tricked Miles into the alley like that, and he couldn't have driven him in. He was dumb but not dumb enough for that. . . . [But] if you caught up with him and asked him to go up there he'd've gone. He was just dumb enough for that. He'd've looked you up and down and licked his lips and gone grinning from ear to ear—and then you could've stood close to him in the dark and put a hole through him with the gun you had got from Thursby that evening." (P. 220)

Thus, Spade infers from the condition of the body and the situation of the killing that the murderer could only have been Brigid. Given these circumstances, there are obvious problems which would arise if the story were told, like Hammett's previous two novels, in a first-person narration: since Spade knows Brigid is guilty from almost the outset of the story, it would be difficult to suppress or camouflage that knowledge. Not only would an early revelation of Brigid's guilt prevent the plot from developing into a classical denouement in which the surprising identity of the murderer is revealed, it would also radically alter our view of Brigid's character during the book's development. Rather than seeing her as an addled, vulnerable young woman whose deceits and evasions are those of a frightened girl trying to hold her own against professional criminals, we would see a calculating killer. But the most striking effect of this change in point of view in *The Maltese Falcon* is that it heightens the mystery of Sam Spade, for it serves to conceal the true nature of his involvement in the case with Brigid O'Shaughnessy. Thus, this third-person narration actually works in much the same way as did the neutral, impenetrable voice of the Op: both narrative techniques keep us at a distance from what is going on in the mind of the detective. Yet there is a crucial difference: in the Op novels, the distanced, objective narrative results from the detective's *own* distanced, objective view of the world, but in *The Maltese Falcon* Hammett uses the third-person approach as a formal device to distance us "artificially" from his main character. For example, in the scene in which Spade is roused from his bed with the news of his partner's death, we are given a neutral reportage of events—an account that is as precise in physical details and movements as it is devoid of insights into the character's mind.

> A telephone-bell rang in darkness. When it had rung three times bedsprings creaked, fingers fumbled on wood, something small and hard thudded on a carpeted floor, the springs creaked again, and a man's voice said: "Hell. . . . Yes, speaking. . . . Dead? . . . Yes. . . . Fifteen minutes. Thanks."
>   A switch clicked and a white bowl hung on three gilded chains from the ceiling's center filled the room with light. Spade, barefooted in green and white checked pajamas, sat on the side of his bed. He scowled at the telephone on the table while his hands took from beside it a packet of brown papers and a sack of Bull Durham. Cold steamy air blew in through two open windows, bringing with it a half dozen times a minute the Alcatraz foghorn's dull moaning. A tinny alarm-clock, insecurely mounted on a corner of *Duke's Celebrated Criminal Cases of America*—face down on the table—held its hands at two minutes past two. (P. 11)

The single word "scowled" in the second paragraph is the only indication of Spade's response—and even "scowled" in this case is not very clear in its implications. Not only does the point of view here, somewhat in the manner of the French New Novelists, purposefully avoid depicting Spade's emotions, it also makes it impossible for the reader to follow Spade's reasoning about the case. Yet the visual point of view remains so resolutely Spade's own that the reader does not realize *who* is dead until three pages later when Sam gazes down at Archer's body. Similarly, every other scene in the novel is dominated by Spade's perspective, but this domination does not lead to a greater understanding of his character—indeed, quite the opposite is true. Thus, point of view in *The Maltese Falcon* is used by Hammett to underscore the mystery surrounding the detective rather than to provide an entry into the character's mind. Rather than the narration illuminating Spade, it keeps him in shadow throughout the novel.

Although the Continental Op is also an enigmatic figure in both

Red Harvest and *The Dain Curse*, there are basic differences between how these two detectives are developed that demonstrate how *The Maltese Falcon* departs from Hammett's earlier works. As we have seen in chapters 2 and 3, Hammett developed the Continental Op as a largely anonymous, emotionless cipher. We discover his character gradually and indirectly by his actions, by his response (or lack of response) to events, and by his choice of language. We are given virtually no physical information except that he is middle-aged and overweight nor any background or personal eccentricities that would help actualize his character. Hammett leaves out the sort of "clues" that would give us insight into the Op and help us understand how he came to be the kind of character he is, at least partly because the Op is not meant to be a "character." He remains, essentially, a voice and a set of attitudes. In *The Maltese Falcon*, however, Hammett carefully sets out to create a vivid, physically striking character. A reader familiar with Hammett's method of presenting the Op will surely be struck with the sharp contrast in the way he opens *The Maltese Falcon*. "Samuel Spade's jaw was long and bony, his chin a jutting v under the more flexible v of his mouth. His nostrils curved back to make another small v. His yellow-grey eyes were horizontal. The *v motif* was picked up again, by thickish brows rising outward from twin creases above a hooked nose, and his pale brown hair grew down—from high flat temples—in a point on his forehead" (p. 3). This first paragraph devotes more lines to Spade's physical appearance than *Red Harvest* and *The Dain Curse* combined provide for the Op. Such physical details are given throughout *The Maltese Falcon*, for Spade's appearance is important to the novel's development in a way that the Op's was not. When Spade undresses early in the novel, for example, we are shown his body's incongruous blend of physical strength and vulnerability. "He took off his pajamas. The smooth thickness of his arms, legs, and body, the sag of his big rounded shoulders, made his body like a bear's. It was like a shaved bear's: his chest was hairless. His skin was childishly soft and pink" (p. 12). Whereas we never know what the Op looks like, how he dresses, or any other elements that would physically identify him, Hammett meticulously describes not only Spade's bodily appearance but also his clothing, his cigarettes, his office and bedroom furniture, and even his facial expressions ("Spade grinned wolfishly, showing the edges of teeth far back in his jaw" [p. 10]).

Clearly, these elaborate details indicate early on that Hammett is much more interested in developing a fuller sense of personality for Spade than he was for the Op. The Op's character was defined almost entirely by abstractions—his code, his epistemological theories, his language. Consequently, Hammett left the Op's actions to speak almost entirely for themselves and used very few of the traditional means of developing personality. In contrast, consider once more the descriptions quoted earlier of what happens when Spade receives the phone call informing him that his partner, Miles Archer, has been murdered (p. 92 of this text). In this passage the physical details of Spade and his environment are sharply defined in an almost classically realistic manner: the details help set the ominous mood of the entire novel (the "moaning" of the Alcatraz foghorn) and provide telling items about Spade's life (the Bull Durham, a tinny alarm clock, a copy of *Celebrated Criminal Cases of America* literally at his fingertips). These are exactly the sorts of details which are conspicuously absent in the Op novels, and their inclusion in *The Maltese Falcon* certainly provides more data with which to "process" Spade. Such physical details are crucial in this novel, for Spade is very much a physical force in *The Maltese Falcon*. Not only is he a man of great strength, but he dominates as well by his emotional and sexual presence in a way that the Op never does.

Although this contrast in the development of character is also illustrated by the difference in their working conditions—the Op's personal anonymity is emphasized by his role as a nameless employee in a large detective agency; Spade's individualism in a small, two-man operation has the opposite effect—both detectives share a strong sense of allegiance to their job. Despite all his personal complexities and idiosyncrasies, Sam Spade is, above all, a very efficient private investigator, a man who has shrewd business sense and loyalty to and respect for his profession. It is significant that in the key scene at the end of the novel, when Spade is explaining to Brigid why he must turn her in, his first three reasons for doing so relate specifically to his job.

> "Listen. When a man's partner is killed he's supposed to do something about it. It doesn't make any difference what you thought of him. He

was your partner and you're supposed to do something about it. Then it happens we were in the detective business. Well, when one of your organization gets killed it's bad for business to let the killer get away with it. It's bad all around—bad for that one organization, bad for every detective everywhere. Third, I'm a detective and expecting me to run criminals down and then let them go free is like asking a dog to catch a rabbit and let it go. It can be done, all right, and sometimes it is done, but it's not the natural thing." (P. 226)

Spade's remarks convey a method of dealing with the world much like the Op's personal code of behavior. At least partially as a result of their awareness of the haphazard, irrational way the universe operates, both men have developed a system of personal conduct that largely ignores the messy business of personal emotions and human morality. Certainly they are both openly suspicious of what they consider foolish romanticism or sentimental feelings, and both attempt to organize their lives along surer, more objectified guidelines. The detective business offers them such guidelines: if someone hires your services, you need not judge the client or the morality of what you are hired to do. As Spade indicates in the following passage, a detective can ignore subtleties of law and morality as long as he is successful in the end:

"At one time or another I've had to tell everybody from the Supreme Court down to go to hell, and I've got away with it. I got away with it because I never let myself forget that a day of reckoning was coming. I never forget that when the day of reckoning comes I want to be all set to march into headquarters pushing a victim in front of me, saying: 'Here, you chumps, is your criminal.' As long as I can do that I can put my thumb to my nose and wriggle my fingers at all the laws in the book. The first time I can't do it my name's mud. There hasn't been a first time yet. This isn't going to be it. That's flat." (P. 184)

Like the Op, Spade prefers to handle his dealings with others in a businesslike manner. For instance, when Joel Cairo enters his office, Spade greets him with the same tone and the same gesture which he used with Brigid. He does not allow the fact that Cairo is homosexual and Brigid an extremely attractive woman to affect his professional demeanor. "Spade rocked back in his chair and asked: 'Now what can I do for you, Mr. Cairo?' The amiable negligence of his tone, his motion in the chair, were precisely as they had been when he had addressed the same question to Brigid O'Shaughnessy the previous day" (p. 44). Likewise, Spade dismisses Brigid's confession that she had lied to them—and thus indirectly caused Miles's death—by reminding her of the professional, monetary basis of his work. "We believed your two hundred dollars. . . . I mean that you paid us more than if you'd been telling the truth . . . and enough more to make it all right" (p. 33). Such things as death and deception, Spade notes calmly, are simply part of the detective's job. "He [Miles] knew what he was doing. They're the chances we take" (p. 34). Even more mercenary is Spade's half-joking remark to Effie that Miles's death may be good for business. "I think we've got a future. I always had an idea that if Miles would go off and die somewhere we'd stand a better chance of thriving" (p. 43). What Spade represents, then, at least on the surface, is a man as ruthlessly dedicated to his profession as the Op is and a man who is confident and efficient in this dedication—a combination of qualities that Hammett felt was an accurate representation of how real-life private detectives wanted to appear. As Hammett describes Spade in the 1934 Modern Library edition of *The Maltese Falcon*, Spade was intended to be just such an ideal hard-boiled detective.

> He is a dream man in the sense that he is what most of the private detectives I worked with would like to have been and what quite a few of them in their cockier moments thought they approached. For your private detective does not—or did not ten years ago when he was my colleague—want to be an erudite solver of riddles in the Sherlock Holmes manner; he wants to be a hard and shifty fellow, able to take care of himself in any situation, able to get the best of anybody he comes in contact with, whether criminal, innocent by-stander or client.[4]

But if Spade embodies the ideal image of the private eye almost perfectly—sexy, tough, capable—there are other aspects of his personality that make him a considerably more complex character than most hard-boiled detectives. Spade's cool efficiency, tough-guy exterior, and code of professional ethics represent standard attributes of our usual notion of the detective. Unlike most other detective writers, however, Hammett goes beyond the standard clichés to explain and justify his detective's *modus operandi*. Both

Spade's personal conduct and his code of professional ethics are shown to evolve from what is a fairly sophisticated philosophical position—a position virtually identical to the Op's view that the universe is composed of a random series of unrelated, often destructive events.[5] Although Spade tries to justify his actions to Brigid on the basis of a simple, primitive system of "I won't play the sap," there is a more complicated motivation also at work. Spade's refusal to be a "sap"—a self-consciously hard-boiled, simplistic avowal—is actually a distillation of a complex view of man's position in the universe and of the options available to him in order to survive. Spade presents these views in an illuminating parable about a past case of his which involved a man named Flitcraft who believed, like most people, that life was "a clean orderly sane responsible affair" (p. 67). Flitcraft, a man with a normal life, family, and job, discovered one day that accident rules one's life when a beam fell from a building and narrowly missed him.[6] As Spade explains it: "He, the good citizen-husband-father, could be wiped out between office and restaurant by the accident of a falling beam. He knew then that men died at haphazard like that, and lived only while blind chance spared them. It was not, primarily, the injustice of it that disturbed him: he accepted that after the first shock. What disturbed him was the discovery that in sensibly ordering his affairs, he had got out of step, and not into step, with life" (p. 66). Life, then, is seen by Spade to be a random affair, and all of its elements that we think are special and meaningful—birth, love, marriage, death—are nothing but accidents of time and circumstance. The fact that Flitcraft reverted to his old ways when he moved to another city is not inconsistent as Spade sees it ("He adjusted himself to beams falling, and then no more of them fell, and he adjusted himself to them not falling" [p. 67]), and Spade believes there is an important lesson to be learned from this episode. He relates this story to Brigid O'Shaughnessy the first time she visits his apartment; the oddly abrupt manner of its delivery—coming as it does in the opening paragraph of a chapter and seemingly unrelated to what has gone on before— suggests the importance he attaches to Flitcraft.

> In his bedroom that was a living-room now the wall-bed was up, Spade took Brigid O'Shaughnessy's hat and coat, made her comfortable in a

padded rocking chair, and telephoned the Hotel Belvedere. Cairo had not returned from the theater. Spade left his telephone number with the request that Cairo call him as soon as he came in. Spade sat down in the armchair beside the table and without any preliminary, without an introductory remark of any sort, began to tell the girl about a thing that had happened some years before in the Northwest. He talked in a steady matter-of-fact voice that was devoid of emphasis or pauses, though now and then he repeated a sentence slightly rearranged, *as if it were important that each detail be related exactly as it had happened.* (P. 63, italics mine)

Brigid's response is one of polite interest ("How perfectly fascinating" [p. 67]), but she does not fully understand what Spade is telling her until the climactic scene when Spade explains why he must turn her in. In this exchange, Spade applies the implications of the Flitcraft story to his own situation: nothing is fixed, no values are absolute unless they are those which you yourself have arrived at in order to survive. A person can count only on oneself; the moment another person is allowed to affect or control you, you are once more at the mercy of forces beyond your control. And, of course, love is the most dangerous demand that can be made on a person, for it can force a man to "play the sap" and abandon those defenses of job and code which are his only means of stabilizing a random, fluctuating world. The overriding fear is that love will not last, and when it goes, you have nothing between you and the devastating knowledge of falling beams.

Because of his fear of being played for a sap, Spade, like all but one of Hammett's heroes (the exception is Nick Charles in *The Thin Man*), retreats into his job and the consolations and securities that it offers. With its clear set of rules and its simple answers to complex questions, Spade's job enables him to survive. But the cost, as with the Op, is high as Hammett sees it. When Spade rejects Brigid's claims that love matters more than anything else, he does so because of a fundamental philosophical, psychological, and linguistic distrust of the concept; after listing eight reasons why he should turn her over to the police, he asks her: "Now on the other side we've got what? All we've got is the fact that maybe you love me and maybe I love you" (p. 227). When this distrust of the abstract concept of love is combined with a distrust of Brigid's motives ("you've counted on me the same as you counted on that with the others," [p. 227]), Spade's decision to turn Brigid in is inevitable. Yet the ramifications of that decision are ambiguous, for such an ending purposefully undercuts the sureties we expect at the conclusion of a mystery novel. Following the emotional scene with Brigid, the police arrive and Spade appears to be completely at ease with his decision to abandon her.

> He looked at Dundy, drew his brows together, leaned forward to peer into the Lieutenant's face, and *burst out laughing.*
> "What the hell's the matter with your little playmate, Tom? He looks heartbroken." *He laughed again.* . . .
> "Cut it, Sam," Tom grumbled. "We didn't think—"
> "Like hell he didn't," *Spade said merrily.* (P. 228, italics mine)

Spade's jocular demeanor in this scene certainly suggests that his decision has been a liberating one—free of the messy, disruptive influence of Brigid and her talk of love, Spade is comfortable and rightly back where he belongs in the masculine comradeship of other detectives and the cheerfully gruff rivalry of maverick private eye against the police. Yet in the final scene back in his office while he is alone with his secretary, Effie—who acts throughout the novel as a kind of conscience figure, as we shall see—Spade appears to be changed. When Effie criticizes his decision by saying, "You did that, Sam, to her?" his defense, based on job and code ("Your Sam's a detective. . . . She did kill Miles, Angel . . . offhand, like that" [p. 229]), does not change her evident repulsion. "She escaped from his arms as if it had hurt her. 'Don't, please, don't touch me,' she said brokenly. 'I know—I know you're right. You're right. But don't touch me now—not now.' Spade's face became pale as his collar" (p. 229). Like Dinah and Gabrielle, then, her final assessment of Spade is that he has given up too much of his own humanity in order to prevail. But Hammett refuses to provide us with a final answer to Spade's decision. He leaves intact his character's ambiguity and mystery by ending the novel not with a jubilant Spade whose fierce insistence on professional and personal honor has been exonerated and who will go on to conquer more villains but with the image of Spade sitting quietly alone at his desk, awaiting the arrival of his partner's wife, Iva, with whom he has had an affair and whom he now despises.

The corridor-door's knob rattled. Effie Perine turned quickly and went into the outer office, shutting the door behind her. When she came in again she shut it behind her. She said in a small flat voice: "Iva is here."

Spade, looking at his desk, nodded almost imperceptibly.

"Yes," he said, and shivered. "Well, send her in." (P. 229)

Despite the similarities in personal philosophy, there is one detail in these last words of the novel—Spade's "shivering" at the prospect of Iva's entrance—that indicates the most important difference between the Op and Spade. We could never imagine the Op "shivering" with emotion in response to almost any situation. With the important exception of the Op's rage in Personville, he seems to have successfully eliminated personal feelings from his dealings with others. There is no romantic involvement between either Dinah Brand or Gabrielle Leggett and the Op despite the attractiveness of these women and their willingness to become involved. The Op's strict allegiance to his job enables him to refuse such involvements and to view such refusals as signs of his principles. His feelings are aroused, of course, after he is attacked in *Red Harvest*, but this is a blind rage at an impersonal enemy— the city of Personville—rather than an emotional response to people he cares about. Significantly, in both *The Dain Curse* and *Red Harvest* the Op neither hates the villain nor loves the heroine; what feelings he does have revolve more around his job than around the people he comes in contact with. With Spade, however, the situation is very different. Spade may well be able to carry through the necessary actions called for by his code, as when he turns in Brigid O'Shaughnessy at the end of the novel, but this is an emotionally wrenching process. By the time the police arrive, Spade has regained control and is able to act the cool professional once more. But during the exchange with Brigid, the intensity of his feelings is obvious. As Brigid frantically works to influence Spade by appealing to his sexuality, his love, and finally his compassion, she makes full use of her considerable talents of persuasion. And even though Spade understands that much or all of what she is saying may be self-serving, he is not unaffected by her performance. His face goes from pale to yellow-white, and when he tells Brigid finally that he refuses to help her, the intensity of his emotions is obvious. "Blood streaked Spade's eyeballs now and his long-held smile had become a frightful grimace. He cleared his throat huskily and said: 'Making speeches is no damned good now.' He put a hand on her shoulder. The hand shook and jerked" (p. 225). The Op is never this moved, for his code has successfully displaced "human foolishness like love"; Spade relies on the code as well, but he struggles against the fierce inner feelings that are so potentially dangerous.

Indications of Spade's inner intensity appear frequently in the novel. Hammett's repeated references to Spade's "Satanic" and "wolfish" qualities are only the most obvious instances. During various important dramatic scenes, Spade's eyes are said to "burn"—in the last scene with Brigid they "burn madly" (p. 226), just as they "burned yellowly" before the two made love for the first time (p. 93). Although Hammett far more frequently emphasizes the *absence* of emotion in Spade's eyes and mannerisms, there are strong indications that such absences are deliberately imposed by Spade, usually either to convey the appearance of icy control to others or to convince himself that he can keep things together internally. For example, during several moments of great tension, Spade's habit of ritualistically rolling a cigarette from his packet of Bull Durham is described by Hammett in elaborate detail. As has been pointed out by critic Irving Malin, these responses should probably remind us of similar attempts by Hemingway's heroes (as with Nick Adams in "Big Two-Hearted River") to maintain their inner composure by exerting physical control of their immediate actions. A good example of such a scene—similar to that in *Red Harvest* when the Op wakes up to find Dinah Brand dead—occurs when Sam wakes to the phone call informing him of his partner's death. In his description of Spade's reaction after he has hung up the phone, Hammett carefully conveys this distance that Spade works to maintain between himself and the world—a distance that Hammett underscores through diction that suggests a detachment even between Sam and his own body parts.

> Spade's thick fingers made a cigarette with deliberate care, sifting a measured quantity of tan flakes down into curved paper, spreading the flakes so that they lay equal at the ends with a slight depression in the

middle, thumbs rolling the paper's inner edge down and up under the outer edge as forefingers pressed it over, thumbs and fingers sliding to the paper cylinder's end to hold it even while tongue licked the flap, left forefingers and thumb pinching their end and lifting the other to Spade's mouth. He picked up the pigskin and nickel lighter that had fallen to the floor, manipulated it, and with the cigarette burning in a corner of his mouth stood up. (P. 12)

For the next several pages, nothing in Spade's action indicates that the report of Archer's death has affected him emotionally. When a cop asks him if he wants to look at Miles's body, Spade's laconic answer surprises even the policeman.

> "Coming down for a look at him before he's moved?"
> Spade said: "No."
> Tom halted astride the fence and looked back at Spade with surprised eyes.
> Spade said: "You've seen him. You'd see everything I could."
> Tom, still looking at Spade, nodded doubtfully and withdrew his leg over the fence. (P. 15)

Later, when a detective tries to give his condolences ("It's tough, him getting it like that. Miles had his faults same as the rest of us, but I guess he must've had some good points too"), Spade's reply—"I guess so"—is said to be delivered "in a tone that was utterly meaningless" (p. 16).

Such responses to his partner's death are, at first, likely to strike us as a shocking departure from the traditional detective's intense sense of loyalty.[7] But we soon begin to realize that this icy control is often only an act, for his exterior calm breaks down on numerous occasions. He is able to maintain his professional calm with Brigid O'Shaughnessy during her second visit to the office and cuts short her show of emotion over Miles's death with a rough, tough-guy dismissal. "Stop it. He knew what he was doing. They're the chances we take" (p. 34). Moments later, however, Spade loses some of his cool demeanor when Brigid makes an emotional appeal to him. "Spade's face reddened and he looked down at the floor, muttering: 'Now you are dangerous'" (p. 37). Throughout his dealings with Brigid, Spade similarly appears to fight for emotional control. When he kisses her for the first time, for instance, we are told that "his face was hard and furious," and moments later when he tries to talk to her, he is "trying to make himself speak calmly" (p. 60). This inner conflict reaches its climax in the final scene with Brigid, when Spade must struggle against his attraction for her.

Spade's running battle with Lieutenant Dundy is another obvious example of his violent emotions. After being forced to stand by indignantly and receive verbal and physical punishment from Dundy, Spade afterwards works himself into a frenzy of outrage that continues out of control for five minutes, only to be ended as abruptly as it began.

> Red rage came suddenly into his face and he began to talk in a harsh guttural voice. Holding his maddened face in his hands, glaring at the floor, he cursed Dundy for five minutes without break, cursed him obscenely, blasphemously, repetitiously, in a harsh guttural voice.
>
> Then he took his face out of his hands, looked at the girl, grinned sheepishly, and said, "Childish, huh? I know, but, by God, I do hate being hit without hitting back." (P. 84)

Following this tirade, Brigid tells him, "You're the wildest person I've ever met" (p. 85),[8] and others in the novel agree with this assessment of Spade's character. Thus when Spade launches into another of his verbal rampages at the young thug Wilmer[9] ("I'll kill him. I don't like him. He makes me nervous. I'll kill him the first time he gets in my way. I won't give him an even break. I won't give him a chance. I'll kill him"), Gutman observes tolerantly, "Well, sir, I must say you have a most violent temper" (p. 115)—a comment which he echoes in the final meeting of all the principals. "You are certainly a most headstrong individual" (p. 180).

This combination of volatility and control reinforces the mystery surrounding Spade, for it makes his character difficult to assess. We are often taken by surprise at ferocity which does not seem called for by the moment and at utter passivity in other situations that would seem to provoke passion. These mercurial moods help make Spade appealing and attractive to other characters in the novel; his personal magnetism is strong enough to develop a kind of bemused tolerance for his moody outbursts and a strong sense of loyalty on the part of those who are drawn to him. Spade's secretary, Effie Perine, provides services that go far beyond those of a typical employer-employee relationship; his lawyer, Mr. Wise, repeatedly is willing to drop everything to assist him; Luke, the house detective at the hotel where Cairo is staying, says at one point to Spade, "I'm willing to go all the way with you all the time" (p. 140). We see similar grudging admiration and even affection in the attitude of Detective-sergeant Tom Polhaus towards Spade and eventually even in that of Gutman, who goes so far as to ask Spade to join them on their trip to Constantinople. "Well, sir, frankly I'd like to have you along. You're a man to my liking, a man of many resources and nice judgment" (p. 216).

The compelling complexity of Spade's character—a blend of passion and controlled coldness, arrogance and humor, and physical intensity—is compounded still further by his own self-conscious posturing. His personality seems to be an endless series of roles and masks. Even when he is completely by himself we cannot be sure we are seeing the "real" Sam Spade, as witnessed by his habit of retreating into ritualized behavior when he is alone to assure himself that he has control over his emotions. Some of Spade's roles, of course, are easy to recognize and analyze, as when he rigidly maintains his composure when threatened by Cairo, Gutman, or the police or when he adopts the blatantly insincere tone of concern with Iva. (Iva herself realizes Spade has only been playing a role with her, as indicated by her bitter complaint to him: "I haven't any rights at all it seems, when you're concerned. I thought I did. *I thought your pretending to love me gave me—*" [p. 62, italics mine].) As a detective, Spade must often rely on his acting ability, much as the Op did, to see him through difficult spots.[10] For instance, when Spade goes back to Gutman to demand that he cooperate with him, he puts on an elaborate and effective show of wild, untamed fury; after speaking to Gutman "in a low furious voice," Spade theatrically throws a glass at the table, smashing its contents over the table and floor, and, following another angry outburst, makes his exit by slamming the door. Throughout this violent outburst, Spade appears to be almost completely out of control and even laughs "crazily" at one point (p. 115). We are given no hint that this has all been an act until the next chapter opens with the following revealing passage:

"Spade rode down from Gutman's in an elevator. His lips were dry and rough in a face otherwise pale and damp. When he took out his handkerchief to wipe his face he saw his hand trembling. He grinned at it and said, 'Whew!' so loudly that the elevator-operator turned his head over his shoulder and asked: 'Sir?'" (p. 116).

This ability to manipulate his actions, facial expressions, and voice to create a specific kind of impression is what finally makes Spade such an enigma. Hammett repeatedly describes Spade creating whatever facial expressions he needs under the circumstances—an ability that effectively masks whatever real feelings he may be having. Consider the implications of the following descriptions:

> He made his eyes dull with boredom. (P. 21)

> His face while he smoked was, except for occasional slight and aimless movements of his lower lip, so still and reflective that it seemed stupid; but when Cairo presently moaned and fluttered his eyelids Spade's face became bland, and he put the beginning of a friendly smile into his eyes and mouth. (P. 49)

> Spade sat on the corner of his desk beside the telephone and rolled a cigarette. His mouth was a hard complacent v. His eyes, watching his fingers make the cigarette, smoldered over lower lids drawn up straight. The door opened and Iva Archer came in. Spade said, "Hello, honey," in a voice as lightly amiable as his face had suddenly become. (P. 105)

Since the reader constantly sees Spade adopting whatever role seems most expedient, it becomes impossible for us to be certain of any of his intentions. One of the most crucial and unsettling examples of this unreadability occurs in the dramatic encounter with Cairo, Gutman, Brigid, and Wilmer near the end of the novel. Spade's seemingly illegal and callous actions—his willingness to assist the criminals in their escape, to share the spoils, and to present Wilmer as a fall guy—seem carried out with sincerity, yet this may all be another act, devised to draw the criminals out and give Spade more details about their crimes. This latter interpretation appears quite likely, since, in a later exchange, Spade sounds very much as if he is leading Gutman on. "A fall-guy is what I asked for, and he's not a fall-guy unless he's a cinch to take the fall. Well, to cinch that I've got to know what's what. . . . I've got to know what happened so I can be sure the parts that won't fit in are covered up" (pp. 199–200). But, in the end, we cannot be certain about anything: was Spade really interested in going in with the criminals? did he really love Brigid or was he just using her to discover the full implications behind Miles's death? is he a man who sustains his integrity in a corrupt world or is he a man who disguises his fears of people and love by an insistence on job and honor?

This theme of deception and illusion is subtly reinforced throughout *The Maltese Falcon* by the novel's setting. As in *The Dain Curse*, the detective is operating in San Francisco, but in this later novel the city plays a far more significant role. In the second chapter, when Spade is called out to view his partner's body, we are told that "San Francisco's night-fog, thin, clammy, and penetrant, blurred the street" (p. 12), while Alcatraz's foghorn serves as an ominous chorus as it sounds "half a dozen times a minute" with its "dull moans" (p. 12). Such an atmosphere is almost gothic in its evocation of mystery and veiled menace and is appropriate not only as a mood setter but also, in a more subtle way, as an indicator of character. During the climactic scene at the novel's conclusion when Spade is explaining to Gutman why a fall guy is needed, he remarks: "This is my city and my game. I could manage to land on my feet—sure—this time, but the next time I tried to put over a fast one they'd stop me so fast I'd swallow my teeth. Hell with that. You birds'll be in New York or Constantinople or some place else. I'm in business here" (p. 185). The reasons why he feels such a strong affinity with "his" city lie in his own character: he understands and accepts the duplicity and corruption that he finds in the city's government because it so accurately reflects his vision of the world.

"Most things in San Francisco can be bought or taken" (p. 56), Spade tells Brigid, and certainly events in the novel support this claim. Although the city lacks the undisguised violence and criminality that marked Personville, San Francisco's slicker, more sophisticated style of politics is just as fundamentally corrupt. The city's district attorney is a more subtle manipulator of the city's courts and police than was Pete Noonan or Elihu Willsson, but his administration seems just as unconcerned with justice. He is eager to resolve the Archer-Thursby murders, but he is also more interested in constructing a dramatic case that will satisfy both newspapers and juries than he is in really arriving at the truth. As with many of Hammett's characters, the district attorney relies on a personal system that will tie up all loose ends, and he seeks confirmation of that system exclusively. When he questions Spade about his involvement in the case, the private detective refuses to cooperate by saying: "You wouldn't want the information I could give you, Bryan. You couldn't use it. It'd plop this gambler's-revenge-scenario for you" (p. 155). Later on, when Sam is explaining to Gutman why they must turn in Wilmer, he reveals a good deal about the operation of San Francisco's legal system.

"Bryan is like most district attorneys. He's more interested in how his records will look on paper than in anything else. He'd rather drop a doubtful case than try it and have it go against him. I don't know that he ever deliberately framed anybody he believed innocent, but I can't imagine him letting himself believe them innocent if he could scrape up, or twist into shape, proof of his guilt. To be sure of convicting one man he'll let a half a dozen equally guilty accomplices go free—if trying to convict them all might confuse his case. That's the choice we'll give him and he'll gobble it up. He wouldn't want to know about the falcon. He'll be tickled pink to persuade himself that everything the punk tells him about it is a lot of chewing-gum, an attempt to muddle things up. Leave that end up to me. I can show him that if he starts fooling around trying to gather up everybody he's going to have a tangled case that no jury will be able to make heads or tails of, while if he sticks to the punk he can get a conviction standing on his head." (P. 189)

San Francisco, then, like everything else in the novel, has a basic undercurrent of deception: even the most carefully regimented and controlled systems—the legal or political systems, for example—can be used and manipulated.

Thus, throughout *The Maltese Falcon* Hammett's intent is to demonstrate that life is too deceptive, too complex, too contradictory, too confused to be "solved." Although Spade is the major example, other characters in the novel illustrate as well that duplicity, fragmentation, and contradiction will always keep people from being explainable, categorizable wholes. Brigid, for example, is a bewildering, enigmatic woman who, like Spade, is undecipherable. Like Dinah Brand in *Red Harvest*, she manipulates her attractiveness to others for her own advantage, but Brigid is even more shrewdly calculating. She pays meticulous attention to her clothes, selecting "two shades of blue . . . because of her eyes" (p. 4). Later when Spade visits her apartment she is wearing "a satin gown of the blue shade called Artoise that season, with chalcedony shoulder-straps, and her stockings and slippers were Artoise" (p. 56); she also affects what Spade calls a "schoolgirl manner" to help create an image of feminine vulnerability and helpless naïveté (p. 57). Brigid acts out a role from the beginning of the novel, and at various times she goes through three separate changes of names.

Spade openly confronts her with her acting in their second meeting; after a long impassioned speech, delivered on her knees, in which she implores his help, Spade answers: "You won't need much of anybody's help. You're good. You're very good. It's chiefly your eyes, I think, and that throb you get into your voice when you say things like 'Be generous, Mr. Spade'" (p. 36). Later he says, "You aren't exactly the sort of person you pretend to be, are you?" (p. 57)—a question that has reverberations for everyone in the novel. Spade even playfully applauds Brigid's masterful performances and offers friendly advice on a few occasions. "You're good. You're very good," he tells her in one scene (p. 36) and then later warns her, "Don't overdo it" (p. 68) when he feels she is hamming it up. In fact, part of Brigid's attractiveness for Spade is that she, like Spade, is constantly acting, constantly lying. She admits to Spade, "I have always been a liar" (p. 90)—a confession that simply confirms what is obvious and makes any assessment of her all the more difficult. Are we to pity her when she tells Spade, "Oh, I'm so tired . . . so tired of it all, of myself, of lying and thinking up lies, and of not knowing what is a lie and what is the truth" (p. 92)? Or is that, too, merely another ploy? At the end of the novel Spade claims that Brigid was, in fact, merely acting out another role ("You came into my bed to stop me asking questions" [p. 224]), and her cold-blooded murder of Miles Archer is an indisputable piece of evidence against her. Yet Brigid acts out her part to the very end, never once abandoning her role as the put-upon victim of circumstances; appropriately, then, the final view of Brigid, as with Spade, is purposefully ambiguous.

> She looked at him, saying nothing. He moved his shoulder and said: "Well, a lot of money would have been at least one more item on the other side of the scales."
> She put her face up to his face. Her mouth was slightly open with lips a little thrust out. She whispered: "If you loved me you'd need nothing more on that side."
> She put her mouth to his, slowly, her arms around him, and came into his arms. She was in his arms when the door-bell rang. (P. 228)

Thus Hammett structures this scene in such a way that no final judgment can emerge. Is Brigid, right up to the very moment the police arrive, trying to change Spade's mind? Or does she hold him even after his decision because she really is in love with him? Is she a cunning, calculating killer whom we must condemn on strict moral grounds? Or should the fact that "Miles . . . was a louse" (p. 225) who "licked his lips" (p. 22) and looked her up and down temper our judgment? Her character, like Spade's, is a perplexing, nebulous mystery.

Although Effie Perine, Spade's secretary, is less dramatically mysterious, she, too, is often difficult to fathom. She seems the opposite of Spade in almost every way—honest, truthful, trustworthy, open—and yet she obviously cares for and respects Spade. Her willingness to serve Spade unhesitatingly is demonstrated on numerous occasions as she cheerfully runs errands that extend her day well beyond normal office hours (after one of these errands she is said to slump down on a couch, "smiling cheerfully up at him through her weariness" [p. 177]) and deals with the irate police, unsavory characters, and bloody corpses that occasionally find their way into the office. At one point she is even willing to inconvenience and possibly endanger both herself and her mother by agreeing to take Brigid into her home. For his part, Spade is obviously appreciative of Effie, constantly patting her shoulder, touching her cheek—once accepting a massage when he has a headache (p. 158)—and on one occasion even rubbing his face against her hip (p. 28). Their emotional and physical intimacy is emphasized in scenes such as the following one, where Effie takes Spade to task for using Iva Archer as he has:

> The girl took his hat from his head and put it on the desk. Then she leaned over and took the tobacco sack and the papers from his inert fingers. "The police think I shot Thursby," he said.
>
> "Who is he?" she asked, separating a cigarette-paper from the packet, sifting tobacco into it.
>
> "Who do you think I shot?" he asked. When she ignored that question he said: "Thursby's the guy Miles was supposed to be tailing for the Wonderly girl."
>
> Her thin fingers finished shaping the cigarette. She licked it, smoothed it, twisted its ends, and placed it between Spade's lips. He said, "Thanks, honey," put an arm around her slim waist, and rested his cheek wearily against her hip, shutting his eyes.
>
> "Are you going to marry Iva?" she asked, looking down at his pale brown hair.
>
> "Don't be silly," he muttered. The unlighted cigarette bobbed up and down with the movement of his lips.
>
> "She doesn't think it's silly. Why should she—the way you've played around with her?"
>
> He sighed and said: "I wish I'd never seen her."
>
> "Maybe you do now." A trace of spitefulness came into the girl's voice. "But there was a time."
>
> "I never know what to do or say to women except that way," he grumbled, "and then I didn't like Miles."
>
> "That's a lie, Sam," the girl said. "You know I think she's a louse, but I'd be a louse too if it would give me a body like hers." (P. 28)

In the moments that follow this exchange, Effie tries to make eye contact with Spade—"bending over for a better view of his face"— suggesting that she is familiar with his evasions and his acting. She finally tells him, "Look at me, Sam," and when he does she directly voices her concern. "You worry me. . . . You always think you know what you're doing, but you're too slick for your own good, and some day you're going to find it out" (p. 29).

Perhaps because of this closeness, Effie is the only character who can influence Spade's actions. Spade, a man who prides himself on his stubbornness and independence (when Detective Polhaus claims that Dundy is "as pigheaded as you are," Spade smiles and announces: "No, he's not. . . . He just thinks he is" [p. 146]), relies on Effie in a way that he does on no one else in making decisions. Early on in the book, he asks Effie's opinion of Brigid— "What do you think of Wonderly?" (p. 43). Not only does Effie offer her opinions about such matters, she also serves as the only sort of conscience that Spade possesses. For example, when he responds to her judgment that Brigid is "all right" by saying: "I wonder. . . . Anyway she's given up seven hundred smacks in two days, and that's all right," Effie primly sits up straight and scolds him. "Sam, if that girl's in trouble and you let her down, or take advantage of it to bleed her, I'll never forgive you, never have any respect for you, as long as I live" (p. 43). Perhaps the best example of Effie's subtle control over Spade occurs when he announces that he is not going out to look for Brigid, who has disappeared while taking an unexplained detour to the docks. The exchange which follows not only demonstrates that Spade is not the emotionless professional he pretends to be but also reinforces Effie's role as Spade's conscience figure:

> She glared at him between tightened lids. "Sam Spade," she said, "you're the most contemptible man God ever made when you want to be. Because she did something without confiding in you you'd sit there and do nothing when you know she's in danger, when you know she might be—"
> Spade's face flushed. He said stubbornly: "She's pretty capable of taking care of herself and she knows where to come for help when she thinks she needs it, and when it suits her."
> "That's spite," the girl cried, "and that's all it is! You're sore because she did something on her own hook, without telling you. Why shouldn't she? You're not so damned honest, and you haven't been so much on the level with her, that she should trust you completely. . . . If you don't go down there this very minute, Sam, I will and I'll take the police down there." Her voice trembled, broke, and was thin and wailing. "Oh, Sam, go!"
> He stood up cursing her. Then he said: "God! It'll be easier on my head than sitting here listening to you squawk." He looked at his watch. "You might as well lock up and go home." (P. 159)

Throughout the novel, Effie shows this kind of support for Brigid, but the basis of her support is never clear. While Spade refers once to her woman's intuition (p. 43), there is no real source for Effie's trust in Brigid—she simply and mysteriously believes in her. Given Effie's intimacy with Sam, we might expect some measure of jealousy on her part, but instead Effie seems as passionately protective of Brigid, whom she has only seen briefly twice, as she is of Spade. After Effie answers a phone call from Brigid, for example, her reaction is hysterical.

> "It was Miss O'Shaughnessy," she said wildly. "She wants you. She's at the Alexandria—in danger. Her voice was—oh, it was awful, Sam! —and something happened to her before she could finish. Go help her, Sam!"
> Spade put the falcon down on the desk and scowled gloomily. "I've got to take care of this fellow first," he said, pointing his thumb at the thin corpse on the floor.
> She beat his chest with her fists, crying: "No, no—you've got to go to her. Don't you see, Sam?" (P. 166)

This uncritical acceptance of Brigid compounds still further the book's mystery: if Effie is the "moral voice" in the novel—and her role as a good woman seems carefully drawn—then what does that say about Spade's rejection of Brigid? When Spade returns to his office and defends himself from Effie's censure by reminding her that Brigid *did* kill Miles, Effie's response is illogical and perplexing. "I know—I know you're right. You're right. But don't touch me now—not now" (p. 229). Thus, like Brigid and Spade, Effie Perine is an enigma: she is a loyal, honest, young working girl who lives with her mother and who defends to the end a thief and a killer.

The thieves in the novel—Joel Cairo, Casper Gutman, and Wilmer—are similarly paradoxical; Hammett builds their characters from varied, often contradictory stereotypes. Gutman, for instance, is a physically grotesque figure whose ringlets and "soap-bubble" body would seem to make him an unlikely villain in a hard-boiled novel.

> Spade went in. A fat man came to meet him. The fat man was flabbily fat with bulbous pink cheeks and lips and chins and neck, with a great soft egg of a belly that was all his torso, and pendant cones for arms and legs. As he advanced to meet Spade, all his bulbs rose and shook and fell separately with each step, in the manner of clustered soap-

bubbles not yet released from the pipe through which they had been blown. His eyes, made small by fat puffs around them, were dark and sleek. Dark ringlets thinly covered his broad scalp. (P. 108)

Gutman's pleasant personality, sense of humor and wit, urbane manner of speech, and tasteful formal dress all undercut the fact that he is a dangerous opponent, for whom treachery and murder come very easy. There is also a strong element of the romantic, dashing adventurer in Gutman. Hammett mitigates his disgusting body and obvious treachery with a quixotic appeal that Spade never has. In the following scene when the falcon is found to be a fraud, Gutman transforms the violent, murderous attempt to steal the falcon into a "quest." He is so persuasive that Cairo is willing to forget his bungling of the theft and his double cross of Wilmer.

> Gutman's jaw sagged. He blinked vacant eyes. Then he shook himself and was—by the time his bulbs had stopped jouncing—again a jovial fat man. "Come, sir," he said good-naturedly, "there's no need of going on like that. Everybody errs at times and you may be sure this is every bit as severe a blow to me as to anyone. Yes, that is the Russian's hand, there's no doubt of it. Well, sir, what do you suggest? Shall we stand here and shed tears and call each other names? Or shall we"—he paused and his smile was a cherub's—"go to Constantinople? . . . For seventeen years I have wanted that little item and have been trying to get it. If I must spend another year on the quest—well, sir—that will be an additional expenditure in time only"—his lips moved silently as he calculated—"five and fifteen-seventeenths per cent."
> The Levantine [Cairo] giggled and cried: "I go with you!" (P. 214)

Joel Cairo and Wilmer are also examples of stereotypes undercut by contradictions. Hammett clearly portrays Cairo as a homosexual who speaks in a "high-pitched thin voice" and sits "primly" with his legs crossed at the ankle (p. 44). But Joel is far from the cowardly sissy that the stereotype suggests. His effeminate appearance belies the spunky, spirited way he stands up to Spade and to the police. When he tries to search Spade's office for the falcon, Spade physically overwhelms him, takes his gun, and knocks him unconscious. When he wakes up Cairo criticizes Spade for striking an unarmed man, asks for the return of his gun, and then calmly turns it once more on Spade. "Cairo pointed the pistol at Spade's chest. 'You will please keep your hands on the top of the desk,' Cairo said earnestly. 'I intend to search your offices'" (p. 53). Cairo's lover, Wilmer, is also a paradox: he seems at first to be a hard-boiled cliché—a tough, hostile hired gun. But this is undercut from the very beginning of the novel by Hammett when he has Spade call the boy a "gunsel." This term, as William F. Nolan points out in his casebook on Hammett, is not, as most people assume, another word for a gunman but is a colloquialism in the homosexual community for a kept man.[11]

The Maltese falcon itself stands as the most central symbol for these deceptions and contradictions and, ultimately, as a symbol of mystery throughout the novel. It represents and underscores the notion that is at the base of character, plot, and theme: things are not as they seem. The falcon provides a unifying thread that ties the novel together from beginning to end. Not only does it work on a symbolic level, however, but it functions on the literal level as well: when the black paint that supposedly masks the gold and jewel-encrusted treasure is scraped away, there remains nothing but the "soft grey sheen of lead" (p. 213). All the deceptions, the violence, and the deaths have come about because the statue's *appearance* belied its reality. "It's a fake," announces Gutman hoarsely when he has examined the bird, and this judgment might well apply to virtually every element we encounter in this novel. Supposedly a *real* falcon exists somewhere, yet even it is a nebulous treasure surrounded by hundreds of years of intrigue and mythic history. Its value is measureless (as Gutman tells Spade, "There's no telling how high it could go, sir, and that's the one and the only truth about it" [p. 135]); even its proper ownership is vague and inconclusive (Gutman says of it, "An article of that value that has passed from hand to hand by such means is clearly the property of whoever can get hold of it" [p. 133]). Thus the Maltese falcon—both the fake statue and the novel—offers a final assertion that mystery is unassailable: it cannot be measured, it cannot be grasped.

5

The Glass Key: A Psychological Detective Novel

— ⋈ —

"You'd be surprised how many things there are you can't understand," he said angrily, "and never will if you keep on like this."

—Ned Beaumont, *in* The Glass Key

Hammett's fourth novel, *The Glass Key* (published in 1931), was written in the same two-year period as the previous works. In his history of the detective and crime novel, *Mortal Consequences*, Julian Symons says of it, "*The Glass Key* is the peak of Hammett's achievement, which is to say the peak of the crime writer's art in the twentieth century."[1] But Robert I. Edenbaum bluntly calls it "Hammett's least satisfactory novel."[2] Such divergent opinion about the novel characterize the peculiar public and critical reception of *The Glass Key*. There are differing opinions about the book's quality and even disagreements about how the book should be classified.[3] Is *The Glass Key* supposed to be a realistic, psychological novel that uses elements of detective fiction in its development? Or is it, like Hammett's other novels, basically a detective novel that happens to rely on certain elements of "serious" traditional fiction? Usually the problems of the book are avoided, and *The Glass Key* is taken as detective fiction simply because it was written by Dashiell Hammett.

But controversies about the book's quality and classification are very understandable, for in many ways *The Glass Key* is Hammett's most frustrating and puzzling work. It is his only book whose main character is not a detective in the traditional sense, and it is also Hammett's closest attempt at creating a conventional psychological novel. Hence, diverging categorizations of the book are responding to different aspects of its hybrid nature. As the previous chapters on *Red Harvest*, *The Dain Curse*, and *The Maltese Falcon* have suggested, the usual elements of detective fiction are frequently manipulated by Hammett to produce effects very different from those usually associated with the genre, but in *The Glass Key*, these mystery aspects—crime, clues, motive analysis, suspense, solutions—are secondary to a more traditional novelistic emphasis on character. Much more so than in the previous works, this novel attempts a psychological understanding of character. Like Sam Spade, Ned Beaumont, the main character, is a mysterious figure, and despite Hammett's emphasis on developing his character, Ned remains even more elusive than his predecessor. To some extent, this creation of a man of mystery is intended, for mystery—the mystery of emotions, motivations, and actions—lies at the center of *The Glass Key*. As in *The Maltese Falcon*, Hammett seeks here to affirm the circumfluent quality of mystery that must always overpower our attempts to order and interpret our lives. Yet *The Glass Key* is a less successful book. The effect of its ambiguity is less artistically satisfying, for Hammett spends too much effort building mystery through character alone and not enough incorporating this sense of mystery in the book's structure and imagery. Ned remains a mystery to us—not because we are convinced, as we were in *The Maltese Falcon*, that all men and women are essentially mysterious but because Hammett does not ever let us see what is going on inside him. *The Glass Key* tries harder than any of the other works to be more than a detective novel, and perhaps because of this strain, it is less successful. Yet there is no mistaking the novel's kinship to Hammett's other works—a kinship which is responsible for most of the book's successes.

The plot of *The Glass Key* bears a number of similarities to that of *Red Harvest*. Like Personville, the small, unnamed city of this novel is a lawless, sometimes violent community of the Prohibition era that is controlled by crooked politicians and warring factions of mobsters. When the novel opens, an upcoming election has disrupted the power balance: Paul Madvig, the gangster who runs the city through his own handpicked political officials, has thrown his support to Senator Henry, a powerful figure in the state's politics, in hope of eventually winning the senator's daughter, Janet. Madvig's position of leadership in the community is challenged, however, when the son of the senator, Taylor Henry, is murdered one night following an argument with Madvig over his sister. Paul's friend and advisor, Ned Beaumont—second in command to Madvig and himself an influential behind-the-scenes figure in the city's operations—volunteers to become a deputy for the city's district attorney so that he can find the killer and stifle the scandal before it can ruin Madvig's slate of candidates. Other factions quickly realize that Madvig's position as a suspect in the murder has weakened his power and influence and begin to seek a means of capitalizing on his vulnerability to gain power for themselves. Soon Madvig's chief gangster rival, Shad O'Rory, openly challenges him for control of the city, and this open warfare and back-room political scrimmaging form the framework for most of the novel's action. Yet this power struggle is secondary to the book's chronicle of the relationship between Madvig and Beaumont and the gradual disintegration of their friendship. Ned begins his investigation of Taylor Henry's death to help his friend, but by the novel's end, when Ned uncovers the fact that it was Senator Henry himself who killed his son, their friendship is over; and it is Ned, not Paul, who gets Janet Henry.

Despite this emphasis on the relationship between Ned and Paul, there remain prominent elements of a traditional detective novel: an unsolved murder, an investigation of clues and motives, and (as in *The Maltese Falcon*) a single revelation of guilt as the book concludes. Like all of Hammett's work this general structure is "traditional" in a superficial sense only, and the novel often departs from these traditional techniques. As in *The Maltese Falcon*, for example, Hammett's method of developing scenes is often deliberately oblique; typically, he thrusts the reader into the middle of an unfolding scene without providing enough background information to allow the reader to fully understand what is happening. Although Hammett gives many individual clues and specific details of the action, the elements are not placed in a context which would allow the reader to understand their significance and to make distinctions between what is essential to the solving of the murder and what is irrelevant. A good example of this type of ambiguous presentation occurs during the opening section of chapter 2, in which Ned arrives in New York. In the two pages which comprise this section, we are given the following information:

> Ned is wearing a hat which doesn't quite fit him.
>
> He is staying at a hotel off Broadway in the Forties.
>
> On his way to his hotel, at Madison Avenue, a green taxicab runs "full tilt" into the one in which Beaumont is riding.
>
> When he registers at the hotel, he is given two telephone-memorandum-slips, both dated that day, one marked 4:50 P.M. and the other 8:05 P.M. When he looks at his watch it is 8:45 P.M.
>
> The earlier slip reads: At the Gargoyle. The later one reads: At Tom & Jerry's. Will phone later. Both are signed: Jack.
>
> He is also given two sealed envelopes without postage stamps.
>
> One of the envelopes contains two sheets of paper covered by bold masculine handwriting, dated the previous day. It reads: She is staying at the Matin, room 1211, registered as Eileen Dale, Chicago. She did some phoning from the depot and connected with a man and girl who live E. 30th. They went to a lot of places, mostly speakies, probably hunting him, but don't seem to have much luck. My room is 734. Man and girl named Brook.
>
> The second envelope contains a sheet of paper, covered by the same handwriting, and is dated the same day. It reads: I saw Deward this morning, but he says he did not know Bernie was in town. Will phone later.
>
> Both messages are signed: Jack.
>
> Beaumont orders a bottle of rye whiskey and drinks steadily until he receives a phone call from Jack.
>
> When he leaves the hotel it is ten minutes past nine o'clock.[4]

Many detective writers, of course, rely on this strategy of presenting the reader with information which initially seems unconnected to the crime but whose relevance is later determined by the detective. But Hammett's method here is crucially different: not only is most of this information unassimilable because no framework has been provided to establish a context, but virtually all of the precise, specific details in this scene prove to be completely irrelevant. For instance, the information that Ned's messages are marked 4:50 P.M. and 8:05, that is 8:45 P.M. when he looks at his watch, and that is precisely 9:10 when he leaves his hotel *appears* to be significant simply because Hammett has bothered to provide it, and influenced by our expectations of the genre, we mark it down as a probable clue of some sort. Similarly, the reader is encouraged to sift through all the rest of the information in this scene. As it turns out, however, only the reference to Ned's hat is relevant to the case at all, and even that detail is only indirectly relevant since it allows Ned to blackmail Bernie into paying off a gambling debt and does not establish anything about who actually *did* murder Taylor. In short, Hammett's oblique presentation, coupled with the strategy of providing numerous irrelevant details that *seem* significant, makes it almost impossible for the reader to draw conclusions about the solution of the murder and to establish the coherency of the plot.

It can be argued that Hammett's handling of plot is much weaker in *The Glass Key* than it was in his earlier books where the plots, no matter how convoluted, are finally bound together. In *The Glass Key*, the entire basis of Ned's solution of the case arises from the fact that Taylor Henry was found with no hat on—a basis that seems both contrived and unconvincing. How, we wonder, does Ned know that the hat is so significant? When Ned reports to Paul moments after he has discovered the body, he already has seized on what will be the only clue that can incriminate the murderer. "Ned Beaumont rose, took steps toward the telephone, halted, and faced the blond man again. He spoke with slow emphasis: 'His hat wasn't there'" (p. 15). More importantly, how does he know that Taylor was even wearing a hat? During an exchange with Janet, he claims that Paul has told him that Taylor was wearing a hat, but as far as we know, Paul never tells him this. Does Ned's line of logic really make sense? Senator Henry races out of the house after his son, too rushed to put on a hat. He kills Taylor (who, despite his hurry to stop Paul, presumably *did* take time to get both a hat and a cane) and afterwards wears his son's hat home in order to disguise the fact that he hurried out of the house. When the final moment of the assignment of guilt arrives, Ned's expla-

nation consequently seems vague and arbitrary; even Ned seems
to sense this in his accusation of Henry.

> "What happened is something like this: when Taylor heard about Paul
> kissing Janet he ran after him, taking his stick with him and wearing
> a hat, though that's not as important. When you thought of what hap-
> pened to your chances of being elected—"
> The Senator interrupted him in a hoarse angry tone: "This is non-
> sense! I will not have my daughter subjected—"
> Ned Beaumont laughed brutally. "Sure it's nonsense," he said. "And
> you bringing the stick you killed him with back home, and wearing
> his hat because you'd run out bare-headed after him, is nonsense too,
> but it's nonsense that'll nail you to the cross." (P. 196)

Of all of Hammett's plots, then, this one seems to be the least
satisfactory from the traditional detective novel's standpoint. Not
only does the solution hinge on an unconvincing analysis of a
missing clue, but the detective solves the case through sheer happenstance—he is convinced from the outset of the hat's significance, yet there seems to be no logical reason for this conviction.
The Op assumes that he did not kill Dinah Brand because the
lights were off when he awoke that morning; Sam Spade knows
the identity of Miles Archer's killer from the position of the body.
Despite the thematic insistence in these books that we can never
know life or people absolutely, there are clues which, when rea-
soned out, can give answers to a "simple" question like who killed
whom. But Ned Beaumont arrives at this solution through a process outside the traditional analysis of clues. He simply knows
with complete assurance that the hat is important—an inductive
awareness that seems inconsistent with Hammett's position on
the difficulties of knowing.

One of the ways in which Hammett disguises the looseness of
the plot is his reliance on hard-boiled detective fiction's stock
pacing devices of quick action, rapid development, and unexpected shocks. This rapid pacing of the novel, enhanced by Hammett's subdivision of major chapters into brief subchapters (a device unique to *The Glass Key* among Hammett's novels), moves
us along so quickly that we probably overlook the irrelevancy of
much of the action in terms of its mystery-solution aspects. For
example, the exciting, quick-paced episode that occurs in New
York in chapter 2 *seems* connected to Ned's investigation, but

when the episode is over, nothing really has been established about Bernie's guilt or innocence. In fact, Ned's visit to New York may have had nothing at all to do with the murder—it may have been motivated only by his desire to get the money which Bernie owes him. We are never certain why the episode is included, even at the end of the book when the solution appears. Thus, much of the novel's action, like the nature of the human relationshps in the book, remains fundamentally mysterious and inexplicable.

One of the reasons why the action of *The Glass Key* is so difficult to follow is Hammett's reliance on the same kind of distanced, objective point of view that he used in *The Maltese Falcon*. Here again, Hammett uses a third-person restricted point of view and confines himself largely to neutral descriptions of what Ned does and sees, along with the presentation of various "objective information"—newspaper reports, letters, physical details of time and place—all presented without authorial commentary or interpretation. William F. Nolan summarized the effect of this distant point of view by saying: "Here Hammett himself wears the Spade mask; we are never allowed inside any of the people he writes about, we see them all once-removed; we are forced to judge them strictly on what they say and do. Hammett never used the objective approach more stringently."[5] Just as it does in *The Maltese Falcon*, this objective approach heightens the detective's inexplicability. For example, the crucial scene in which Ned stubbornly refused to help O'Rory in his plan to discredit Paul is described as follows:

> Ned Beaumont stood up. His face was pallid and damp with sweat. He looked at his torn coat-sleeve and wrist and at the blood running down his hand. His hand was trembling.
>
> O'Rory said in his musical Irish voice: "You would have it."
>
> Ned Beaumont looked up from his wrist at the white-haired men. "Yes," he said, "and it'll take some more of it to keep me from going out of here." (P. 82)

Throughout this scene and the one that follows in which Ned is horribly beaten, we are given no indication as to what is going on in Ned's mind: is he defying O'Rory because of the way he has been treated, because of loyalty to Paul, or because of pride in himself and his ability to "stand anything I've got to stand" (p.

5)? Although this point of view distances us from all the characters, it makes Ned even further removed than the others by an inventive use of names: Ned Beaumont is referred to throughout the novel only as "Ned Beaumont," never "Ned," never "Beaumont." The effect of this technique is to inject an odd kind of formality between character and narration and between character and reader that makes Ned seem even further removed.

There is one aspect of the novel, however, that is not marked by mystery and ambiguity: the depiction of political corruption. Not surprisingly, most of the critics who have praised *The Glass Key* as Hammett's finest novel do so because they admire his unrelenting presentation of the American political system—a view that is made more unsettling and terrible by its seemingly utter objectivity. For example, Martin Seymour Smith, in calling the book "Hammett's most successful novel," says that "*The Glass Key*, apparently a simple murder story, is an indictment of American urban politics only because it sets out *not* 'to take a stand.'"[6] Just as he did in *Red Harvest*, Hammett portrays corruption in *The Glass Key* in a deceptively flat, neutral manner. As in the earlier novel, the setting provides the backdrop for examples of personal, social, and political decay. The city in which the action takes place is purposely anonymous, with no individuality emerging at all except for the references to a few street names. Although modeled on Baltimore, this city, like Personville, could be anywhere in America. Hammett's depiction of corruption in this later novel, however, is even more disturbing. There is more violent action and actual death in his first novel, but the scene in which Ned is beaten and the one in which Shad O'Rory is killed are far more savage than any comparable scenes in *Red Harvest*. The effect of this brutality is even greater in *The Glass Key* because there is no outside reference—like that of the Op in *Red Harvest*—to use as some sort of measure. Here no outsider provides a normative view to suggest that we are witnessing a special, isolated instance of corruption. Ned Beaumont operates in a landscape of absolute decay which, somewhat like the landscapes of science fiction novels, seems both familiar and alien. It is familiar in the sense that we recognize the elements of greed, violence, and immorality which are embodied in the expected stereotypes: gangster chieftains, a self-serving district attorney, policemen on the take, sadistic thugs. But the absence of any outside judgment—someone to say, "This city is corrupt and evil," as the Op did in *Red Harvest*—leads to this bleak vision of the ultimate urban nightmare in which people accept and expect violence and corruption as the rule rather than the exception.

Specific examples of this corruption are easy to find in the presentation of the novel's secondary characters. District Attorney Michael Farr, for instance, is almost a caricature of a groveling, frightened puppet of his superiors. As a lackey for Paul, Farr is concerned only with keeping his job by making sure that law and city government never interfere with the profitable business of running the city. When Ned begins an explanation of his actions, Farr stops him with the comment: "That's all right, Ned. It's none of my business what you and Paul do" (p. 50). Farr's attitude that illegal activities are routine matters which can easily be overlooked if they further one's own interests is apparently shared by most of the other public officials in the city. The exchange between Ned and Paul following Ned's visit to New York clearly shows how crime in this novel is viewed by everyone concerned as being just like any other business.

> Ned Beaumont returned to his chair. "Anything happen while I was gone?" he asked as he picked up the half-filled cocktail-glass standing behind the silver shaker on the table at his elbow.
>
> "We got the muddle on the sewer-contract straightened out."
>
> Ned Beaumont sipped his cocktail and asked: "Have to make much of a cut?"
>
> "Too much. There won't be anything like the profit there ought to be, but that's better than taking a chance on stirring things up this close to election. We'll make it up on the street-work next year when the Salem and Chestnut extensions go through." (P. 58)

Similarly, the police force of the city is completely controlled from Madvig's office and owes its loyalty not to law enforcement but to Madvig personally. The police's complete lack of concern for law is portrayed in an exchange between Ned and Paul; anxious to "knock Shad loose from our little city" because he is "tired of having him around," Paul orders the police to close down most of Shad's speakeasys in town. Ned's answer to this suggestion is revealing. "You're putting Rainey [the city's police chief] in a tough spot. Our coppers aren't used to bothering with Prohibition-enforcement. They're not going to like it very much" (p. 58).

As an ongoing commentary on the decay of law and order, we have the Tim Evans case. Evans has murdered a man, but because of his connections with Madvig, he expects to be released with all charges dropped—and apparently he will be after the election is over. His case provides a kind of counterpart to Madvig's own dilemma in being accused of Taylor Henry's murder; Madvig's fate, like Evan's, hinges on the election—not on his guilt or innocence. As Ned Beaumont comments to Janet Henry, it is political control, not justice, that will determine the outcome for Madvig.

> Ned Beaumont nodded and spoke with calm certainty: "If he loses the election, loses his hold on the city and state government, they'll electrocute him."
>
> She shivered and asked in a voice that shook: "But he's safe if he wins?"
>
> Ned Beaumont nodded again. "Sure."
>
> She caught her breath. Her lips trembled so that her words came out jerkily: "Will he win?"
>
> "I think so."
>
> "And it won't make any difference then no matter how much evidence there is against him, he'll—" her voice broke, "—he'll not be in danger?"
>
> "He won't be tried," Ned Beaumont told her. (P. 137)

Thus throughout *The Glass Key* Hammett shows how political systems are run by men whose only interest is in their own power; nowhere do we see even the pretense on their part of civic duty or responsibility. Even the city's newspaper, *The Observer*, which does speak out against the corruption of the Madvig regime, is operating from its own self-serving basis: it pretends journalistic objectivity, but because it is owned by the rival political faction, it is merely a tool being used against Madvig. As Ned explains to Opal, the daughter of Madvig, the dizzying connections and back-scenes maneuverings of the anti-Madvig forces result in one certainty—that truth is being subordinated to political influence.

> She addressed him in a low voice between lips that barely moved to let the words out: "They wouldn't dare say such things if they were not true."

"That's nothing to what'll be said before they're through. . . . Politics is a tough game, snip, the way it's being played here this time. *The Observer* is on the other side of the fence and they're not worrying much about the truth of anything that'll hurt Paul. . . . Mathews does what he's told to do and prints what he's told to print." (P. 103)

This kind of absolute corruption has filtered down throughout the system, from the very top—Senator Henry, "one of the few aristocrats left in American politics" (p. 9)—to the most minor city official. The common citizen is ignored or is held in contempt by those in power; the only impact that the individual citizen can have is when he or she joins a powerless mass of voters who, although theoretically free to vote as they see fit, are actually manipulated and wooed by dishonest and self-serving politicians. Short of the most blatantly illegal act—in this case, the murder of a senator's son on the streets of a city—public officials are free to act as they wish so long as they have the power over police, newspapers, and rival factions to disguise or suppress the truth. Both Ned and Paul view the populace with distrust and condescension; the most succinct expression of the attitude of the public officials towards their constituency is found early in the book in the following exchange between them:

"Tim's wife's going to have a baby next month," Ned Beaumont said.
Madvig blew breath out in an impatient gust. "Anything to make it tougher," he complained. "Why don't they think of those things before they get in trouble? They've got no brains, none of them."
"They've got votes."
"That's the hell of it," Madvig growled. (P. 11)

Ned's practical reply to Madvig's assessment of the public's stupidity—"They've got votes"—provides an important clue as to why he has risen so rapidly in the city's power structure. Ned Beaumont is presented as a practical individual above all, a man who has figured out that the world is filthy and corruptible and who has developed a means of efficiently operating within it. As with all of Hammett's major characters, we know little about Ned Beaumont, although, like Sam Spade, he is given a variety of vivid, defining details such a his nervous habits of playing with his mustache and chewing his nails, his style of dress, his room's appearance, his taste in music. Once again, however, Hammett gives his major character almost no background—"I never told anybody where I came from," Ned tells O'Rory when asked if he came from New York (p. 76). Physically Beaumont is unlike either Spade or the Op. There are few specific details about his appearance except for a brief description in chapter 3. "Ned Beaumont leaving the train that had brought him back from New York was a clear-eyed erect tall man. Only the flatness of his chest hinted at any constitutional weakness. In color and line his face was long and elastic" (p. 46). As William F. Nolan has suggested in his casebook on Hammett, this physical description of Ned as a tall, lean man with a mustache who suffers from some sort of lung disorder, coupled with such vices as gambling and drinking, makes Ned sound a great deal like Hammett himself.[7]

Though his physical characterization is meager, Ned Beaumont is given more personality traits than the Op or even Spade; his character is, in fact, more traditionally developed. Since Ned is not really a detective, his presence in scenes is not necessarily that of an investigator. Those expectations we have of Spade and the Op because they are private detectives—toughness, shrewdness, cool efficiency—do not apply to Ned, and he must emerge without the conventions of the private eye to provide character traits. In almost all of his exterior qualities, Ned bears little resemblance to Hammett's earlier heroes; certainly the fact that Beaumont has a strong sense of proper etiquette and decorum is a striking departure from the portrayals of Spade or the Op, who pride themselves on their direct, unaffected response to social situations. Beaumont is a man of striking incongruities: a gambler, a hard-drinker, and a crony of gangsters, crooked officials, and thugs, he also plays the piano, bows when introduced to ladies, and advises his friends about what gift is proper under what circumstances ("You know more about this kind of stuff than I do," acknowledges Madvig [p. 10]). Although Ned enjoys affecting a rude exterior—"You can't go by my manners," he tells Janet Henry at one point, "They're always pretty bad" (p. 95)—he is actually very polished and well mannered in an almost courtly way. Despite the often unsavory situations and people which he must deal with, he is a man very much concerned with being a proper gentleman and with maintaining decorum. There is, for example, a dandyish quality in his tastefully decorated room ("It's delightful," judges Janet Henry. "I didn't know there could be any more of these left in a city as horribly up to date as ours has become" [p. 141]) and in his knowledge of social graces and proper dress. "You oughtn't to wear silk socks with tweeds," Ned fussily admonishes Madvig while they are in the midst of a heated discussion of Paul's receiving illegal kickbacks from city officials, and when Madvig protests that he likes "the feel of silk," Ned cuts him off with the quick retort, "Then lay off tweeds" (p. 58). Later in this same conversation, we are told that "Ned Beaumont put his glass on the table and touched his lips with a white handkerchief taken from the outer breast-pocket of his coat"—a fastidious gesture hardly imaginable of the Op or Spade which he repeats in a subsequent confrontation with O'Rory (p. 66). Ned knows when it is to his advantage to pretend to be crude (as it usually is in his dealings with the urban political machinery), but his predilection for the aristocratic often emerges. For instance, in discussing Paul Madvig with Janet Henry one evening, Ned drops his pose of the unschooled, bumbling roughneck to ridicule both her and himself. "He smiled at her. His smile was very young and engaging, his eyes shy, his voice youthfully diffident and confiding, as he said: 'I'll tell you what makes you think that, Miss Henry. It's—you see, Paul picked me up out of the gutter, as you might say, just a year or so ago, and so I'm kind of awkward and clumsy when I'm around people like you who belong to another world altogether—society and roto-sections and all—and you mistake that—uh—*gaucherie* for enmity, which it isn't at all.'" (p. 95).

Ned's awareness of decorum in various circumstances—from reassuring a minor employee with appropriate diction and tone ("I'll put it to him [Madvig] as hot as I can and you ought to know he'll go the limit, but he's in a tough spot right now" [p. 4]) to revising a formal thank-you note so that it reads "be able someday to show my gratitude more clearly" rather than "some day be able to more clearly show my gratitude" (p. 98)—is extremely useful in his role as Madvig's chief advisor. Beaumont is the most politically shrewd character in the novel; having arrived in the city only eighteen months before, he is now consulted by Madvig about all major politically strategic decisions and always seems to know the best way to handle business problems. After their first major confrontation with O'Rory, Madvig senses that he has mishandled the situation and asks Beaumont for advice on where he went wrong. Ned replies with an elaborate and carefully considered analysis which illustrates his superior understanding of politics and personalities.

> Ned Beaumont said: "All right. . . . Shad'll fight. He's got to. You've got him in a corner. You've told him he's through here for good. There's nothing he can do now but play the long shot. If he can upset you this election he'll be fixed to square anything he has to do to win. If you win the election he's got to drift anyhow. You're using the police on him. He'll have to fight back at the police and he will. That means you're going to have something that can be made to look like a crimewave. You're trying to re-elect the whole city administration. Well, giving them a crime-wave—and one it's an even bet they're not going to be able to handle—just before election isn't going to make them look any too efficient. They—"
> "You think I ought'to've laid down to him?" Madvig demanded, scowling.
> "I don't think that. I think you should have left him an out, a line of retreat. You shouldn't have got him with his back to the wall." (Pp. 69–70)

Clearly, Madvig relies on Ned's judgment and respects his ability to analyze situations. After asking Ned's advice about how best to deal with an unfriendly business associate—"How far do you think I ought to go with M'Laughlin this first time?" (p. 93)—Paul later entreats Ned: "I wish you'd go see M'Laughlin. . . . You can handle him if anybody can" (p. 152). Although Paul does not always accept Ned's advice, usually with disastrous consequences, he continues seeking it throughout the novel.

Another of Ned's traits—and the most striking departure from Hammett's earlier detectives—is his sense of humor. Like Raymond Chandler's Philip Marlowe, Ned Beaumont is a wisecracker, a man who often offers one-liners at the least expected moments.

> "Can't you be wrong?" Whiskey demanded.
> "Sure," the man in bed [Ned] confessed. "Once back in 1912 I was. I forget what it was about." (P. 73)

"A copper found you crawling on all fours up the middle of Colman Street at three in the morning leaving a trail of blood behind you."

"I think of funny things to do," Ned Beaumont said. (P. 91)

The nurse, looking at him with contemptuous eyes, said sarcastically: "We've had to keep policemen in front of the hospital to fight off all the woman that've been trying to see you."

"That's all right for you to say," he told her. "Maybe you're impressed by senators' daughters who are in the roto all the time, but you've never been hounded by them the way I have. I tell you they've made my life miserable, them and their brown roto-sections. Senators' daughters, always senators' daughters, never a representative's daughter or a cabinet minister's daughter or an alderman's daughter for the sake of variety—never anything but—Do you suppose senators are more prolific than—" (P. 92)

"Do stop it. You're worse than the Airedale Paul used to have."

"I'm part Airedale," he said, "on my father's side." (P. 106).

Given the overall tone of the novel, this kind of humor might appear to be misplaced, but when carefully considered, it suggests another important aspect of Ned's character—his desperate attempt to maintain control and keep his inner feelings hidden whenever they might betray his vulnerability. Like Chandler's Marlowe, Ned constantly finds himself placed in threatening situations, and to survive, he must disguise his own feelings and motives and convince others that he is the master of the situation. For both Marlowe and Beaumont, *verbal* control is often all that can be mustered; by telling jokes about themselves and their circumstances, they manage to indicate, however feebly, that things have not overwhelmed them, that they control their problems enough to joke about them. These jokes control and also allow Ned to disguise his real feelings. Very much like the Op and Spade, Ned Beaumont remains a mystery to all of the people he comes in contact with, even to his closest friend, Paul Madvig, and the woman he eventually goes away with, Janet Taylor. Thus Ned's actions, his motivations, and especially his emotions are even more impenetrable than those of his predecessors because the basis of his character cannot be fixed or interpreted by the notion of job. The job code that provided Spade and the Op with a system of values and, in a quite basic way, a guide for existence provided us as well with an entry into the mystery of their characters. Ned's

system, based on gambling, winning, and luck, is more vaguely
sketched and does not play as prominent a role in the novel as did
the issue of job in the earlier works. There is only one passage of
any length that develops Ned's attitude toward gambling, and even
it fails to illuminate his character in the way that Spade's discussion of job did in *The Maltese Falcon*.

> "I've got to get this guy. I've got to. . . . Listen, Paul: it's not only the
> money, though thirty-two hundred is a lot, but it would be the same if
> it was five bucks. I go two months without winning a bet and that gets
> me down. What good am I if my luck's gone? Then I cop, or think I do,
> and I'm all right again. I can take my tail out from between my legs
> and feel that I'm a person again and not just something that's being
> kicked around. The money's important enough, but it's not the real
> thing. It's what losing and losing and losing does to me. Can you get
> that? It's getting me licked. And then, when I think I've worked out
> the jinx, this guy takes a Mickey Finn on me. I can't stand for it. I'm
> licked, my nerve's gone. I'm not going to stand for it. I'm going after
> him." (P. 23)

There are, of course, certain insights that can be gained through
analysis of Ned's gambling code (and in a later discussion, I will
address these), but Ned's attitude toward winning and losing tells
us less about him than does the Op's attitude toward job. With so
few clues to go on as to the basis of his character, then, Ned is
almost undecipherable. At the very outset of the novel, Madvig
complains to Ned in a voice which contains "affection and exas-
peration": "What gets into you, Ned? You go along fine for just so
long and then for no reason at all you throw an ing-bing. I'll be a
dirty so-and-so if I can make you out" (p. 8). Paul's inability to
"read" Ned is probably the most telling indication of the mystery
that lies at Beaumont's core, and his frustrations are regularly voiced
throughout the rest of the book in such comments as:

> "Don't anything ever suit you? Some more of your God-damned
> foolishness?" (P. 67)

> "You crazy son of a bitch." (P. 71)

> "Ned! Don't anything ever look right to you?" (P. 153)

As was the case with both Spade and the Op, Beaumont's inner secrecy is kept intact by his ability to act, to create a mask which hides what is really going on inside him. Hammett repeatedly suggests that Beaumont is manipulating his voice and facial expression, especially his eyes, in order to disguise his emotions. In the very opening scene with Paul, Ned's ability to act out roles and cover up inner feelings is graphically illustrated by the following descriptions:

> Ned Beaumont made his eyes blank. . . . His eyes, by the time he was facing Madvig squarely again, had lost their shocked look. (P. 6)

> Spots of color appeared in Ned Beaumont's lean cheeks. He smiled his nicest smile. (P. 8)

> "How far have you got with her?" he asked in a voice that expressed nothing of what he might have been thinking. (P. 9)

> Ned Beaumont grinned crookedly at the blond man and made his voice drawl. (P. 10)

This kind of acting is evident in all of Ned's dealings with people, and Hammett creates numerous scenes that establish a sharp juxtaposition between his outer mask and inner feelings. For instance, when Janet Henry visits Ned in the hospital after he has been beaten, Hammett describes Ned waiting for her entrance by saying: "Ned Beaumont took a long breath. His eyes were shiny. He moistened his lips and then pressed them together in a tight secretive smile, but when Janet Henry came into the room his face was a mask of casual politeness" (p. 93). Similarly, on the two occasions when Ned visits the district attorney's office, Hammett concludes both scenes by revealing that Beaumont's demeanor with Farr has been only a role. "He went out grinning, but stopped grinning when he was outside" (p. 151); "Ned Beaumont signed the paper. 'This isn't nearly so much fun as I thought it was going to be,' he complained cheerfully. . . . Outside he grimaced angrily" (p. 175).

One of the implications we can draw from these many references to Ned's role playing is that he has more in common with Sam Spade's fierce, emotional character than with the Op. Like Spade, Ned at times seems to lose his composure completely. When

Paul and Ned confront one another and eventually come to blows, it is Ned's intense but unexpected anger that dominates the scene.

> Madvig drank beer, ate a pretzel, started to drink again, set his seidel down on the table, and asked: "Was there anything on your mind—any kick—besides that back in the Club this afternoon?"
> Ned shook his head. "You don't talk to me like that. Nobody does."
> "Hell, Ned, I didn't say anything." (P. 69)

> Madvig was up behind him immediately, with a hand on his shoulder, saying, "Wait, Ned."
> Ned Beaumont said: "Take your hand off me," He did not look around.
> Madvig put his other hand on Ned Beaumont's arm and turned him around. "Look here, Ned," he began.
> Ned Beaumont said: "Let go." His lips were pale and stiff.
> Madvig shook him. He said: "Don't be a God-damned fool. You and I—"
> Ned Beaumont struck Madvig's mouth with his left fist. (Pp. 70–71)

Ned acts irrationally in several scenes, and in two instances his loss of personal control is so thorough that he becomes like an animal. The most dramatic example of this behavior occurs when he is being beaten by Shad O'Rory's hired thugs—a scene that is surely the most brutal created by Hammett in all his fiction. Ned responds to his punishment by repeatedly getting up, only to be knocked down again, a mindless, mechanical response that is apparently motivated by the "dull hate" he directs towards his attackers (p. 85). Likewise, in the scene that follows Mathews's suicide in which Ned goes for help, he again appears to be acting almost unconsciously, compelled to continue by some inner, primitive drive. When he finally arrives back with assistance, his actions are completely irrational.

> "All right," he said speaking with difficulty. "I want to talk to you alone."
> Eloise Mathews ran over to him. "You killed him!" she cried.
> He giggled idiotically and tried to put his arms around her.
> She screamed, struck him in the face with an open hand.
> He fell straight back without bending. The red-faced man tried to catch him, but could not. He did not move at all after he struck the floor. (P. 133)

While these intense, emotional qualities seem much like those of Sam Spade, Ned exhibits other traits that are uncharacteristic of Hammett's earlier detectives. Spade, as Hammett publicly stated, was intended to be a type of "dream detective," a perfect embodiment of passion, inner control, and intelligence. Hammett, therefore, never placed him in situations where these qualities would be insufficient to maintain the upper hand, but in *The Glass Key* Hammett develops a fundamentally different type of hero— a man who, despite bravery and intelligence, is often the victim rather than the master of circumstances. Unlike Spade's cool comportment under any circumstance—he can calmly roll a perfect cigarette after hearing of his partner's death—Beaumont's personal habits constantly betray a nervousness that is foreign to Hammett's other heroes. The clearest depiction of this nervous quality is seen after Ned receives a mysterious, anonymous message.

> Scowling, he returned each to its envelope and put them in his pocket, only to take them out again immediately to reread and re-examine them. Too rapid smoking made his cigar burn irregularly down one side. He put the cigar on the edge of the table beside him with a grimace of distaste and picked at his mustache with nervous fingers. He put the messages away once more and leaned back in his chair, staring at the ceiling and biting a finger nail. He ran fingers through his hair. He put the end of a finger between his collar and his neck. He sat up and took the envelopes out of his pocket again, but put them back without having looked at them. He chewed his lower lip. (P. 57)

While Spade's physical strength and cunning help him to master any situation, Beaumont is often placed in circumstances where control in any meaningful sense becomes impossible. The beating at Shad O'Rory's place, for example, is an inevitable result of the physical odds against him—being out numbered and in enemy territory, bravery and intelligence become irrelevant. Despite his stubborn willingness to endure as much punishment as O'Rory's thugs can administer, Beaumont eventually breaks down when left alone and tries to commit suicide. Hammett's description of this scene, rendered in his typically neutral prose, is a horrifying portrayal of a brave man pushed beyond the limits of personal control—limits which Spade and the Op are never forced to confront.

> Going on hands and knees into the bathroom when he had regained consciousness after the last of these beatings, he saw, on the floor behind the wash-stand's pedestal, a narrow safety-razor blade red with the rust of months. Getting it out from behind the pedestal was a task that took him all of ten minutes and his nerveless fingers failed a dozen times before they succeeded in picking it up from the tiled floor. He tried to cut his throat with it, but it fell out of his hand after he had no more than scratched his chin in three places. He lay down on the bathroom floor and sobbed himself to sleep. (P. 87)

Thus, while both Spade and the Op are men whose personal code allows them to operate successfully in an unpredictable, often brutal universe (though Hammett does question the morality of this "success"), Beaumont's ability to control his destiny is limited, partially because of his own nature but more fundamentally because the world is simply more overpoweringly destructive in *The Glass Key*. Hammett was careful to give both Spade and the Op a kind of personal code, based on expediency and survival rather than on morality and truth, that allowed them to withstand the hazards of the world. But in *The Glass Key*, the world is not only presented as being corrupt and destructive, but Hammett creates a character who is more vulnerable to personal violation. The shift here can be seen in Beaumont's personal code which is not the same as that of Spade or the Op. The early codes share a view of the world that is best summarized in Spade's Flitcraft anecdote; they center around job and absolute control of oneself as a practical means of dealing with the world's absurdities. As long as the hero follows this code, he feels protected from personal disintegration and pain, and, on the whole, he is right, for, in each encounter with the world, he manages to keep his code and sense of personal integrity. Beaumont's code, however, is at once more simple and more pessimistic in its orientation: its clearest expression is his remark to Paul early in the novel, "I can stand anything I've got to stand" (p. 5). What is unique to Ned's code and is missing from the Op's and Spade's is the implication that the world is going to get to you in one way or another and that all you can do is learn to brace yourself and take the punishment. In other words,

Beaumont's code is not designed to protect him from anything or even to allow him to generate practical solutions which will momentarily provide a sense of coherence. Rather, it contains a basic acceptance of human vulnerability: no matter how successfully one maneuvers in the world and no matter what superior qualities one has—bravery, humor, intelligence, dignity, persistence—one can never be fully secure from potential destruction.

Although we are not given any direct insights into the underpinnings of Beaumont's code, as we were with the Op's various musings on the nature of the detective or with Spade's Flitcraft parable, it seems evident that Ned shares the basic belief of Hammett's earlier detectives that the world is *not* a sane, orderly affair. One indication of this view occurs when he angrily tells Opal Madvig, "You'd be surprised how many things there are you can't understand" (p. 109). The fact that Ned is a gambler by profession suggests a belief that chance underlies the basic operations of life,[8] but like all gamblers, he is also willing to try any system of order, no matter how apparently irrational, if he feels he can use it to win. Thus, when Janet Taylor asks him if he believes in dreams, Ned responds with a particularly revealing answer. "I don't believe in anything, but I'm too much of a gambler not to be affected by a lot of things" (p. 169). Precisely because Ned *does not* believe in anything, winning or losing becomes all-important to him, for loss and gain are about all that can be determined with surety. Ned is realistic enough to realize that he is going to lose sometimes, and when he is losing, he wants to face up to things with a kind of dignified resignation, epitomized in his "I can stand anything I have to stand" comment. Although Ned is willing to face up to anything he has to face up to, it is also a crucial part of his personal philosophy that he refuse to accept any unpleasantness that can be avoided. Because he believes that the world operates randomly and, in keeping with this belief, he lives the life of a gambler, he insists that a man must take advantage of any good fortune that comes his way. If a man is to preserve his dignity and sense of worth, he must demand his winnings when they are due him—to do otherwise is, in Spade's words, to "play the sap" for others. Like both Spade and the Op, then, Ned Beaumont is a man who governs his life by an allegiance to an abstract ideal—an ideal which is a variation of the business ethic that was so much a part of their philosophy. Significantly, at the book's climax, Ned re-phrases this notion that one must be willing to accept whatever payment the world demands—*if* the payment is due. Thus he re-fuses to allow Senator Henry to forgo his debt to society by com-mitting suicide. "No. You'll take what's coming to you" (p. 198). And moments later, he replies to Janet Henry's question about whether or not he despises her by irritably commenting: "I don't despise you. Whatever you've done you've paid for and been paid for and that goes for all of us" (p. 201).

There is an obvious connection between the defensive qualities of Ned's code and his willingness to absorb punishment with such restraint. When Jeff Gardner, O'Rory's hired thug, repeatedly com-ments on Ned's beatings that Ned "likes this" (pp. 84, 176) and that he is "a God-damned massacrist" (p. 176), there may be more than a hint of truth to what he says. There are several instances in which Ned seems to set himself up to be brutalized. This is apparent not only in his long ordeal with Jeff and Rusty but also in the bar scene in New York, when he knowingly confronts Ber-nie despite Jack's advice that "this isn't a hell of a good spot to go up against him if he's got friends here" (p. 31). There is no hard evidence to support the view that Ned actually derives some sex-ual pleasure out of the punishment he absorbs, although Jeff im-plies as much when he talks about "me and my sweetheart" going upstairs to "rehearse our act" (p. 177). There is, however, a strong suggestion of sexuality in the sadistic enjoyment Jeff receives in punishing others. The scene in which O'Rory is slowly strangled to death by Jeff is, in fact, charged with sexual undertones, several of which point to a certain complicity of Ned and Jeff in a sado-masochistic relationship; after trying "to embrace" O'Rory when he comes into the room, Jeff decides to strangle him when he pulls out a gun.

Jeff turned his head over his shoulder to grin at Ned Beaumont. The grin was wide, genuine, idiotically bestial. Jeff's little red eyes glinted merrily. . . .

Ned Beaumont said: "I don't want anything to do with it." His voice was steady. His nostrils quivered.

"No?" Jeff leered at him. . . . He ran his tongue over his lips. "He'll forget. I'll fix that."

Grinning from ear to ear at Ned Beaumont, not looking at the man whose throat he held in his hands, Jeff began to take in and let out long slow breaths. His coat became lumpy over his shoulders and back and along his arms. Sweat appeared on his ugly dark face.

Ned Beaumont was pale. He too was breathing heavily, and moisture filmed his temples. He looked over Jeff's lumpy shoulder at O'Rory's face.

O'Rory's face was liver-colored. His eyes stood far out, blind. . . . Grinning at Ned Beaumont, not looking at the man whose throat he held, Jeff spread his legs a little wider and arched his back. (Pp. 182–83)

It seems evident in this scene that Ned is identifying with O'Rory's pain and experiencing some sort of sexual arousal from watching it. One explanation of these masochistic tendencies in Ned can be traced back to his code's admonition that he be ready to stand what must be stood; given this attitude, it should not be surprising that Ned can derive a certain amount of personal satisfaction that his character is strong enough to bear up under the most trying conditions—in this case, witnessing death itself without turning away.

Having established these fundamental qualities of Ned's personality and code, we now arrive at the most important aspect of his character: a basic inscrutability which is stronger than even Sam Spade's or the Op's. Even after we have analyzed Ned's personality traits and examined his code—a process we normally expect would lead to a psychological understanding of his character—it is almost impossible to decipher the meaning of his actions or to understand what motivates him. In compiling questions that we *cannot* answer about his motivation, we find a list of virtually all the major issues in the book.

What is the basis of Ned's friendship with Paul?
Why does Ned refuse to answer O'Rory's questions about Paul?
What specifically causes the breakup between Ned and Paul?
Why does Ned refuse Paul's offer to reestablish their friendship?
Why does Ned go away with Janet at the end of the novel?

These questions clearly lie at the center of the novel's development, and the fact that it is impossible to answer them is the major source of critical objections to the novel. Critics like William F. Nolan who view the novel as Hammett's weakest see the undecipherability of Ned's actions as a serious defect, and in the following rather petulant analysis of the beating scene, Nolan implies that such ambiguity keeps us from knowledge that Hammett needed to provide:

> We see Beaumont picked up by Madvig's political enemies; he is offered money by Shad O'Rory to betray Madvig. Beaumont seems to go along with the idea, accepting the money. But he wants to leave; O'Rory wants him to stay. On this physical basis, not on any apparent moral one, Beaumont throws the money at O'Rory. Hammett then delivers one of the most brutal sequences ever written, wherein Beaumont is beaten back from the door again and again by O'Rory's apelike henchman, Jeff. Shad wants the information on Madvig, but Beaumont refuses to speak. He is beaten savagely until, to quote Jeff, "It ain't no good now. He's throwed another joe." (Meaning he is no longer conscious.) They bring him to, keep beating him. In his blood-weary state Beaumont tries to kill himself. He is finally found by police and taken to a hospital. Did he suffer this agony out of loyalty to his friend, or because his ego was threatened? Would he have walked out with O'Rory's money and laughed about it with Madvig, or would he have sent O'Rory the damaging information he wanted? Or is Beaumont really "a damned massacrist" as Jeff calls him? We don't know. Hammett does not tell us. There is much he does not tell us.[9]

Yet such condemnation of the novel on grounds that Ned Beaumont is an ambiguous figure seems to ignore the fact that ambiguity in *The Glass Key* is for Hammett a logical manifestation of mystery, just as it was in *The Maltese Falcon*. We cannot untangle Ned's motives because, finally, we cannot know Ned. In a lengthy essay discussing Hammett and his work, David Bazelon criticizes what he believes is a failed attempt by Hammett to break away from the confining characterization associated with a detective hero. Pointing out that *The Glass Key* is "his chief attempt at a genuine novel," Bazelon argues that although Ned Beaumont is Hammett's "closest, most serious projection . . . we never know whether Beaumont's motive in solving the murder is loyalty, job-doing, or love. . . . This ambiguity reflects, I think, Hammett's difficulty in writing an unformularized novel—that is, one in which an analysis of motives is fundamental."[10] This criticism, however, seems misplaced: *The Glass Key* is not a flawed work because its main character is ambiguous but because Ned's ambiguity is less skillfully controlled, less cohesively worked into the structure of the rest of the novel, and less a result of Hammett's construction as it is a result of his ignoring Ned's inner life.

Perhaps the most puzzling of all aspects of *The Glass Key* has to do with the relationship between Ned and Paul. Given Paul's background and limited intelligence, it is somewhat difficult to understand what attraction he holds for Ned or how he inspires such firm loyalty. Although he is the most influential figure in the city, Madvig is basically a simple, instinctive leader who believes that force is the best way to exert power. His background suggests a sort of mythic American hero who began in the lower ranks "running errands for Packy Flood in the old Fifth" (p. 70) and who now has the respect of others because he has been willing to use his power ruthlessly. Madvig his risen to the top through instinct and common sense; his source of strength—and weakness—lies in his singlemindedness of purpose and in a simplicity of vision that reduces life's complexities to a specific problem that can be attacked. The system developed by Madvig is simple: when you encounter any opposition you go after it with every means at your disposal until it has been crushed. When Ned suggests that perhaps more subtle methods might work better, Madvig replies: "I do know fighting—my kind—going in with both hands working. I never could learn to box and the only times I ever tried I got licked. . . . I don't know anything about your kind of fighting. . . . All I know is when you got somebody cornered you go in and finish them. That system's worked all right for me so far" (pp. 62, 70). Such a simplistic system, of course, has obvious drawbacks, and Paul has apparently realized the need for other approaches in some of his dealings. Because he recognizes that Ned understands complexities in politics that he cannot, Paul respects and admires Beaumont, and beyond these professional considerations, he seems to have genuine affection for his friend.

The attraction of Paul for Ned, however, is more difficult to understand. In nearly every respect the two men are polar opposites: Paul is tall, blond, and powerfully built with large shoulders and fists; Ned is tall but lean, with dark hair and eyes and a "constitutional weakness." More importantly, the men are opposites in character. Paul is loud, confident, simple, and cheerful while Ned is laconic, intellectual, complex, and self-doubting. Part of Ned's attraction could be based on gratitude for Paul having helped him out when he needed it. More fundamentally, however, Ned appears to be drawn to Paul's larger-than-life, simpler-than-life vision, even though he himself is often critical of it. His boss may be childish, deluded, and even foolish, Ned seems to feel, but even these delusions seem somehow healthy and substantial. Ned believes so strongly that a person must face squarely whatever the world gives one that he must admire Paul's willingness to confront challenges bravely and directly. Even after he has broken with Madvig, Ned is quick to agree with Jack's assessment that Paul has "more guts than all the rest of them put together," and he adds ruefully, "He has and that's what's licking him" (p. 172).

Given the firm bond that exists between Ned and Paul, a bond which seems truly remarkable if Ned's motive in suffering at O'Rory's hands was based on loyalty, a basic question in the book's development is why Ned is so intractable in his anger after their fight. Ned explains the basis of their fight by telling Janet Henry that "things were said that can't easily be unsaid" (p. 159), but what were these things? The argument between the two men culminates in the following passage:

> Madvig said: "That's enough." He stood erect, a big blond man whose eyes were cold blue disks. "What is it, Ned? Do you want her yourself or is it—" He jerked a thumb carelessly at the door. "Get out, you heel, this is the kiss-off."
> Ned Beaumont said: "I'll get out when I've finished talking."
> Madvig said: "You'll get out when you're told to. You can't say anything I'll believe. You haven't said anything I believe. You never will now."
> Ned Beaumont said: "Oke." He picked up his hat and overcoat and went out. (P. 158)

A careful analysis of this scene suggests that there are a number of things that may have contributed to the vehemence of Ned's reaction. One or all of the following factors may have been involved: (1) Paul's accusation that Ned wants Janet for himself; (2) Paul's insult of calling Ned "a heel"; (3) the fact that Paul orders Ned around—"You'll get out when you're told to"; (4) the announcement that "this is the kiss-off"; (5) Paul's questioning Ned's honesty in a conclusive way—his present honesty, his past and future honesty. In addition, (6) there is the vague, puzzling remark "or is it—" which seems so potentially important in much the same way that Dan Rolfe's "there is no—" comment was in *Red Harvest*. Is Paul asking him if Ned might not want *Paul* for himself? We cannot be certain what the reference is to nor can we be certain about anything in this exchange. Other than Ned's comment that "things were said," the only other references made to this crucial scene are his ambiguous remarks to Janet that although he is "sorry" about the fight, "I wouldn't have gone a step out of my way to avoid it" (p. 160) and his comment that even if Paul decides that Ned is right later, "That won't make any difference between him and me now" (p. 161). Considering the close ties which unite these two men when the book opens—ties reinforced by Ned's closeness to Paul's family—Ned's violent reaction to these remarks and his adamant refusal to accept what appears to be a genuine apology from Paul (p. 204) seem difficult to gauge. A possible explanation may lie in Ned's apparently precarious sense of self-worth: when Paul, a trusted friend, questions Ned's worth and trustworthiness, Ned's sensitivity to this issue, evident in his earlier remarks to Paul about how important it is for him to be "a winner" again, creates a strong reaction. But obviously even this explanation is inconclusive.

In some ways, Ned's relationship to Janet Henry creates a mystery even more difficult to fathom than the Ned-Paul friendship. Throughout much of the novel, Ned and Janet are at odds with one another since she is anxious to prove that Paul has murdered her brother. But in spite of their respective, stubborn loyalties, it is also evident that there is some sort of attraction between them. Ned, for example, is said to wear a "tight secretive smile" just before Janet comes to visit him at the hospital; afterwards he tells his nurse to take away part of the fruit Janet has brought him so that it will appear he has eaten some. Not only does he write her a polite thank-you note for her gifts and concerns, he also cares enough about the sort of impression he is making to write a second, more grammatically correct copy. For her part, Janet is just as clearly drawn to Ned. Even when Ned is deliberately cruel to her, as when he harshly tells her that "whoever killed your brother did the world a favor" (p. 145), Janet quickly forgives him and responds sympathetically. "Almost immediately the horror went out of her face and she sat upright and looked compassionately at him. She said softly, 'I know. You're Paul's friend. It hurts'" (p. 145). Still, Janet's sudden decision to run off with Beaumont in the last few pages of the novel must certainly come as a surprise to the reader. There has been no real exchange of love on their part up to this point, and it seems significant that even as they make their decision to depart together Janet does not say she loves Beaumont nor does he express any kind of affection for her. Their exchange is, in fact, unromantic and remarkably distant, considering the matter at hand.

> She asked in a dry constricted voice: "And you don't like me because—?"
> He did not say anything.
> She bit her lip and cried: "Answer me!"
> "You're all right," he said, "only you're not all right for Paul, not the way you've been playing with him. . . ."
> "You despise me," she said in a low hard voice. "You think I'm a whore."
> "I don't despise you," he said irritably, not turning to face her. "Whatever you've done you've paid for and been paid for and that goes for all of us. . . . I have to say good-bye now."
> A startled light came into her eyes. "You're not going away?"
> He nodded. "I can catch the four-thirty."
> "You're not going away for good?"
> "If I can dodge being brought back for some of these trials and I don't think that'll be so hard."
> She held out her hand impulsively. "Take me with you."
> He blinked at her. "Do you really want to go or are you just being hysterical? . . . It doesn't make any difference. I'll take you with me if you want to go. . . . If you're going get packed. Only what you can get in a couple of bags. We can send for the other stuff later, maybe." (Pp. 200–201)

This cool exchange is followed, on the last page of the novel, by Paul arriving at Ned's apartment to apologize and say goodbye. When Ned tells him that "Janet is going away with me," Paul is visibly shocked and "clumsily" leaves the room (p. 204). The novel concludes with Janet looking at Ned while he sits and stares "fixedly at the door" (p. 204). Thus, *The Glass Key* ends in an enigmatic scene whose "real" meaning Hammett purposefully leaves unresolved. As was also true in *The Maltese Falcon*, the conclusion to *The Glass Key* comes without supplying answers to basic questions about the main characters. Are we to assume that Ned and Janet have fallen in love during the course of the novel's action? What does Janet's "high-pitched unnatural laugh" in response to Ned's agreement to take her with him (p. 201) really indicate? Does Ned take Janet away to save Paul? Does he feel she is, in fact, a monster as she claims (p. 171) and thus sacrifices himself for Paul? Such ambiguity is central to *The Glass Key*: people cannot understand each other nor can they ever understand themselves. In an important passage near the end of the novel, Janet Henry and Ned discuss this difficulty in knowing oneself.

> She nodded miserably. "I hated him [Paul]," she said, "and I wronged him and I still hate him." She sobbed. "Why is that, Ned?"
> He made an impatient gesture with one hand. "Don't ask me riddles."
> "And you," she said, "tricked me and made a fool of me and brought this on me and I don't hate you."
> "More riddles," he said. (Pp. 199–200)

Not surprisingly, Ned and Janet have no better luck interpreting their subconscious emotions than their conscious ones. When they tell each other their dreams—an opportunity of sorts to illuminate the "clues" their psyches offer—they reveal much of themselves and their attitudes, but these revelations seem to do little to advance their understanding. Janet openly manipulates her dream so that it has a happy ending, and later on when she reveals the truth, Ned dismisses it with "that was only a dream. . . . Forget it" (p. 202). Ned tells her his dream first. "I was fishing . . . and I caught an enormous fish—a rainbow trout, but enormous— and you said you wanted to look at it and you picked it up and threw it back in the water before I could stop you" (p. 169). While several readings are possible here, one in particular seems likely, especially given the content of Janet's dream: Ned's sexuality, the "enormous fish," is rejected, thrown back into the water, by Janet. She dismisses the dream, denying its implications. "It was a lie. . . .

I won't throw your trout back" (p. 169). When she in turn tells her dream, however, she reveals an attitude that seems to confirm the underlying thrust of Ned's dream. In her dream, she and Ned are walking through the forest hungry and lost. They come across a house, but it is locked up with bars over the windows; peeking through to the inside, they see a huge table covered with all kinds of delicious foods. They find the key to the door under the mat, but when they unlock it, hundreds of snakes are inside and come slithering toward them. They manage to relock the door before the snakes get to them and then climb on the roof where Ned leans down and turns the key to open the door; they watch as the snakes slither away and then climb down to feast on the food. After she finishes telling her dream—one that certainly suggests an abhorrence of sexuality, a fear of the phallus at the same time that it shows Janet is desperate to have her "hunger" satiated—Ned confronts her with "I think you made that up" (p. 170), and she admits that part of the dream is made up. Later on, she tells him the truth: when they found the key to the house, it was made of glass and shattered before they could relock the door. The snakes poured out over them and she woke herself screaming. Thus, the key here brings them disaster, and if we apply the most literal association to the word—that is, a key as clarification and truth—we are left with an unavoidable reading: the truth (behind emotions, sex, or murders) cannot save or redeem but can only reveal. And what is revealed can be more painful and destructive than the mystery itself.

What this dream suggests about Janet's attraction for Ned and her revulsion for Madvig is that the former is desirable because his sexuality is not forceful. As opposed to Madvig's animal physicality and strength, Ned's passions are all inward and restrained. Despite the fact that he appears to be more self-conscious than Janet, there is no indication that the "meaning" of these dreams is any clearer to him nor does he understand his motivations and fears any better than she. He is just as fully a victim of his own confused passions and self-destructive values. He says he believes in nothing, yet he is in fact so fiercely committed to his own vision of himself and the world that he leaves the Madvig family—presumably the only bonds he has with people—for a principle that even he does not seem to fully understand. In the process he abandons a "sister," a "mother" for whom he clearly feels great affection, and, most importantly, Paul—a friend, "brother," and perhaps lover.

In a world where emotions are so hopelessly tangled, relationships become impossible to sustain. Normal ties between people—those based on family, romantic love, or friendship—simply cannot hold because they assume a coherency of emotion that is impossible to maintain. Parent-child relations seem especially vulnerable: Opal Madvig hates her father and tries to destroy his reputation; Senator Henry is willing to prostitute his daughter to lure support for his candidacy from Paul; and, of course, Henry kills his own son. Relationships based on love fare no better: Bernie Despain runs out on his lover, Lee Wilshire, when his gambling debts become due; Taylor Henry is having a torrid affair with Opal Madvig but is also seeing several other women on the sly; Eloise Mathews is willing to torment her husband by seducing Ned Beaumont right before his eyes.

As with *The Maltese Falcon*, then, deception, incongruity, and paradox are the dominant forces in *The Glass Key*. Hammett reinforces the thematic significance of these elements by skillfully incorporating them into the details of the text: Jeff, an "apish" man, has "remarkably beautiful white teeth" that are false and Shad O'Rory possesses "a musical Irish voice" (p. 82). Rusty, one of the sadistic thugs who helps beat Ned, is described as being "a rosy-cheeked boy with sandy hair" (p. 82). Senator Henry, the chief murderer, is "one of the few aristocrats left in American politics" (p. 9). O'Rory's dog, Patty, is a huge English bulldog who initially presents a deceptively lazy and good-natured appearance with her "waddle" and her "morose eyes" (p. 77)—so much so that Ned calls her a "nice pooch." But on O'Rory's command, she viciously rips Ned's arm. In the scene in which Ned is beaten Hammett creates a strange, disquieting contrast that makes the violence all the more vivid—a bloody, disfigured Ned wakes up in a room that sounds more appropriate for a little girl than for a prisoner in a gangster's house. "His face was swollen and bruised and blood-smeared. Dried blood glued his shirt-sleeve to the wrist the dog had bitten and that hand was caked with drying blood. He was in a small yellow and white bedroom furnished with two chairs, a table, a chest of drawers, a wall-mirror, and three white-framed

French prints beside the bed. Facing the foot of the bed was a door that stood open to show part of the interior of a white-tiled bathroom" (p. 83).

Thus, *The Glass Key*, like *The Maltese Falcon*, is adamant both stylistically and thematically in its insistence that people are as inexplicable as the world in which they live. But despite this similarity in outlook, *The Glass Key* is not as effective in incorporating its theme into the structure and imagery of the work. Ambiguity certainly pervades the novel, as has been shown, but the ambiguity that is fascinating in Sam Spade—the delicate handling by Hammett of the metaphysical and metaphorical relationship between the conventions of detective fiction and of a larger, more complicated inquiry into human systems and the need for personal truth—is more diffused, less sharply focused in Ned Beaumont. Unlike *The Maltese Falcon*, where the idea of mystery is complemented and illuminated by the *structure* of the mystery novel, *The Glass Key* attempts to develop mystery through the structure of a psychological novel. Hammett's efforts are less successful in the later work because its mystery is achieved primarily by avoiding the notation of people's thoughts—a notation that is the very essence of the psychological novel and whose absence, at a very minimum, has the perverse effect of turning *The Glass Key* into a sort of "antipsychological" novel. It may well be that Hammett is deliberately upsetting what we expect from a psychological novel in order to underscore his point about the ambiguity of human motivation and psychology; in each of his three earlier novels, Hammett undercut the conventional expectations of the detective novel to establish his point about *worldly* ambiguity, and in *The Glass Key* his intent may have been similar, to manipulate the conventions of the psychological novel in order to underscore the notion of *personal* ambiguity. But Hammett produces his effect primarily by *avoidance* in *The Glass Key* and not, as in his earlier novels, by skillfully manipulating conventions to undercut their usual implications. It would have been possible for Hammett to present his point about human motivation by playing the psychological novelist's game and *still* turning the rules of this game on their head for his own purposes—that is, the more legitimate approach would seem to have been to make Ned and the other characters appear ambiguous and incoherent and to still present us with a portrait of their inner lives. He could have made Ned just as inconsistent—perhaps even more so—and yet more convincing by giving him the inner life that would demonstrate Hammett's point rather than seeming to avoid confronting it. Consequently, the reader of *The Glass Key* is likely to sense that Hammett was unable to face up to the full implications of his view of people.

6

The Thin Man: The Detective and the Comedy of Manners

— ► ◄ —

"I don't believe it," she [Nora] said. "You made it up. There aren't any people like that. What's the matter with them? Are they just the first of a new race of monsters?"
"I just tell you what happens; I don't explain it."
— *from* The Thin Man

In 1934, at the age of thirty-nine, Dashiell Hammett published his last novel, *The Thin Man*, a work characterized by John G. Cawelti as a "novel of a high society and urban sophistication."[1] Certainly the witty, urbane charm and good-natured decadence of its main character and narrator, Nick Charles, seem far removed from the stoic grimness and metaphysical despair found in the detectives of *Red Harvest*, *The Glass Key*, *The Maltese Falcon*, and *The Dain Curse*. There are any number of possible explanations for the change in tone and approach to character development: Hammett's first four works were produced during a three-year period from 1927 to 1930; *The Thin Man*, however, was written some three years later. In the three years separating *The Glass Key* from *The Thin Man* (the longest gap between any two novels by Hammett) his personal situation changed dramatically. Like many successful writers of the day, Hammett went to Hollywood where he became involved in the parties, drinking, and women that a celebrity's life offered; it was also during this period that he met Lillian Hellman. Critics have taken the immersion of *The Thin Man* in details of the fast life, along with its wit and

148

new (for Hammett) lightness of tone, as evidence of artistic deterioration and loss of seriousness.[2] Such judgments, based on the notion that literature to be serious must be solemn and didactic, seem out of place for any Hammett work and are particularly unsuited to *The Thin Man*, which merges hard-boiled fiction with a comedy of manners. This chapter will attempt to show the artistic unity and seriousness of intent that control Hammett's last major work.

The lightness of tone which dramatically distinguishes *The Thin Man* from all the rest of Hammett's work is the product of various factors, including the way Hammett develops the setting. New York City, like Personville, San Francisco, and the unnamed city in *The Glass Key*, is presented as a city accustomed to political and judicial corruption, but in *The Thin Man* this corruption is presented more as farcical incompetency than as a willful, calculated attempt to subvert law and order. Indeed, we often recognize in Nick Charles an amused appreciation for the ironies implicit in the legalistic corruption. For example, after a man is apprehended in his and Nora's hotel room by the police, Nick tells us that the "coppers worked him over a little just for the fun of it,"[3] yet these same policemen later adopt a policy of scrupulous attention to regulations as they refuse to allow the prisoner a drink because "it's against the law to give a prisoner a drink or drugs except on a doctor's say-so" (p. 29). In most instances when public figures manipulate the law there is little sense of malevolent corruption being exposed, as there was in Hammett's earlier works; rather, there is the suggestion that the police and the district attorney are following a simpler, more commonsensical code than the fussy complexities of the law allow. The chief detective, John Guild, for example, has no interest in prosecuting a man for a crime like bigamy, which he considers to be a personal matter ("I never believe in hounding a man over things that are none of my business" [p. 114]).[4] Even the victim of a police beating, who tells Nora, "You got to expect it" (p. 105), is willing to excuse the technical illegality of the police's actions as long as he feels he has himself performed well. "It's all right as long as it takes two or three of 'em to do it" (p. 105). A similar presentation of this good-sportsman relationship between criminals and the legal establishment can be seen when Nick meets Studsy Burke, a man he was responsible for sending to prison; Burke greets Nick's introduction of Nora by good-naturedly saying: "A wife. Think of that. By God, you'll drink champagne or you'll fight me" (p. 69).

As these examples suggest, despite the presence of real murders, brutality, and corruption, *The Thin Man*'s portrayal of these elements is much lighter and less grim than in Hammett's previous fiction. Certainly there is no equivalent here to the relentless, dehumanizing corruption of the Op novels, the cold, grotesque portrayal of violence in *The Maltese Falcon* or the sickening scene of Ned's beating in *The Glass Key*. Indeed, there are often strong undercurrents of farce in Hammett's portrayal of the police's attempt to act like policemen. In the following exchange between Guild and a bungling detective assigned to watch an apartment, there is a slapstick style which makes the characters seem more likely to be appearing in a Thorne Smith novel—or even in a Marx Brothers movie—than in a novel by Hammett:

[Guild]: "Go ahead, Flint, let's have it."
Flint wiped his mouth with the back of a hand. "He's a wildcat for fair, the young fellow. He don't look tough, but, man, he didn't want to come along. I can tell you that. And can he run!"
Guild growled: "You're a hero and I'll see the Commissioner about your medal right away, but never mind that. . . . What'd he do in the apartment?"
"He didn't have a chance to do nothing. I—"
"You mean you jumped him without waiting to see what he was up to?" Guild's neck bulged over the edge of his collar, and his face was as red as Flint's hair.
"I thought it best not to take no chances."
Guild stared at me with angry incredulous eyes. I did my best to keep my face blank. He said in a choking voice: "That'll do, Flint. Wait outside."
The red-haired man seemed puzzled. He said, "Yes, sir," slowly. "Here's his key." He put the key on Guild's desk and went to the door. There he twisted his head over a shoulder to say: "He claims he's Clyde Wynant's son." He laughed merrily.
Guild, still having trouble with his voice, said: "Oh, he does, does he?"
"Yeah. I seen him somewhere before. I got an idea he used to belong to Big Shorty Dolan's mob. Seems to me I used to see him around—"
"Get out!" Guild snarled, and Flint got out. (Pp. 152–53)

Hammett builds several other scenes out of similar burlesque elements—as, for instance, when Nick knocks Nora out while scuffling with Morelli—and in relying on such devices he considerably lightens the mood of *The Thin Man*.

Not only is the setting of *The Thin Man* presented in such a way as to lighten Hammett's portrayal of urban corruption, but the tone is also moderated by the presence of several minor characters who have little or nothing to do with the plot's murder story. This wealthy, leisured cast of characters—augmented by numerous topical references to current songs ("Rise and Shine," "Eadie was a Lady"), popular entertainers (Jack Oakie and Oscar Levant, the latter appearing somewhat disguised as a piano player named "Levi Oscant"), and national events—opens up a new dimension of social satire and comedy of manners that is almost completely lacking in Hammett's previous work.[5] In the course of describing several cocktail parties attended by Nick and Nora, Hammett presents numerous characters who could not be related to this case—an obvious break with the conventions of most hardboiled novels which decree that even minor characters must have some bearing on the case. Thus, we have Hammett's detective presented very much within a social world—a world of parties, wealthy friends who seem to have no professions, and evenings spent at the theater. Unlike any of Hammett's other fiction, *The Thin Man* is considerably more interested in creating a perspective on a segment of contemporary life where murder and criminality are an aberration, not the rule. These portraits, then, are not done to advance the case but to satirize the lives of the wealthy. However, it is also crucial to realize that, finally, this portrayal *does* fit into the larger scheme of the book, for in several of the seemingly irrelevant scenes involving these people (as with the Edges' cocktail party and its unpleasant aftermath at the Quinns [pp. 95–100]) we see the novel's important motifs of cannibalism, of destruction for the mere pleasure of it, of the stripping of others being developed in a social rather than a criminal context.

In developing the action of *The Thin Man* Hammett switches rapidly back and forth between the world of the wealthy, decadent characters mentioned above and the more usual lowlife world of the police and common criminal types found in most hard-boiled fiction. However, since an important aspect of the novel's development is its comedy-of-manners technique, it is appropriate that the plot is much more like that of a classical detective story than that of a hard-boiled one. The artifice of the comedy of manners is simply more compatible with the more genteel, civilized artifice of the classical detective story than it is to the viscerally realistic methods of most hard-boiled fiction. A gangster element is present in *The Thin Man* and some of its most effective scenes involve the hard-boiled underworld friends of Nick Charles, but the essential elements of the plot are derived primarily from the classical formula: a wealthy family, a limited number of suspects, a dilettante detective, and an inept—rather than corrupt—police force. Compared to the complexities of *Red Harvest* and *The Dain Curse* the plot here is relatively simple and focused. The narrator and main character of the novel, Nick Charles, arrives in New York City with his wife, Nora, and his pet schnauzer, Asta, to spend their Christmas holidays. Nick, a private detective for the Trans-American Detective Agency before his marriage to Nora, accidentally meets the daughter of a former client, Clyde Wynant. Years before, Nick had worked on a case that involved Wynant (a wealthy scientist and inventor) and one of his assistants, Charles Rosewater, who, because he believed Wynant had stolen one of his inventions, physically threatened Wynant and his family. The earlier case ended with no real resolution when Rosewater disappeared, but in the meantime, Nick had become familiar enough with the family to know that Wynant was having an affair with his secretary, Julia Wolf, and to have a brief affair with Wynant's wife, Mimi. As *The Thin Man* opens, Nick runs into Dorothy Wynant (the daughter) in a hotel bar; we soon learn that Wynant, who is now divorced and estranged from his family, has been out of town for several months and that he has been in contact only with his lawyer and Julia Wolf. Two days later, Julia is murdered and her body is discovered by Mimi Wynant, who had come to the apartment hoping to reach her former husband through the secretary. Despite the immediate suspicion that falls on Wynant, he stays in hiding, ostensibly to protect the secrecy of his latest scientific project; he communicates to his lawyer, Macaulay, and to Nick through a series of letters, telegrams, and telephone calls (although, significantly, these phone calls are made only to Macaulay). As Nick becomes reluctantly involved in the case, he grows convinced that Wynant is innocent of both Julia Wolf's murder and the subsequent murder of a petty criminal and stool pigeon, Arthur Nunheim. When the police discover a body in the basement of Wynant's laboratory—a body that has been there for several months and whom they assume to be still another murder victim of Wynant's—Nick solves the case: it is Wynant's body under the laboratory and the obvious identity of his murderer, as well as that of Julia Wolf, is the person who claims to have spoken with Wynant just recently—the lawyer, Herbert Macaulay.

One of the more apparent differences between Hammett's method of plot development in *The Thin Man* and that of his earlier novels is the fact that the pacing of his later novel is considerably more leisurely. We have little sense here, as we did in *Red Harvest, The Dain Curse,* or *The Maltese Falcon,* of breakneck speed of action, of murders and violent events rapidly accumulating, of labyrinthine connections proliferating which are beyond our power to understand. Somewhat like the cocktail parties which occupy so much narrative space in the first half of the novel, the plot of *The Thin Man* develops without haste or urgency and with little or no suspense; Hammett is even willing to halt the narrative flow completely to insert his long, central parable about cannibalism into a cocktail party scene. Another factor which contributes to the lack of suspense in the novel has to do with the nature of the murders themselves. All happen off the page— one has happened months before—and there is rarely any sense of physical threat to Nick or to any other major participant in the novel. Thus there are few scenes of real drama; ironically, the most singly dramatic scene is probably the one where Nick and Nora face Shep Morelli in their apartment—but, as it turns out, this has little to do with the case. Indeed, the most crucial difference between the plot development here and that of earlier Hammett novels is the fact that Nick remains, for the most part, much less directly embroiled in the violence and dangers of the case itself. It is also important that, because of Nick's relationship with Nora, there is never the possibility of his becoming romantically involved with any of the case's participants—a possibility that adds a considerable dimension of dramatic tension to each of the earlier novels.

In *The Thin Man* Hammett decides to return to the first-person narration that he employed in his first two novels. As in all of his fiction, Hammett takes considerable delight in portraying collo- quial speech, although here Nick's position as a "middleman" between high and low cultures allows Hammett even more free- dom than usual to mimic a wide variety of voices. But Hammett's use of Nick as a narrator has several important differences from the way in which he used the Op. Nick's narrative voice contains none of the peculiar, unemotional, coldly objective qualities of the Op's voice; rather than neutral, dispassionate descriptions of things and events which give little clue to the observer's attitudes or emotions (as was the case with the Op's narration), Nick Charles's voice is quick to reveal personal attitudes, draw conclu- sions about others, create interpretations. His narration appears less constrained by the need to mask himself and his feelings. This difference in Hammett's handling of point of view is imme- diately apparent in the first words of the novel, in which the re- laxed, rather ironic tone of Nick's narration is obvious. "I was leaning against the bar in a speakeasy on Fifty-second Street, waiting for Nora to finish her Christmas shopping, when a girl got up from the table where she had been sitting with three other people and came over to me. She was small and blonde and whether you looked at her face or at her body in powder-blue sports clothes, the result was satisfactory" (p. 13). These two different narrative styles reveal, of course, important differences in the personalities of the two detectives: the Op is a lonely, utterly private individual whose devotion to duty results from a fundamental fear of what the outside world (and those who inhabit it) can do to someone who is foolish enough to "open up"; Nick, meanwhile, is consid- erably more open (with us and with other characters in the novel), as might be expected of a man who has established a happy, ful- filling relationship with his wife. Although just as aware as the Op of the metaphysical limitations of human reason—a point to be raised in more detail later in this chapter—Nick seems less personally fearful of allowing us to see him making judgments. Consequently, we feel we grow to know Nick as his narrative pro- gresses, whereas the Op remains always masklike, mysterious. On the other hand, Hammett does not take this narrative involve- ment so far as to violate the central premise of all detective stories—withholding the identity of the criminal until the most dramatically effective moment—for we are hardly made privy to *all* of Nick's thought processes. Although Nick is more willing than the Op to share his opinions about people and events, he does not reveal his specific reasoning about the case itself.

This shift to a more open, personal narrative distinguishes *The Thin Man* from other Hammett novels, but Nick Charles is still much like the earlier detectives. In the climactic scene in which Nick accuses Macaulay of the murders of Wynant and Julia Wolf, Nick tells us that the desperate lawyer "started to move." Nick's response is that of the quintessential Hammett hero. "I did not wait to see what he meant to do, but slammed his chin with my left fist. The punch was all right, it landed solidly and dropped him, but I felt a burning sensation on my left side and knew I had torn the bullet-wound open. 'What do you want me to do?' I growled at Guild. 'Put him in cellophane for you?'" (p. 181). The instinctual decisiveness, the physicality, and the tough-guy wisecrack that mark this incident could have been that of the Op or Sam Spade or Ned Beaumont. And yet, there is one very obvious difference between Nick and his fictional predecessors: he left the world of private detecting, gangsters, and violence and has taken up with a woman. Indeed, not only has Nick retired as a private detective, he now has no job whatsoever. After having examined in the previous chapters the significance placed by Hammett's heroes on their jobs—the way the individual identified with his vocation—the importance of this change should be obvious: unlike the Op or Spade, Nick has found something that is more important to him than his job. From the very opening of the novel, with Nick "leaning against the bar . . . waiting for Nora to finish her Christmas shopping" (p. 3), the domesticating influences of Nora are evident—certainly it is difficult to imagine the Op or Sam Spade proceeding in a case with a schnauzer named Asta in tow. Yet it is also significant that Nick's decision to give up his job as a private eye was his own. We might expect his retirement to have been the result of Nora's influence—either a wife's aversion to the dangers and demands of her husband's job or a wealthy woman's ability to make him financially independent of work—but Nick quit for his own undisclosed reasons. Early on in the novel, Nora asks Nick, "Don't you ever think you'd like to go back to detecting once in a while just for the fun of it?" Nick's reply—"It's nothing in my life" (p. 13)—suggests an important change in the Hammett hero.

As with all of Hammett's previous detectives, Nick's background is sketchy: forty-one years old at the time of the novel's action (1933) and a veteran of World War I, Nick was an operative in New York City of the Trans-American Detective Agency (a "former ace" of the agency according to a newspaper story [p. 24]) until 1927 when he married Nora, a wealthy heiress from San Francisco. In many respects, Nick's transition from a working-class private detective to a leisured, comfortable life is as classic an American success story as Jay Gatsby's. His father, a Greek immigrant, had been processed through Ellis Island, where officials changed his name from Charalambides to Charles. Thus, there is a storybook quality to Nick's life, complete with his finding fortune and love out West, that contrasts sharply with the lives of Hammett's other heroes—all of whom, even Ned Beaumont, are committed to solitary lives of social exile. But despite this important change from hard-boiled detective to an inhabitant of society's affluent upper class, there remains much in Nick that is reminiscent of earlier detectives. There is an easiness about him, a cheerful willingness to go along with Nora's bossing—"'You're a sweet old fool. Don't read that here now.' She took the newspaper away from me and stuck it out of sight behind the radio" (p. 13)—but there is also an underlying toughness about him that no amount of domestication seems able to dispel. Nick may have gladly retired from detective work ("I'm not a private detective any more," he tells John Guild, "I'm not any kind of detective" [p. 44]), but when the Wynant case keeps intruding into his private life, his reaction is the same kind of direct, forceful, personal response that the Op made in *Red Harvest*. Following an encounter with Shep Morelli, an old friend of Julia Wolf, in which Nick is shot, he explains his reasons for becoming involved in the case to Nora in almost exactly the same terms that led the Op to remain in Personville. "I didn't want to get mixed up with these people—still don't—but a fat lot of good that's doing me. Well, I can't just blunder out of it. I've got to see" (p. 30). Later in the same scene he adds: "I've been pushed around too much. I've got to see about things" (p. 31). Nick's participation in the case is, of course, less intensely personal than the Op's, and his conduct is correspondingly far from the "blood simple" frenzy that precipitated so much of the violence in *Red Harvest*.

If Nick's motives in the Wynant case seem similar to those of earlier Hammett detectives—a refusal to be "pushed around" or to "play the sap"—his detective methods as well are familiar. As is true of all hard-boiled detectives, Nick is hardly able to proceed in this case in a direct, inductive manner; like the Op and Spade, Nick is well aware that the deceptive nature of appearances makes drawing hard-and-fast conclusions nearly impossible. Somewhat like the Op, who says he likes "to stir things up," Nick seems to realize that oftentimes the best way to proceed in a case is to create some kind of action and then see if he can make sense of things. As he explains to Dorothy Wynant: "I'm just fumbling around. . . . I don't know what I'm going to do because I don't know what's being done to me. I've got to find out. I've got to find out in my own way" (p. 32). It is also significant that, like the Op and Spade, Nick often resorts to lying as a means of making this "fumbling around" produce results. From the opening of the novel, when Dorothy Wynant is recalling the time years before when Nick worked for her father, there are references to this lying. When she asks Nick, "Remember those stories you told me? Were they true?" his reply—"Probably not" (p. 4)—is a revealing one, for like his fellow Hammett detectives, Nick Charles is a man who fully understands the utility of lying in the process of attempting to arrive at the truth.

Yet Nick's lies and manipulations are presented in a somewhat different light from the Op's or Sam Spade's. He does sometimes lie and create masks for himself, as all successful private detectives must, but because his devotion to duty and job are much less total than was the case with Hammett's earlier detectives, he shows a correspondingly greater willingness to drop his lies and pretenses when not forced to adopt them. Indeed, we often sense with Nick that his lies are less an attempt to trick people to gain the upper hand in a situation than they are an expression of his recognition that people rarely want the truth nor are they willing to accept it when it is given them. Mimi Wynant is right when she tells Nick that he is "the damnedest evasive man" (p. 22), but Nick's evasiveness frequently appears to derive from compassion for others and not (as with the Op or Spade) from a deep-seated *fear* of others. A good example of this sympathetic evasiveness occurs in a scene when Nick brings his drunken, passed-out friend, Harrison Quinn, home to Quinn's wife, Alice. Her irritated reaction is obvious—"She looked wearily at Quinn and spoke wearily: 'Bring it in'" (p. 99)—yet she is also anxious to know if her husband has been out all evening with Dorothy Wynant. Nick's reluctance to criticize Harrison and to hurt Alice's feelings is revealing.

> "Where'd he pass out this time?" she asked with not much interest. She was still standing at the foot of the bed, brushing her hair now.
> "The Edges'." I unbuttoned his pants.
> "With that little Wynant bitch?" The question was casual.
> "There were a lot of people there."
> "Yes," she said. "He wouldn't pick a secluded spot." She brushed her hair a couple of times. "So you don't think it's clubby to tell me anything. . . . It's none of my business, Nick, but what do people think of me?"
> "You're like everybody else: some people like you, some people don't, and some have no feeling about it one way or the other."
> She frowned. "That's not exactly what I meant. What do people think about my staying with Harrison with him chasing everything that's hot and hollow?"
> "I don't know, Alice."
> "What do you think?"
> "I think you probably know what you're doing and whatever you do is your own business."
> She looked at me with dissatisfaction. "You'll never talk yourself into any trouble, will you?" She smiled bitterly. (Pp. 99–100)

Nick's evasiveness and lies are often the result of a keen appreciation of the ironies and paradoxes of social interplay. For example, when Nora asks why he had not told Studsy Burke, a former convict, that he had quit the detective business, Nick replies: "He'd've thought I was trying to put something over on him. . . . To a mugg like him, once a sleuth always a sleuth, and I'd rather lie to him than have him think I'm lying" (p. 72). Nick understands that often people ask for the truth when what they really want is confirmation of their own wishful thinking, and he is more willing than Hammett's other detectives to go along with this need. In the following exchange with Dorothy Wynant, when Nick's evasion fails to appease her, he supplies her with the answer that she is hoping for—but openly acknowledges that he is doing so:

> She raised her head and laughed, but when she asked, "Do you think I take after Mama much?" she was serious.
> "I wouldn't be surprised."
> "But do you?"
> "You want me to say no. No." (P. 23)

Nick is sensitive to the kinds of social lies that one hears every day. Even when reporting the most casual deceptions of social intercourse, Nick notes the subtle discrepancies between what we say and what we feel. In the following scene, a friend of theirs, Larry Crowley, is discussing Harrison Quinn's infatuation with Dorothy Wynant:

> Larry said: "He's nuts over the girl, isn't he? He told me he was going to divorce Alice and marry her."
> Nora said, "Poor Alice," sympathetically. She did not like Alice.
> Larry said: "That's according to how you look at it." He liked Alice.
> (P. 97)

From the lies of a criminal seeking to hide his guilt to the petty social lies of his own circle of friends, Nick is bothered and frustrated by the constant need to "solve" puzzles—whether it be to uncover the identity of a murderer or to uncover the real feelings of his friends. And this, more than the danger and demands of the detective business, seems responsible for his leaving the profession. In a significant remark to Nora when she asks him what is bothering him, he answers: "Things . . . riddles, lies, and I'm too old and too tired for them to be any fun. Let's go back to San Francisco" (p. 132).

Perhaps because Nick has left the often unpleasant business of private detecting, he is a much more likable and humane character than any of Hammett's other heroes. Even those characters who typically would be expected to despise the private eye—the cop and the criminal—display more than a passing acceptance of Nick. John Guild, a staid and rather unimaginative policeman, calls on Nick for advice throughout the novel, and despite suspicions that Nick is not always open with him, Guild clearly respects the former detective's abilities. "I think you're a smart detective. I want to listen to what you got to say" (p. 75). Studsy Burke, the former convict whom Nick helped send to prison, is similarly impressed. When a friend of his, Shep Morelli, needs someone to talk to about his involvement with Julia Wolf, Burke suggests that he go to Nick because "Nick might not maybe sell his own mother out" (p. 70), and given the natural animosity of the criminal for the law, such an understated recommendation should be taken as high praise. Throughout the novel, characters ask Nick's opinions on a variety of subjects—from Alice Quinn to Shep Morelli to John Guild and the Wynants, people regularly come to Nick for answers and help.

Although Nora jokingly claims this reliance on her husband is owing to the fact that "everybody trusts Greeks" (p. 14), people seem drawn to Nick simply because he refuses to judge them. As with all Hammett heroes, there is a quality of detachment about Nick, yet unlike the Op, Spade, or Beaumont, his is not a detachment that comes from drawing away from people as much as it is a deliberate effort to treat himself and others lightly. Nick is the wittiest of the four detectives. Although there is some humor in all of Hammett's other novels, *The Thin Man* has a comic tone which persists in spite of the murders, the brutalization of Dorothy Wynant, the unhappiness of Alice Quinn. Nick's comic spirit is consistent—he is not like Ned Beaumont who can be very funny at one moment and almost neurotically intense the next. At times, Nick's humor is simply gay and silly, as in this scene with Nora:

> Nora sighed. . . . "I'll give you your Christmas present now if you'll give me mine."
> I shook my head. "At breakfast."
> "But it's Christmas now."
> "Breakfast."
> "Whatever you're giving me," she said, "I hope I don't like it."
> "You'll have to keep them anyway, because the man at the Aquarium said he positively wouldn't take them back. He said they'd already bitten the tails off the—" (P. 14)

And it can be used as a means of dealing with fear and danger. When Shep Morelli breaks into their bedroom and threatens them with a gun, Nick asks: "Do you mind putting the gun away? My wife doesn't care, but I'm pregnant and I don't want the child to be born with—' (p. 25). Such wisecracking is a large part of Nick's style, but its importance goes beyond a desire to entertain others: it is a means of defusing and disarming the danger and the ugliness around him. His final reference to the Wynant case is characteristic of his insistence that nothing, not even murder and violence, should be taken too seriously. When Nora suggests that they leave for San Francisco the next day since the case is over, Nick replies: "Let's stick around awhile. This excitement has put us behind in our drinking" (p. 180).

Like his humor, Nick's drinking is an important aspect of his character. There are numerous references to drinking, and these are cited in the critical work of both William F. Nolan and David Bazelon as a major indication of Nick's moral dissipation: a *real* hero does not drink with Nick's frequency, enthusiasm, and enjoyment. Yet such condemnation (Bazelon refers to the drinking as "the weakness of mere self-indulgence, the weakness of deliberate unconsciousness")[6] has a moralizing tone that is not only removed from the evidence of the text but also contradicts the current medical view of alcoholism. Nick drinks often, but his narrative is always lucid. And even from the point of view of the other characters, his drinking seems to be a minor consideration; a policeman like John Guild would hardly respect Nick's opinion as much as he does if he thought him a drunkard nor, for that matter, would any of the other characters. At one point in the novel, when Mimi Wynant tells her daughter that she drinks too much, she retorts, "I don't drink as much as Nick" (p. 22), yet this fact does not deter either one from relying on his judgment and abilities. Nick seems to drink all the time (in an early scene, he repeatedly asks Nora for a drink, and when she tells him, "Why don't you have some breakfast first," he answers, "It's too early for breakfast" [p. 9]), but his drinking never makes him ugly, cruel, or hostile, nor does it seem to affect his ability to function competently as a detective. During one scene in the early part of the novel when his drinking seems more frequent, Nora tries to talk seriously to Nick about helping Dorothy Wynant. When he insists that he can do nothing, she sighs, "I wish you were sober enough to talk to" (p. 14), but what follows this remark is, in fact, a scene in which Nick exercises perfect control. Dorothy Wynant arrives at their apartment drunk and hysterical and tells them a story about buying a gun in a speakeasy, illustrating her story by waving a gun about. The same man who, moments earlier, is supposedly too drunk to talk to disarms the girl, analyzes the situation, and correctly points out Dorothy's real fears. "All she was trying to tell you was that she was afraid Jorgensen was waiting to try to make her when she got home and she was afraid she was drunk enough to give in" (p. 18).

Despite the amount of alcohol Nick consumes, he never appears to be in a drunken state nor does he drink when actively working on the case. This is a reversal from the presentation of drinking in most hard-boiled detective fiction. The typical hard-boiled detective often has a scene in which he sits alone in his office, escaping the pain of his case through bourbon—the Op has such a session in *Red Harvest*, for example, when he drinks a combination of gin and laudanum in order to forget his part in Personville's violence. In the case of Nick Charles, however, Hammett's references to drinking are more often good-natured and joking: when Nora asks him how he feels, he answers, "Terrible, I must've gone to bed sober" (p. 43). Nick does drink at all times of the day and night, yet alcohol does not seem to be a destructive influence in his life—he can drink often and enjoy the effects of liquor without harming his relationship to others or his own mental faculties.[7] But the main emphasis in *The Thin Man* on alcohol and drinking cannot be ignored, for its role in the novel is a complex one. On the one hand, drinking is presented as fun—the standard clichés that alcohol can heighten one's experiences and make them more enjoyable, exhilarating, and humorous certainly hold true for Nora and Nick. To some extent it is this sense of carefree fun and frivolity that makes *The Thin Man* such a delightful book. Yet there is another side to drinking and alcohol and another side to the charm of *The Thin Man*: drinking is a means of dulling and blurring an often ugly and brutal world. It is significant that the only time in the novel where Nick's need for a drink seems desperate ("For God's sake, let's have a drink" [p 32.]) occurs in a scene in which Dorothy Wynant tells of being beaten regularly by her mother while her stepfather watches. As a later discussion will suggest, the world that often seems so gay with parties, drinking, repartee, and an abundance of leisure time is, in fact, often a world of unhappiness and cruelty, and the pain of living in such a world is mitigated for Nick and Nora by alcohol.

Although alcohol helps Nick cope with the world, it is finally Nora who stabilizes his life and provides him with a sense of self-fulfillment. Her presence in *The Thin Man* means that Nick does not have to live in the absolute isolation of Hammett's other heroes. In almost every respect, Nora is the ideal mate. She is brave (her response when Nick knocks her out during the confrontation with Morelli is "you damned fool . . . you didn't have to knock me cold. I knew you'd take him, but I wanted to see it" [p. 27]); she is funny (when Studsy Burke convinces Morelli to apologize for his attack on Nick, Nora murmurs, "Old Emily Post Studsy" [p. 104]); and perhaps most importantly, she accepts and appreciates Nick ("I love you, Nicky, because you smell nice and know such fascinating people" [p. 112]). Rather than trying to socialize Nick, Nora enjoys those qualities that set him apart from others. Despite the difference in their ages—she is twenty-six while Nick is forty-one—Nora often stands up to Nick. At the same time, however, she trusts his judgment: when Nick asks her why she does not think Wynant killed Julia Wolf, she answers with a surprised "because you don't" (p. 144). In addition, Nora has a vitality and an eagerness for the next moment that appeals to Nick. During the scene in which Morelli threatens them with a gun, Nick comments as he looks over at her, "She was excited, but apparently not frightened: she might have been watching a horse she had a bet on coming down the stretch with a nose lead" (p. 129).

Although Nora's spirit and intelligence are a large part of her appeal, it may be finally her decency that is most important to Nick. In a world which seems to be populated by the cruel, the vicious, or the hopelessly neurotic, Nick can look to Nora for stability, support, and sanity. In a scene typical of Hammett's ability to create understated yet powerful tensions, we see this tie between them graphically illustrated. The scene takes place in the Wynant apartment just after the police have departed. Nick and Nora are also preparing to leave when Dorothy, obviously disturbed and frightened at the prospect of being left alone, announces that Gilbert knows the identity of the killer. The exchange which follows is fraught with psychological violence as well as the threat of actual physical violence; in the midst of this confusion and tension, Nick's response to Nora's presence is extremely revealing.

> Mimi said, "Now, Dorry, don't let's have one of those idiotic dramatic performances."
> Dorothy said: "You can beat me after they's gone. You will." She said it without taking her eyes off mine. Mimi tried to look as if she did not know what her daughter was talking about.
> "Who does he know killed her?" I asked.
> Gilbert said: "You're making an ass of yourself, Dorry, you're—"
> I interrupted him: "Let her. Let her say what she's got to say. Who killed her, Dorothy?"
> She looked at her brother and lowered her eyes and no longer held herself erect: "I don't know. He knows." She raised her eyes to mine and began to tremble. "Can't you see I'm afraid?" she cried. "I'm afraid of them. Take me away and I'll tell you, but I'm afraid of them."
> Mimi laughed at me. "You asked for it. It serves you right. . . . I wish you wouldn't baby her so, Nick. It only makes her worse. She—"
> I asked Nora: "What do you say?"
> She stood up and stretched without lifting her arms. Her face was pink and lovely as it always is when she has been sleeping. She smiled drowsily at me and said: "Let's go home. I don't like these people. Come on, get your hat and coat, Dorothy."
> . . . Nora stepped between Mimi and Dorothy. I caught Mimi by a shoulder as she started forward, put my other arm around her waist from behind, and lifted her off her feet. She screamed and hit back at me with her fists and her sharp high heels made dents in my shins.
> Nora pushed Dorothy out of the room and stood in the doorway watching us. *Her face was very live. I saw it clearly, sharply: everything else was blurred.* (Pp. 128–29, italics mine)

In this scene Nora provides for Nick an element of familiarity, stability, and common sense in the midst of an otherwise bewildering, violent confrontation. Certainly the fact that Nick turns to Nora for advice in this crucial situation—"What do you say?"— suggests his reliance on her. But it is the climactic moment of recognition for Nick, of seeing Nora's face as a clear, sharp, "very live" image when everything else—the violence and cruelty of Mimi, and pathetic helplesness of Dorothy and Gilbert, the sheer ugliness of the situation—is blurred, that best demonstrates what Nick feels for Nora.

The scene just cited also provides a good example of the subtle, understated approach relied on by Hammett to present the nuances of Nick and Nora's relationship. Obviously Nick and Nora are not intended to be an overtly romantic couple; indeed, Hammet characteristically avoids almost all sentiment and all of the romantic rhetoric in presenting a marriage which appears to be as affectionate and successful as theirs is. Nick and Nora *are* very much an idealized couple, yet Hammett develops their relationship in much the same understated, unemotional language that he used in his other fiction. The suspicion of sentimentality, the aversion to abstract and rhetorical language, and the reluctance to trust any word or deed not founded in irony or in concrete, immediate experience make traditional love scenes impossible. Indeed, they display a casual, almost dispassionate attitude in their remarks when they comment upon each other to outsiders, although such remarks carry a considerable amount of implicit affection. In the following exchanges, both are scrupulous in avoiding sentimental rhetoric or any hint of "love" language:

> I distributed the drinks and sat down beside Mimi. She said: "Your wife's lovely."
> "I like her." (P. 20)

> "You like Nick a lot, don't you, Nora?" Dorothy asked.
> "He's an old Greek fool, but I'm used to him." (P. 22)

> Macaulay said: "She's grown up to be something to look at." He cleared his throat. "I hope your wife won't—"
> "Forget it. Nora's all right." (P. 142)

During scenes in which Nick and Nora are alone together, this understated display of affection is still very much the basis of their relationship. Both, for example, enjoy teasing each other and both enjoy silly verbal games which frequently refer self-consciously to Nora's maternal treatment of Nick. Nora, who is twenty-six, asks, "What's worrying you now, son?" and Nick, who is forty-one, responds in kind, "What's a clue, Mamma?" (pp. 132–33). Nick rarely refers to Nora in his narrative unless it is to report on her physical actions or her conversations, nor does he comment on his feelings for her. One exception occurs in a scene with John Guild, who earlier said of Nora, "There's a woman with hair on her chest" (p. 27); when Guild later tries to apologize for this remark, Nick tells us, "Nora can smile very nicely. She gave him one of her nicest smiles. 'Mind? I liked it.'" (p. 29).

Lillian Hellman, to whom *The Thin Man* is dedicated and who was the basis for Nora, was once asked if she liked the character of Nora. She responded: "Yes. It's an affectionate portrait of a woman; but what pleased me more than anything else was that it was an affectionate pair of people. A man and woman who amused each other and got along."[8] This simple summation of the relationship seems appropriate, for both Nick and Nora clearly love and enjoy one another. Hammett creates numerous scenes throughout the novel that do convey their love and mutual appreciation. A good example of such a scene occurs at the end of the opening chapter, when Nora returns from her shopping to see Dorothy Wynant and Nick talking together; after introductions are made, Dorothy leaves and we are told:

> We found a table. Nora said: "She's pretty."
> "If you like them like that."
> She grinned at me. "You got types?"
> "Only you, darling—lanky brunettes with wicked jaws."
> "And how about the red-head you wandered off with at the Quinns' last night?"
> "That's silly," I said. "She just wanted to show me some French etchings." (P. 5)

Throughout the novel, the chapters frequently end with this sort of teasing, almost ritualistic exchange between Nick and Nora. Such chapter endings are effective, for they dramatically underscore the good-natured, affectionate relationship that Hammett is anxious to establish.

Despite, however, this warm and positive bond between Nick and Nora, *The Thin Man* is marked by other interpersonal relationships which are as destructive and perverted as any in Hammett's other novels. The malevolence of the Dain family in *The Dain Curse* is perhaps more dramatic since familial murder is committed, but the Wynants, and especialy Mimi, have a capacity for psychological violence that may be even more disturbing. When Nick describes the family to Nora, her response is one of incredulity. "I don't believe it. . . . You made it up. There aren't any people like that. What's the matter with them? Are they the first of a new race of monsters?" (p. 94). And Mimi does, in fact, seem truly monstrous: throughout the novel, her sole concern is for the Wynant fortune, and to protect her interests, she is willing to suppress evidence, blackmail her former husband, and use both herself and her daughter as sexual bait. According to Nick, "Mimi's poison" (p. 15)—an assessment that is more than borne out by her self-serving lies, by her attempts to manipulate her own son and daughter, and by her complete disregard of moral or ethical considerations. She beats Dorothy so badly that her back is "crisscrossed by long red welts" (p. 32), and at times, she becomes so violent that she can bring on a seizure from hysterical rage. Nick describes such a seizure: "Mimi's face was becoming purple. Her eyes protruded, glassy, senseless, enormous. Saliva bubbled and hissed between clenched teeth with her breathing, and her red throat—her whole body—was a squirming mass of veins and muscles swollen until it seemed they must burst" (pp. 129–30).

The rest of the Wynant family seems only slightly less "monstrous." Dorothy is a frightened, neurotic young woman who tells Nick early in the book that she likes neither her father, her mother, nor her brother (p. 10) yet is dominated by all three. Convinced that her father is insane, she fears for her own sanity as well, and that fear, according to Nick, has "got her doing figure eights" (p. 38). Like her mother, she has a propensity towards violence. Once at a party at which Harrison Quinn teases Dorothy, she becomes hysterical. "'Shut up! Shut up, you drunken fool!' Dorothy began to beat his face with both hands. Her face was red, her voice shrill. 'If you say that again I'll kill you'" (p. 98). More often, however, Dorothy is the victim of violence—a victim of either her mother's beatings or men's sexual molestations. In this respect, she is much like Gabrielle Leggett, for like Gabrielle, Dorothy is young, pretty, and vulnerable to both emotional and physical attacks. She is both afraid of and attracted to her handsome stepfather, and there are several suggestions that he has approached her. But perhaps more important are the thinly veiled references to Nick and

Nora that she was abused as a child. On three different occasions in the book, she tries to tell Nick of something that happened to her as a little girl—something she feels would enable him to understand her better (pp. 34, 131, 132). The exact nature of the trauma is never explained, but clearly we are intended to think it involved incest—perhaps with her father. Her brother, Gilbert, once abruptly asked Nick, "You'll think it's a funny question: is there much incest?" (p. 160). Yet the result of this abuse is not rejection or rebellion but a sort of masochistic dependency on her mother. Her mother may beat her and use her as sexual bait to enlist the aid of Nick, but Dorothy still kisses her on the mouth and then watches as Mimi checks in her compact-mirror to see that her lipstick has not been smeared (p. 21). The complete inexplicability of her relationship to Mimi seems most apparent in her last words of the novel. When Nick tells Dorothy that her father is dead, she sobs, "I want to go home to Mama" (p. 172).

Gilbert Wynant is similarly attached to his mother and sister. When Nick—in his attempts to keep Mimi from attacking Dorothy—becomes himself involved, he must fight Gilbert as well. Gilbert tries to defend his mother with "clumsy, ineffectual blows" (p. 129) that must have been humiliating to him, and yet afterwards, when Mimi calms down, she treats his efforts with derision and ridicule. "She began to laugh. 'Oh, Gil, did you really try to protect me? And from Nick?' Her laughter increased" (p. 130). In many respects, Gilbert is a foolish figure with all of his prattling questions to Nick about criminology, drugs, cannibalism, incest, and self-inflicted pain, but he still emerges as the best of the Wynants. Faced with the cruelty and ugliness of his family, he tries to understand why they act as they do. His fascination with Freudian analysis seems to be a means of objectifying and dealing with their unpleasant and often contemptible actions. Gilbert is, in fact, an obvious and often amusing parody of a Freudian who views people in terms of mother-fixation, dromomania, and kleptomaniac impulses (p. 60). Nick—who maintains that "I'm not a psychoanalyst. I don't know anything about early influences. I don't give a damn about them" (p. 131)—is skeptical of Gilbert's theories but sympathetic towards the young man himself. When Gilbert asks Nick what he thinks of him, Nick replies, "You're all right . . . and you're all wrong" (p. 160)—a rather ambiguous assessment that seems to fit Gilbert. The means by which Gilbert tries to understand his family may be wrong (as closed systems always are in Hammet's novels), but the motive behind his attempts to explain their neuroses and cruelties seems to be one that is rare in the Wynant family: he cares about his sister and mother. Despite the contempt and ridicule with which they often treat Gilbert, he remains loyal and protective.

Not only are the parent/child relationships crippling and confused, the relations between men and women are equally twisted and hard to fathom. *The Thin Man*, like all of Hammett's novels, is filled with misalliances in which love leads to pain and ultimate betrayal. Clyde Wynant leaves his wife for Julia Wolf, yet according to Shep Morelli her motives were purely economic. "She figured maybe he'd be worth more for a long pull than for a quick tap and a get-away, so she give him the business and wound up with a steady connection" (p. 109). Mimi's next husband, Chris Jorgensen, is actually Rosewater, the man who years before had threatened the Wynant family. He had abandoned his wife to marry Mimi to avenge himself on Wynant and get part of the family fortune. Even secondary characters carry through this theme of twisted love. Alice and Harrison Quinn have a marriage of economic and social convenience that seems to make them both unhappy. Even more dramatic is the relationship between Arthur Nunheim and his girlfriend: at one point, he threatens her with "all right . . . put your mouth in and I'll pop a tooth out of it" (p. 78), yet moments later when she storms out of their apartment, he begs Guild: "Let me go. . . . Let me bring her back. I can't get along without her. . . . I've got to have her" (pp. 79–80).

Thus, Hammett's presentation of interpersonal relationships in *The Thin Man* is, despite the novel's lighter tone, just as bleak as in his earlier novels. With the important exception of Nick and Nora, the characters here suffer a similar fate—greed, betrayal, and manipulation seem a part of all human relationships. The fact that there is less physical brutality in this book is finally irrelevant, for this is a novel of psychological violence and willful cruelty. The long section on cannibalism in the middle of the story seems to be a parable of this deliberate pain. Gilbert Wynant, with his eccentric interests in human aberration, asks Nick if there have been many cases of cannibalism in the United States. Nick answers by handing him a copy of *Duke's Celebrated Criminal Cases of America* (the same book that was on Spade's nightstand in *The Maltese Falcon*) and pointing out a passage entitled "Alfred G. Packer, the 'Maneater,' Who Murdered His Five Companions In the Mountains of Colorado, Ate Their Bodies And Stole Their Money" (p. 61). In this four-page account, we learn the story of Packer and his five companions who become lost in the wilderness in the winter of 1873. Facing starvation, the six men become involved in a grisly confrontation over who should eat whom. One by one, they turn on each other until only Packer is left to continue the journey back to civilization—a journey during which he subsists mainly on the flesh of his friends. When he finally makes his way to a trading post, he disposes of the strips of flesh, but his story of the experience is questioned. In his confession, the most horrifying aspect of the account is revealed. "When I espied the Agency from the top of the hill, I threw away the strips I had left, and I confess I did so reluctantly as I had grown fond of human flesh, especially that portion around the breast" (p. 65).

After reading the section from the casebook, Gilbert returns the text to Nick, apparently unaffected by the account.

> Gilbert, book in hand, came over to us. He seemed disappointed in the story I had given him. "It's very interesting," he said, "but if you know what I mean, it's not a pathological case." He put an arm around his sister's waist. "It was more a matter of that or starving."
>
> "Not unless you want to believe him," I said. (Pp. 67–68)

What Gilbert has failed to understand is, of course, the real horror of the story: atrocities can occur out of necessity, but out of sheer human perversity we can learn to enjoy them. Just as Sam Spade used his Flitcraft story as a means of telling Brigid his belief in a random universe, Nick seems to be using the Packer story as a means of illustrating to Gilbert an ugly and disturbing lesson: people can inflict pain on others or can enjoy the pain *of* others simply because, like Packer, they have "grown fond of human flesh." Even some of the minor scenes demonstrate this savagery. In the following scene, Tip Edge, a friend of Nick and Nora, has just come upon the end of the fight between Dorothy and Harrison, both of whom are crying:

We had what audience there was. Tip came running, her face bright with curiosity. "What is it, Nick?"

I said: "Just a couple of playful drunks. They're all right. I'll see that they get home all right."

Tip was not for that: she wanted them to stay at least until she had a chance to discover what had happened. She urged Dorothy to lie down awhile, offered to get something—whatever she meant by that— for Quinn, who was having trouble standing up now. (P. 99)

More dramatic perhaps are the scenes between Alice and Harrison Quinn in which they tear at one another or the instances in which Mimi seems to get some kind of mindless enjoyment out of tormenting her children, but this notion of wanton cruelty and pleasure in that cruelty exists throughout *The Thin Man*. It seems an appropriate symbol for the book that Macaulay, after killing Clyde Wynant, pours lye on the body, stripping away the flesh.

Just as Hammett's development of interpersonal relationships in *The Thin Man* echoes that found in his earlier works, so too does he retain his concern here with metaphysical issues. These issues lack the prominence they had in the earlier works and are usually introduced in a more playful manner, but when we peel away some of the banter from Nick and Nora's conversations about the nature of truth and our methods of arriving at knowledge and hypothetical systems, we find a similar metaphysical skepticism emerging from Nick as we did from the Op and Spade. Nick also indicates on several occasions that he takes a pragmatic, fundamentally skeptical attitude about truth: we can explain *what* happens, he suggests, but never *why*—or, as he puts it bluntly at one point, "I just tell you what happens; I don't explain it" (p. 94). Very much like the Op's practical approach to detective work, Nick continually emphasizes that his role is to juggle facts, to shift them around until a coherent picture emerges; once this picture is developed the detective need not concern himself with its relationship to *truth* but only with its ability to present an explanation which fits the facts. This emphasis is very obvious in the long exchanges between Nick and Nora in the novel's concluding chapter: Nora listens to Nick's elaborate hypothesis about the case and contiually attempts to pin Nick down as to the "truth" of his theories; Nick's response to these attempts is extremely revealing.

[Nora]: "Then you're not sure he—"

"Stop saying that. Of course we're sure. That's the only way it clicks. Wynant had found out that Julia and Macaulay were gypping him and also thought, rightly or wrongly, that Julia and Macaulay were cheating on him—and we know he was jealous—so he went up there to confront him with whatever proof he had, and Macaulay, with prison looking him in the face, killed the old man. Now don't say we're not sure. It doesn't make any sense otherwise. . . ."

"But this is just a theory, isn't it?"

"Call it any name you like. It's good enough for me."

"But I thought everybody was supposed to be considered innocent until they were proved guilty and if there was any reasonable doubt, they—"

"That's for juries, not detectives. . . ."

"But that seems so loose."

"When murders are committed by mathematicians," I said, "you can solve them by mathematics. . . . Macaulay wasn't silly enough to think Nunheim was to be trusted even if he paid him, so he lured him down to this spot he had probably picked out ahead of time and let him have it—and that took care of that."

"Probably," Nora said.

"It's a word you've got to use a lot in this business. . . . Now are you satisfied with what we've got on him?"

"Yes, in a way. There seems to be enough of it, but it's not very neat."

"It's neat enough to send him to the chair," I said, "and that's what counts." (Pp. 173–74)

As should be evident from the context of the passage just cited, Hammett largely uses Nora as a type of classical detective figure to develop this contrast between absolute and relative truth. Nora, then, is the person who believes in an ordered, coherent, fully understandable world in which all human action is explicable; Nick, meanwhile, simply does not believe in such a rational order and contents himself with arriving at solutions which fit the facts. "I always thought detectives waited until they had every little detail fixed in—" Nora once tells Nick (p. 179), and at one point she uses this philosophy to examine step-by-step and eliminate from consideration all the possible suspects in the case; this performance, based on induction and logic, is an exact replica of the conventional moment in classical detective fiction when the detective ticks off each participant in the case and explains why he or she could not possibly be the culprit (leading of course to the final assignation of guilt).

[Nora]: "Now don't make fun of me; I've thought about it a lot. It wouldn't be Macaulay, because he's using him to help shield whoever it is and—"

"And it wouldn't be me," I suggested, "because he wants to use me."

"That's right," she said, "and you're going to feel very silly if you make fun of me and then I guess who it is before you do. And it wouldn't be either Mimi or Jorgensen, because he tried to throw suspicion on them. And it wouldn't be Nunheim, because he was most likely killed by the same person, and furthermore, wouldn't have to be shielded now. And it wouldn't be Morelli, because Wynant was jealous of him and they'd had a row. . . . I tried to throw out my personal feelings and stick to logic. Before I went to sleep last night I made a list of all the—"

"There's nothing like a little logic-sticking to ward off insomnia. It's like—"

"Don't be so damned patronizing. Your performance so far has been a little less than dazzling." (P. 145)

Nora's last comments here are right, of course—as is true of all the cases handled by Hammett's detectives, Nick's performance is not "dazzling," the way we would expect a classical detective's to be. Unlike such detectives, Nick, Spade, the Op, and Beaumont are all forced to operate in a chaotic, violent, dehumanizing universe which simply cannot sustain the notion of final truths or "logic-sticking." It is a tribute of sorts to all of Hammett's detectives that none despair in the face of this vision, that all have devised a means of carrying on in such a world, and that all do manage—through courage, persistence, luck, and their own undeniable detective skills—to arrive at solutions which work. Hammett suggests that such solutions may only be a thrust at the truth and not the truth itself. But the act of creating these solutions is all we can ask of a modern human.

7
Conclusion

— ⌣ —

For ten years he was able to do what almost no other writer in this genre has ever done so well—he was able to really write, to construct a vision of a world in words, to know that the writing was about the real world and referred to it and was part of it; and at the same time he was able to be self-consciously aware that the whole thing was problematical and about itself and "only" writing as well. For ten years, in other words, he was a true creator of fiction.

—*Steven Marcus*

When Gertrude Stein returned to the United States and began her celebrity tour, she told a friend that she wanted to meet two Americans: Charlie Chaplin and Dashiell Hammett. In *Everybody's Autobiography* Stein explained why she was so eager to meet a man whose background, tastes, temperament, and writing seem so fundamentally different from her own. "I never was interested in cross word puzzles or any kind of puzzles but I do like detective stories. I never try to guess who has done the crime and if I did I would be sure to guess wrong but I liked somebody being dead and how it moves along and Dashiell Hammett was all that and more."[1]

Through ten years of writing and five novels, Dashiell Hammett did just what Stein described: he made something "more" out of a type of writing traditionally expected to be less than literature. People typically read detective fiction "to guess who has done the crime" and because they are intrigued by "somebody being dead"—and hard-boiled novels offer a consistency of form, style, and content that enables them to be read quickly, easily, undiscriminatingly. What is perhaps most striking about Dashiell Hammett's work is that his novels succeed so well on this level, yet, at the same time, they can be probed and analyzed until they yield a sharp, brilliant vision of fiction and the world. There is a complex substructure in each of Hammett's novels that operates symbolically, metaphysically, and metafictionally. To enjoy his novels, one need not address this substructure; to appreciate Hammett's achievement as a writer, one must. His first novel, *Red Harvest*, is a clear example of this. The most exciting, physical, and energetic of his works, *Red Harvest* is a study of personal systems, of ethical responsibility, of the individual's impotence against an overwhelming destructiveness of corruption, chaos, and death, yet all this is subtly woven into dramatic action that thrilled audiences of pulp, sensationalized fiction. Unlike Raymond Chandler's novels, which seem to demand a serious treatment by their readers, Hammett's never insist that weightier matters are at hand. The result is an ongoing sense of revelation in Hammett: once a reader perceives there is something "more" to the action-filled, violent whirl of motion and death that marks *Red Harvest*, a pattern of increasing complexity appears. The Continental Op seems a character much like those in other hard-boiled works, but once the reader makes the most casual observations about the unheroic qualities in the Op's nature, the entire focus of the novel shifts and suddenly *Red Harvest* is charged with a disquieting potential for reversal and transmutation. What begins as a traditional detective story, in which the detective will prevail over forces of evil and chaos, ends with the reader questioning not only the "goodness" of the hero but also the means by which he triumphed—or if he triumphed at all. If the Op is not the hero we expect him to be—and certainly such expectations lie at the heart of the genre—then what is he? Thus, there is an important leap in our perception of the fiction we are reading. The murder mystery we read to pass the time is transformed into an intricate inquiry into the morality and expediency of personal systems.

Similarly, *The Dain Curse* changes as we gain insights into what the book is about. Perhaps more than in any of his other works, this novel has an innovative cleverness that manages to shape and control the outrageous plot and makes it somehow feasible. The excesses of plot (labyrinthine connections, melodrama, multiple murders) are, in fact, self-consciously drawn, and even more so than in *Red Harvest* there is a vivid moment of revelation when the connection between these elaborately sensational plots and the epistemological discussions of the Op and Fitzstephan becomes apparent. Yet again this substructure—the level at which the novel becomes a metafictional analysis of the detective novel—connects to, but does not supersede, the integrity of the work as popular fiction. At the same time, once the reader becomes aware of the implications of the exchanges between the Op and Fitzstephan, even the mundane aspects of the novel take on new significance. This technique of "reconsideration" is built into the plot on every level. When we learn at the end that Fitzstephan is the killer, there are obvious implications for the plot: we must see the struggle on the stairway between Owen and Alice Dain in a new light; the events that occurred during the gothic night in the temple must be reinterpreted; the attempt to rescue the kidnapped Gabrielle involved different factions than we first perceived. But the denouement brings an even more complex reassessment of the novel's metafictional qualities: how does Owen's "guilt" affect his position as spokesperson for traditional fiction? Since we now see that his earlier arguments with the Op were predicated by the need to mask his guilt, how are we to view his insistence on order and form?

In *The Maltese Falcon* a similar shift at the end again forces us to reevaluate the characters and the relationships among them. When we lern that Brigid is Miles Archer's murderer, the knowledge alters our perception of what has happened in the novel, but this change is only the most obvious manifestation of the book's central theme: things are not as they seem. This idea, symbolized more clearly by the fake statue, is woven so skillfully into the novel that virtually every element of the plot's structure comes into question. This is Hammett's most intricate work, for he manipulates detail, characterization, and plot until the very concept of mystery emerges as the central point of the book. The harder we try to understand the nature of the conflict in order to determine guilt, innocence, and motivation—the way we would in other detective novels—the more mysteries proliferate. And once the notion of ambiguity occurs to us, we find it everywhere—from a blond satan as detective-hero to a dashing and romantic gentle-man crook who is also treacherous and grotesquely fat to a ho-mosexual hired gunman—until the novel achieves a dizzying ef-fect that makes solution and analysis turn upon one another, canceling out surety and undercutting our attempts to under-stand the meaning of anything at all. Thus on the simplest level of plot, we do not understand the mystery (did, for instance, Spade ever contemplate going in with the crooks? would his actions have been different if the falcon had been real?), nor can we assign meaning on a more complicated level of metafiction and the metaphysical implications (what fictional category does Spade be-long to? Brigid? did Hammett create a mystery that has no solu-tion or did he give us a solution that revolves around mystery?).

This exploration of mystery—the mystery behind people's ac-tions and the mystery of people themselves—is also central to *The Glass Key.* On one level the book is an exposure of political corruption in America, but it is also an ambitious exploration of the psychological novel. It is usually read as an indictment of urban American politics—a devastating account of the bank-ruptcy of American democracy. But this ostensible subject is an overlay of sociological interest that covers a more complex in-quiry into a broader notion of government: how do we govern the affairs of our own minds? how do we govern our own emotions? Just as the elaborate system of elections, of checks-and-balances, and of laws designed to from an orderly, rational society fails to keep order, so too do individual attempts to control our own psy-chology. Thus the social and political chaos that abounds in *The Glass Key* is the inevitable result of an individual chaos brought about by personal fragmentation and the inability to understand ourselves and others. By his denial of psychological clues that might explain, clarify, and solidify character, Hammett implies that a coherent, consistent, self-aware course in life is indeed a fiction—one perpetrated by the traditional novelist—that simpli-fies and glosses over the essential mysteries of consciousness.

While Hammett's last novel, *The Thin Man,* is viewed by some as a retreat from such "serious" considerations, it may well be his most subtle and, in certain ways, his most controlled work. The glib lightness of the tone, the playful humor, and the warmth that exists between Nora and Nick create an atmosphere that seems far removed form the tortured fatalism of *The Glass Key. The Thin Man* is a stylish, urbane novel that deals more blithely than usual in hard-boiled detective fiction with the grubbier aspects of crime, but as with all of Hammett's books, this outward appearance belies what lies beneath—a stark and stubborn insistence on the human capacity for cruelty and "cannibalism." The book works successfully on a lighter level, and we can be amused by the eccentricities of the Wynant family and the social lives of the wealthy, yet if we step back we see something else at work that is not amusing and is not so light. The first of these perspectives exists exclusive of the second—Hammett never insists that his reader must look beyond the obvious meaning of his novels. But the second perspective—not only is the world neither charming nor gay, it is painful, destructive, and personally divisive—depends upon the first, for the reverberations between the outward cheerfulness and the inner chill give an unexpected edge to the entire novel.

All five novels have in common, then, this capacity to provide "more" for the reader of hard-boiled detective fiction—more complexity of ideas and more technical artistry. Yet, given the predisposition to dismiss this genre of popular fiction as inconsequential literature, why did Hammett write only in this form? Was he hesitant to attempt a "serious" novel because he doubted his skill? Did he write detective fiction only because of happenstance? Most puzzling of all, why would a writer who insisted so resolutely on the ultimate mystery of the human experience work within the very medium most committed to solving and eliminating mystery? The answer seems to lie in Hammett's conviction that the notion of mystery's supremacy is best illustrated by showing its power to withstand our attempts to dismantle it. Solutions are offered in Hammett's work—we know at the end who killed whom—but his novels are concluded not in dissipation of mystery but by reaffirmation of the limits of reason. Life *is* mystery—it cannot be explained, it cannot be understood, it cannot be categorized. Yet we search for motives that will define human behavior and seek retribution on those who defy the structures set up to maintain the illusion of order; we want, above all, systems of justice that reassure us that there are measures for human conduct, and we construct laws, ideologies, and fictions to dispel our fear that life is a random fluctuation and each one of us is alone in its maelstrom. For Hammett the greatest mystery is human consciousness—how we know, how we think we know, how we lead our lives thinking life is a "clean orderly sane responsible affair" (*The Maltese Falcon*), p. 66).

Hammett's life presents its own kind of mystery and certainly part of the attraction people feel for his art is interwoven in their fascination for the creator. Biographical assessment is difficult and often contradictory, but certain configurations emerge. He was a sick man most of his adult life, and because of this constitutional weakness, his mental life took precedence over a physically active one. He read widely and continuously; with no formal schooling past age thirteen, he educated himself in the arts, science, mathematics, and history. Clearly he was an intellectual— his was a life of the mind. And although this may have been imposed on him by his poor health, in many ways it was a life that agreed with him. By the accounts of Hellman and others, he appears to have been deeply uncomfortable around most people. He was constantly puzzled by what he considered the inexplicability of men and women: why people's actions and words were so often disconnected from their thoughts and feelings. This sense of confusion around others, this unease, may have been the main reason why he drank so much; it certainly suggests why he was so reclusive and private a person. Yet even though it was difficult, sometimes painful for Hammett to share communion with people, he had a profound feel for humanity and worked much of his life for causes he believed were most closely allied with promoting freedom. His own personal psychology (a product of a not-so-happy home and the chance experiences life had dealt him) may have made it difficult to spend time with individuals, but he cared enough about people in the abstract to spend six months in a federal prison when he believed their freedoms were being threatened.

Given the strength of his commitments, why then did he stop writing? At the end of the unfinished *Tulip*, Pop (a slightly fictionalized Hammett) says, "If you are tired you ought to rest, I think, and not try to fool yourself with colored bubbles."[2] That might be the answer Hammett would have offered to our question, but other, more entangled reasons suggest themselves. Simply stated, his fiction was taking him in one direction—toward a vision that the world and people are essentially beyond understanding, beyond control—while his politics were taking him in another. As a Marxist, he believed in the pursuit of economic and personal freedom; a cohesive, meaningful world was possible and all his political efforts worked towards that end. As an artist, however, he saw human endeavor in a different light. He was carried by his fiction to an aesthetic and philosophical position that life *is* chaos and random transformation. Any attempt to systematize what is essentially an eclectic experience into a single focus will fail and rightfully so: by "sensibly ordering" our affairs, we get "out of step, and not into step with life" (*The Maltese Falcon*, p. 66). Thus, his deeply-felt political convictions clashed with his artistic beliefs. This "answer" to why he quit writing seems likely, but it is not conclusive—after all, what was Hammett's art all about if not the idea that there are no single solutions? What is true is that, before he left writing, Dashiell Hammett created works of fiction that continue to speak to us of the way we live and the way we think even as they entertain.

Notes
Bibliography
Index

Notes

—— ⌒ ——

1. Dashiell Hammett and the Hard-Boiled Detective Genre

1 Raymond Chandler, *The Simple Art of Murder* (New York: Ballantine, 1977), p. 17.

2 Richard Layman, *Shadow Man: The Life of Dashiell Hammett* (New York: Harcourt, 1981), p. 6. Diane Johnson has recently completed the authorized biography with a tentative publishing date of Oct. 1983. William F. Nolan's *Dashiell Hammett: A Casebook* (Santa Barbara: McNally, 1969) and Peter Wolfe's *Beams Falling: The Art of Dashiell Hammett* (Bowling Green: Bowling Green Univ. Popular Pr., 1980) both discuss his life and work. Biographical material on Hammett is interspersed throughout Lillian Hellman's *An Unfinished Woman* (New York: Bantam, 1974), *Pentimento* (New York: Signet, 1973) and *Scoundrel Time* (New York: Bantam, 1977) as well as in her introduction to *The Big Knockover* (New York: Vintage, 1972).

3 Dashiell Hammett, "The Gutting of Couffignal," in *The Big Knockover*, ed. and with an introduction by Lillian Hellman (New York: Vintage, 1972), p. 34.

4 Layman, p. 11.

5 Layman, p. 15.

6 Nolan, p. 18.

7 Nolan, p. 19.

8 In this account, either Hellman or Hammett is mistaken in combining the Frank Little murder with the lynchings at Everett, Washington. The Everett murders took place on Nov. 5, 1916; Frank Little was assassinated near Butte, Montana, on July 31, 1917. Although both were acts of violence directed against union organizers, they were not connected.

9 Hellman, *Scoundrel Time*, p. 45.

10 Layman, p. 28.

11 Layman, p. 75.

12 Hellman, *Knockover*, p. xiv.

13 This publishing information is summarized in the "Checklist" of Hammett's works found in Nolan's *Casebook*, pp. 138–45.

14 Nolan, p. 78.

15 For an excellent study of these and other issues, see George J. Thompson, "The Problem of Moral Vision in Dashiell Hammett's Detective Novels," Diss., Univ. of Connecticut, 1971.

16 Hellman, *Scoundrel Time*, p. 41.

17 Hellman, *Unfinished Woman*, pp. 228–29.

18 At the conclusion of his testimony, the following exchange took place between Hammett and the chairman, Joseph McCarthy:

> THE CHAIRMAN: May I ask one further question: Mr. Hammett, if you were spending, as we are, over a hundred million dollars a year on an information program allegedly for the purpose of fighting communism, and if you were in charge of that program to fight communism, would you purchase the works of some 75 Communist authors and distribute their works throughout the world, placing our official stamp of approval upon those works?
> Or would you rather not answer that question?
> MR. HAMMETT: Well, I think—of course, I don't know—if I were fighting communism, I don't think I would do it by giving people any books at all.
> THE CHAIRMAN: From an author, that sounds unusual.

> Cited by Layman, p. 232.

19 Joseph T. Shaw, ed., *The Hard-Boiled Omnibus* (New York: Simon and Schuster, 1946), p. viii.

20 Shaw, p. vii.

21 In his unfinished autobiographical novel, *Tulip* (written in 1952 but not published until the posthumous edition of some of his short stories, collected in *The Big Knockover*), Hammett deals with this problem of reason and order that is found throughout his detective novels. In this fragment of a novel, Pop—clearly Hammett himself—has retreated to a friend's farm in New England after being released from prison. There he enjoys the pleasures of country life as well as reading widely in mathematics and physics until his peace is broken by the reappearance of Tulip, a man he has known for several years. Tulip is obsessed with the idea that Pop should write his autobiography and has, in fact, led most of his adult life under the prevailing desire to produce colorful, histrionic material. Pop refuses and tries to make Tulip understand why by telling him that all the events, the people, the memories of his own life have resulted in "only one brief and

fairly pointless story about a quiet lunger going to Tijuana for a placid day's outing" (p. 345). Yet Tulip persists because of, as one of the characters in the story points out, "his preoccupation with congruity. He devotes considerable attention to the various theories that a some-what consecutive—though not necessarily chronological attention—course of events—no matter how dissimilar they may seem—gives life—or any life, for that matter, including perhaps most importantly his own—a—or it may be the—form" (p. 351). Pop/Hammett recognizes in Tulip's need to have him "sort out the beads and string them for him" (p. 351) the longing for order that most people share.

22 Nolan, p. 149.

23 Dashiell Hammett, review of *The Death of Cosmo Revere*, by Christopher Bush, *New York Evening Post*, May 24, 1930, sec. 4, p. 3, col. 4.

24 R. A. Knox, *Literary Distractions* (New York: Sheed, 1958), p. 188.

25 G. K. Chesterton, *The Spice of Life* (London: n.p., 1967), pp. 16, 17, 19, 20.

26 A. E. Murch, *The Development of the Detective Novel* (Port Washington, N.Y.: Kennikat Pr., 1968), p. 11.

27 Julian Symons, *Mortal Consequences* (New York: Schocken, 1973), p. 10.

28 Symons, p. 12.

29 W. H. Auden, *The Dyer's Hand and Other Essays* (New York: Random, 1962), p. 158.

30 John G. Cawelti, *Adventure, Mystery, and Romance* (Chicago: Univ. of Chicago Pr., 1976), p. 149.

31 Any reader who can follow the plot of a Chandler novel is a very careful reader indeed, and to guess its outcome would be miraculous. During the filming of *The Big Sleep*, Howard Hawks and Humphrey Bogart got into an argument about the death of the chauffeur; they could not figure out whether it had been a murder or a suicide. They sent a telegram to Chandler, but his reply was that he did not know either. See Raymond Chandler, *Raymond Chandler Speaking* (Boston: Houghton, 1977), p. 221.

32 Cawelti, p. 146.

33 Dashiell Hammett, *Red Harvest* (New York: Vintage, 1972), p. 79. All subsequent reference to this novel will be to this edition, with page references included parentheticaly in the text.

34 Cawelti, p. 146.

35 Chandler, *Simple Art of Murder*, p. 16.

36 Cawelti, p. 155.

37 Carroll John Daly, "The False Burton Combs," in *The Hard-Boiled Detective* (New York: Vintage, 1977), p. 4.

38 James Cain, *Three of a Kind* (New York: Knopf, 1943), p. x.

39 Russell Nye, *The Unembarrassed Muse: The Popular Arts in America* (New York: Dial, 1970), p. 255.

40 Symons, p. 136.

41 Cited by Nye, p. 257.

42 Mickey Spillane, *My Gun Is Quick* (New York: American Library, 1950), p. 6.

43 George Harmon Coxe, "Murder Mixup," in *The Hard-Boiled Omnibus*, p. 187.

44 Lester Dent, "Tropical Disturbance," in *Murder—In Spades* (New York: Pyramid, 1969), p. 99.

45 Raymond Chandler, *The Little Sister* (New York: Ballantine, 1976), p. 39; *The Big Sleep* (New York: Ballantine, 1975), p. 5; *The High Window* (New York: Vintage, 1976), p. 34.

46 Nye, p. 256.

47 Cawelti, p. 156.

48 John Paterson, "A Cosmic View of the Private Eye," *Saturday Review*, Aug. 22, 1953, p. 8.

49 Raymond Chandler, *The Long Goodbye* (New York: Ballantine, 1953), p. 204.

50 Cawelti, p. 144.

51 An interesting treatment of this debate over the morality of hard-boiled detective fiction is William Ruehlmann's *Saint With a Gun* (New York: New York Univ. Pr., 1974).

52 "Hammett Eulogized by Lillian Hellman," *New York Times*, Jan. 13, 1961, sec. 1, p. 29, col. 1.

2. *Red Harvest*: The Detective as Cipher

1 The criticism of our political system that runs throughout *Red Harvest* is obvious and is noted in all critical assessment of Hammett and his work. The more complex treatment of the failures of *personal* systems, however, has been largely overlooked. There have been no critical articles that deal specifically with *Red Harvest*, and the few paragraphs devoted to the novel in general works on detective and popular fiction (for example, Russel Nye's *The Unembarrassed Muse* and Julian Symons's *Mortal Consequences*) all fail to point out the dramatic irony which is at work. Only two critics question the heroic stature of the Op and the validity of his system: William Ruehlmann, who does so for moralistic reasons outside the evidence of the text, and David Bazelon, who addresses the inadequacies of the Op's system but who assumes that Hammett was unaware and uncritical of the failure of the detective's professional code.

2 Fitzgerald, of course, created a similarly ironic view of the West in *The Great Gatsby*.

3 It is therefore appropriate that when the Op walks the streets in his dream late in the novel (pp. 149–51), he walks streets which represent all of America: "I walked streets hunting for her, half the streets in the United States, Gay Street and Mount Royal Avenue in Baltimore, Colfax Avenue in Denver, Aetna Road and St. Clair Avenue in Cleveland, McKinney Avenue in Dallas, Lemartine and Cornell and Avory Streets in Boston, Berry Boulevard in Louisville, Lexington Avenue in New York until I came to Victoria Street in Jacksonville, where I heard her voice again, though I still could not see her" (pp. 149–50).

4 As I will later emphasize, *Red Harvest* even eliminates the usual clearcut distinction between "good guys" and "bad guys," for the Op's complicity in the lawlessness and violence in Personville makes him as guilty as anyone else in the novel.

5 Donald Ogden Stewart, ed., *Fighting Words* (New York: Harcourt, 1940), pp. 56–57.

6 Nolan, p. 49.

7 Nolan provides a detailed summary of the Op's appearances in *Black Mask* in his chapter "*Black Mask* and the Birth of the Op," pp. 21–33.

8 It is no accident that of the seventeen motion pictures adapted from various Hammett stories and novels (including the three versions of *The Maltese Falcon* and the five movies created about Nick and Nora Charles), none deal with the Op (although the movie *Roadhouse Nights* was supposedly based on *Red Harvest*, it actually has little to do with the plot). *The Dain Curse*, a 1976 made-for-television movie, appears to be an exception, for it does have an Op figure, but he has been transformed into "Hamilton Nash"—a character clearly based on Hammett himself, whom James Coburn, the star of the film, physically resembles. What this suggests is obvious: the Op does not translate into a film character very well unless his identity is transformed by the grafting of some specific identity (like that of Hammett) onto his own.

9 Nolan, p. 26.

10 This posture of casualness is certainly inconsistent with Lillian Hellman's remarks about the writing of *The Thin Man* in her introduction to *The Big Knockover*. "Life changed: the drinking stopped, the parties were over. The locking-in time had come and nothing was allowed to disturb it until the book was finished. I had never seen anybody work that way: the care for every word, the pride in the neatness of the typed page itself, the refusal for ten days or two weeks to go out even for a walk for fear that something would be lost" (p. xvii).

11 Throughout *Red Harvest* the Op is a man of many identities; early in the novel when asked by Bill Quint who he is, the Op tells us: "I got out my card case and ran through the collection of credentials I had picked up here and there by one means or another. The red card was the one I wanted. It identified me as Henry F. Neill, A.B. seaman, member in good standing in the Industrial Workers of the World. There wasn't a word of truth in it" (p. 7).

12 This is precisely the narrative strategy currently being employed by such contemporary fiction writers as Thomas Pynchon and Joseph McElroy. In her reminiscences about Hammett in *An Unfinished Woman*, Lillian Hellman comments several places about Hammett's obsession with facts (see, for example, pp. 230–42).

13 The preference of hard-boiled audiences for this lone-wolf figure was recently dramatized with their reaction to the highly successful television series "Mannix." This show had a poorly rated first season when the detective was part of a large, computerized agency, but when Mannix's role was changed to that of a lone operator, the show's ratings improved.

14 Chandler, *Little Sister*, pp. 198–99.

15 Carroll John Daly, *The Hidden Hand* (New York: Grosset, 1929), p. 11.

16 The Op's membership in an organization should *not*, however, be taken as a sign of socialization, for his relationship to the agency is hardly familial or even personal. His job gives the Op certain bureaucratic guides that define procedures, standardize paper work, and establish the extent of his commitment to a case. But the agency itself is nothing more than an impersonal structure whose design is based on the most efficient means to go about the business of catching criminals; as a business enterprise, it possesses no morality or emotion in its approach to crime. The head of this structure, the Old Man, is amoral and emotionless. If the Op successfully moves up the corporation ladder, if he successfully emulates the model, then he too will eventually come to be like the Old Man "with his gentle eyes behind gold spectacles and his mild smile, hiding the fact that fifty years of sleuthing had left him without any feelings at all on any subject" (from "The Scorched Face" in *The Big Knockover*, p. 91). The Old Man, the embodiment of the professional operative, is a figure who appears sporadically throughout the series as a kind of ghost-of-things-to-come for the Op and as a living realization of where the philosophy of the agency will take you. To the people who worked under him, "He was also known as Pontius Pilate, because he smiled pleasantly when he sent us out to be crucified or suicidal" (*Red Harvest*, p. 108). His response to the Op's report that a woman has been murdered is de-

scribed by the Op in "Fly Paper" as being, "'Indeed,' as if I had said it was raining, and he smiled with polite attentiveness while I told him about it" (*Knockover*, p. 50).

17 Paul Cain, *Fast One* (New York: Doubleday, 1933), p. 304.

18 Carroll John Daly, *The White Circle*, (New York: Clode, 1926), p. 186.

19 Daly, *The White Circle*, p. 175.

20 Raoul Whitfield, *Green Ice* (New York: Knopf, 1930), p. 28.

21 Whitfield, p. 16.

22 Dashiell Hammett, *The Dain Curse* (New York: Vintage, 1972), p. 204. All subsequent reference to this novel will be to this edition, with page references included parentheticaly in the text.

23 The Op's attitude towards his job can best be seen in "The Gutting of Couffignal," a 1925 short story. A portion of this story has already been cited in chapter 1. In the larger passage that follows, the Op is explaining his attitude about his work to a female criminal who attempted to win her freedom through bribery and sexual overtures to the Op:

"Let me straighten this out for you," I interrrupted. "We'll disregard whatever honesty I happen to have, sense of loyalty to employers, and so on. You might doubt them, so we'll throw them out. Now I'm a detective because I happen to like the work. It pays me a fair salary, but I could find other jobs that would pay more. Even a hundred dollars more a month would be twelve hundred a year. Say twenty-five or thirty thousand dollrs in the years between now and my sixtieth birthday.

"Now I pass up about twenty-five or thirty thousand of honest gain because I like being a detective, like the work. And liking the work makes you want to do it as well as you can. Otherwise there'd be no sense to it. That's the fix I am in. I don't know anything else, don't enjoy anything else, don't want to know or enjoy anything else. You can't weigh that against any sum of money. Money is good stuff. I haven't anything against it. But in the past eighteen years I've been getting my fun out of chasing crooks and tackling puzzles, my satisfaction out of catching crooks and solving riddles. It's the only kind of sport I know anything about, and I can't imagine a pleasanter future than twenty-some years more of it. I'm not going to blow that up. . . . You think I'm a man and you're a woman. That's wrong. I'm a manhunter and you're something that has been running in front of me. There's nothing human about it. You might just as well expect a hound to play tiddly-winks with the fox he's caught." (*Knockover*, p. 34)

24 Mickey Spillane, *My Gun is Quick* (New York: New American Library, 1950), p. 17.

25 Maxwell Grant, *The Living Shadow* (London: New English Library, 1976), p. 23.

26 Review of *Red Harvest*, by Dashiell Hammett, *New Statesman*, July 27, 1929, p. 500.

27 It is appropriate that it is Dan Rolff who pronounces this moral judgment on Dinah, for he is the only character in the novel to display any sense of morality. He is physically weak and ineffectual when compared to the rest of Personville, yet the Op seems to have a greater respect for him than for most of the other people he encounters there. After Dinah slaps Dan several times, the Op hits Dan a few times himself and explains: "I poked him to give him back some of his self-respect. You know, treated him as I would a man instead of a down-and-outer who would be slapped around by girls" (p. 78). Later on, when Dinah and the Op are literally bidding against one another over the price she should get for turning over Whisper Thaler, Dan tries to protest. Once again, Dinah overcomes him physically and, before he collapses to the floor, he says "wearily," "There is no—" (p. 101). This enigmatic sentence is purposefully ambiguous—there is no "justice"? no "morality"? no "respect for human decency"?—but clearly it is intended as some sort of moral judgment. In typical fashion, Hammett leaves this issue open, for to complete such a judgment would have added some degree of abstract sentimentality to the scene and to the book. One could, incidentally, make a convincing argument that the Dan Rolff character is, to some extent, based on Hammett himself: Dan certainly displays a concern for moral commitment that Hammett's own life often revealed, and both suffered from tuberculosis.

3. *The Dain Curse*: The Epistemology of the Detective Story

1 This is not to suggest, however, that the issue of the Op's job does not appear at all in this novel. There are several instances where the Op's insistence on job—and his lack of human emotion—appears in *The Dain Curse*, as well. For several examples where the Op seems to respond coldly to the human reality of the case while rationalizing his lack of emotion as being "job-oriented," see pp. 43, 60, 135, and 168.

2 This interest in epistemology is, for the most part, missing in *Red Harvest*, and since most critics regard Hammett's second novel as merely a sequel to the first, very little attention has been paid to the issue. There are no critical articles that deal solely with *The Dain Curse*, but the most valuable general discussion is Steven Marcus's introduction to *The Continental Op*. Although the discussion does not pertain specifically to either *Red Harvest* or *The Dain Curse*, it does provide an insightful analysis of the metaphysical impulse in

Hammett's work. Marcus focuses on how Hammett integrates his metaphysical/metafictional interests with the detective novel format. As Marcus details the usual pattern of the Op's cases, the Op is typically called to the scene of a crime or a potential crime where he is met by conflicting stories, motives, and accusations. Different versions of "reality" have been constructed by different characters—some with the clear intention of creating confusion, some merely the result of ignorance or prejudice—and as detective, the Op's job is "to deconstruct, decompose, deplot and defictionalize that 'reality' and to construct or reconstruct out of it a true fiction, i.e., an account of what 'really' happened" (New York: Vintage, 1975), p. xix. Marcus goes on to point out, however, that this process does *not* lead to the omnipotent unveiling of a final truth, as ordinarily happens in other hardboiled detective fiction, but to the replacing of myriad illusions of reality with a single vision—the Op's.

> What happens in Hammett is that what is revealed as "reality" is a still further fiction-making activity—in the first place the Op's, and behind that yet another, the consciousness present in many of the Op stories and all the novels that Dashiell Hammett, the writer, is continually doing the same thing as the Op and all the other characters in the fiction he is creating. That is to say, he is making a fiction (in writing) in the real world; and this fiction, like the real world itself, is coherent but not necessarily rational. What one both begins and ends with, then, is a story, a narrative, a coherent yet questionable account of the world. (Marcus, p. xxi)

3 Hammett also gains a certain amount of verisimilitude by setting this section in San Francisco, for he undoubtedly relied on the fact that most of his readers would feel California was the most likely place for a cult such as this one to take root (the Jim Jones tragedy of 1978 only reinforces this conviction). Within the novel itself, there are two specific references to this popular association of California and "kooky cults": at one point Collinson comments of the Temple of the Holy Grail that "it's the fashionable one just now. You know how they come and go in California" (p. 36); later the Op agrees with this assessment. "They brought their cult to California because everybody does, and picked San Francisco because it held less competition than Los Angeles" (p. 97).

4 Although few hard-boiled detective novels carry the gothic atmosphere as far as does *The Dain Curse*, it is important to note that these gothic elements exist in other forms in the genre. There has always been an obvious connection between classical detective fiction and the gothic thriller, beginning with Poe and Doyle (especialy

The Hound of the Baskervilles), but with hard-boiled fiction, these gothic elements are transformed by an urban twentieth century sensibility. The mysterious, all-powerful villain who controls those around him from his solitary country estate becomes a czar of organized crime who lives in the city he rules. The monster often becomes the city itself, uncontrollable and threatening. But in almost all hard-boiled fiction, these gothic elements are rendered as inconspicuously as possible; Hammett, however, blatantly exploits them. And in that exploitation, he insists once more on the artifice of his own fiction.

5 Hammett skillfully leaves even the Op's final solution open to question; a reader may well wonder if there might not be *some* elements of truth in Gabrielle Leggett's "confession"—she claims *she* is the real murderer and supplies a surprisingly coherent explanation of all that has happened considering the fact that she is in the throes of morphine withdrawal symptoms (pp. 196–97). It would be easy enough, if we took her story seriously, to disregard Owen Fitzstephan's confession since it is just possible that he is in love with her; horribly mutilated by the bomb blast, Owen might well have decided to take a chance by confessing to the crime himself, especially since he felt he had an excellent chance to "beat the rap" (which he basically does, by reason of insanity).

6 This method is fairly common and has been employed with great success on the television series "Columbo," although there the tables are turned since the detective—and the viewers—know who is guilty, while the criminal is not aware of this.

7 Hammett makes fun of newspapers' tendency to fictionalize events for mere sensation's sake throughout his fiction. In this novel, Fitzstephan comments, for example, that he needs "direct" news of events, "instead of having to depend on what I can get out of you [the Op] and what the newspapers imagine their readers would like to think had happened" (p. 96).

8 The Op makes another disparaging comment about Owen's tendency to romanticize people and events when he says: "So you read newspapers? What do you think he is? King of the bootleggers? Chief of an international crime syndicate? A white-slave magnate? Head of a dope ring? Or queen of the counterfeiters in disguise?" (p. 21).

9 For a complete treatment of this analogy between readers of traditional fiction and detectives, see William Spanos's "The Detective and the Boundary: Some Notes on the Postmodern Literary Imagination," *boundary 2* 1 (Fall 1972):147–68.

10 The Op also has no illusions about the role of "truth" in our court systems. When Gabrielle's lawyer, Madison, asks the Op at one point if he thinks Gabrielle actually believes one of his hypotheses, the Op

snaps: "Who said anybody believes it? I'm just telling you what we'll
go into court with. You know there's not necessarily any connection
between what's true and what you go into court with" (p. 188).

4. Ambiguity in *The Maltese Falcon*

1 Hammett toys with the implications of names throughout *The Maltese
Falcon*. Casper Gutman's name, for example, refers both to his obes-
ity (gut-man) and to his function in the novel—"Casper" is a deriva-
tive of "Jasper" which means "the lord of the treasure" in old French.
2 Dashiell Hammett, *The Maltese Falcon* (New York: Vintage, 1972),
p. 195. All future reference to this book will be to this edition, with
page references inserted parenthetically in the text.
3 This inability to defend oneself against the forces of violence is most
vividly dramatized by Hammett in his next novel, *The Glass Key*, in
which his main character, Ned Beaumont, is ruthlessly and terribly
beaten by two sadistic thugs after he has been kidnapped.
4 Dashiell Hammett, "Preface," in *The Maltese Falcon* (New York:
Modern Library, 1934), p. ii.
5 Steven Marcus summarizes the major implications of this world view
when he comments of Spade's personal philosophy that it is based on
"the ethical irrationality of existence, ethical unintelligibility of the
world . . . life is inscrutable, opaque, irresponsible, and arbitrary . . .
human existence does not correspond in its actuality to the way we
live it" (p. xvii).
6 As Marcus notes in a footnote, it can hardly be an accident that when
Hammett chose a new name for Flitcraft (he adopts it after he leaves
his wife) it is the same as that of the famous American philosopher,
Charles Peirce (with the vowels reversed) (p. xviii). Peirce was engaged
in speculations very similar to the epistemological views of Flitcraft,
which are later adopted by Spade.
7 A classic example of this conventional loyalty is developed by Mickey
Spillane in *I, The Jury*.
8 Cf. Brigid's comment to Spade later in the novel, "You know you do
such wild and unpredictable things that—" (p. 223).
9 Spade's violent and seemingly irrational hatred for Wilmer is difficult
to account for; it may partially lie in Spade's disdain for the young
hoodlum's homosexuality, though Spade seems tolerant enough about
Cairo. There is an intricate but puzzling homosexual motif that runs
throughout *The Maltese Falcon*: its development ranges from Effie's
"boyish qualities" (cf. Spade's comment to her, "You're a good man,
sister") to various ambiguous double entendres (the hotel detective
to Spade, "I'm willing to go all the way with you all the time" [p.

140]) to the elaborate symbolism of guns and other phallic objects that can be found in many scenes. It is difficult to judge the importance of this homosexual reading of such elements; it may be merely another of the ways in which Hammett adds complexity and ambiguity to the novel, while undercutting our conventional expectations.

10 There is even an element of deception in the relationship between Spade and Effie—as with Spade's repeated questions to Effie about whether or not she still supports Brigid (he *knows* Brigid is the murderer) and Effie's evident sense of betrayal by Sam at the novel's end.

11 Nolan, pp. 64–65.

5. *The Glass Key*: A Psychological Detective Novel

1 Symons, p. 139.

2 Robert I. Edenbaum, "The Poetics of the Private Eye: The Novels of Dashiell Hammett," in *Tough Guy Writers of the Thirties*, ed. David Madden (Carbondale: Southern Illinois Univ. Pr., 1968), p. 142.

3 In his casebook on Hammett, Nolan cites a comment by Raymond Chandler in which Chandler notes of *The Glass Key* "an effect of movement, intrigue, cross-purposes" and "the gradual elucidation of character, which is all the detective story has any right to be about anyway" (p. 74). Yet Cawelti in his work comments that it "goes beyond the detective story altogether to become a study in political power and corruption" (p. 163).

4 Dashiell Hammett, *The Glass Key* (New York: Vintage, 1972), pp. 28–30. All future reference to this work will be to this edition with page references given parenthetically in the text.

5 Nolan, p. 69.

6 Martin Seymour Smith, *Who's Who in Twentieth Century Literature* (New York: McGraw, 1977), p. 149.

7 Nolan, p. 69.

8 Cf. Hammett's own written comment, "If you have fooled around with crap games as much as I have, you know what chance can do to the laws of probability." Cited by Nolan, p. 71.

9 Nolan, pp. 69–70.

10 David T. Bazelon, "Dashiell Hammett's 'Private Eye,'" *Commentary* 7(5):471.

6. *The Thin Man*: The Detective and the Comedy of Manners

1 Cawelti, p. 165.

2 The sources of critical dissatisfaction with *The Thin Man* vary, but it is interesting to note how consistently critics return to the notion that the changes in Hammett's personal life had irreparably damaged

his writing powers and had caused his last novel to be hurriedly and carelessly put together. This assumption that Hammett's personal life made it impossible for him to create an aesthetically unified novel in *The Thin Man* is hinted at by William F. Nolan's comments.

What, on the surface, is amusing and fresh in the published version simply reflects Hammett's own decay as an individual and as a writer. The discipline which held him to the typewriter was largely gone; the drinking was constant; the man could no longer believe in, nor write about, detectives who resisted life's pleasures to get a case solved. . . . This novel reflects the author's own uncertainty in his career; it foreshadowed the long years of creative silence ahead; after *The Thin Man* just three new short stories appeared (all in 1934). (P. 88)

An even clearer expression of this attitude can be found in David T. Bazelon's essay, "Dashiell Hammett's 'Private Eye,'" in a 1949 *Commentary* issue, where he states:

We can assume this alliance between our deep desires and a carefully defined world *on paper*, intellectually; but can it be *lived*? Or, a less ambitious question, can it subserve the creation of an aesthetically unified novel?

In the case of Hammett, the answer apparently is no—not without great distortion. For Hammett, in *The Glass Key*, got only as far as the experience of the vital need of knowing (beyond the horizon of the job). He then collapsed—quite completely, instead of following his literary problem where it was leading him, he preferred to follow his new-found Hollywoodism down whatever paths of pleasure *it* might take him. He postponed the attempt to resolve those problems with which life had presented him. But it was, it could be, only a postponement, and after a few years he came upon Stalinism—that fake consciousness, fake resolution, perfect apposite of Hollywoodism—and created the t's of his lost art.

Nick Charles, the hero of *The Thin Man*, spends more time drinking than solving crimes. If he does his job at all, it is only because Nora, his wife, eggs him on for the sake of her own excitement. Nick is as indulgent of his wife's whims as he is of the bottle's contents. Ned Beaumont's weakness, which was at least to some degree a product of moral consciousness, becomes in Nick Charles the weakness of mere self-indulgence, the weakness of deliberate *unselfconsciousness*; thus literal drunkenness becomes a symbol of that more fundamental drunkenness that submerges the individual in commercialized culture and formularized "progressive" politics. (Bazelon, *Commentary* 7[5]:472).

It should be pointed out here that Bazelon's essay, written at the height of the Communist-scare period in America, is very obviously prejudiced in its assessment of Hammett owing to Hammett's Stalinist sympathies.

As these two representative quotes indicate, it has been extremely difficult for critics of Hammett to analyze *The Thin Man* objectively and not be influenenced by a moralistic condemnation of Hammett's life in Hollywood (the "Hollywoodism" of alcohol and too many women) and his politics (Communism). Such critics choose to ignore the strong evidence that Hammett worked on *The Thin Man* with precisely the same obsessive diligence and artistic control as he had with his earlier works. As Lillian Hellman suggests in her memoirs of Hammett during this period, it was certainly *not* the case that Hammett had weakly allowed Hollywood to destroy his artistic integrity: "I had known Dash when he was writing short stories, but I had never been around for a long piece of work. Life changed: the drinking stopped, the parties were over. The locked-in time had come and nothing was allowed to disturb it until the book was finished. I had never seen anybody work that way: the care for every word, the pride in the neatness of the typed page itself, the refusal for ten days or two weeks to go out even for a walk for fear something would be lost" (Hellman, *Knockover*, p. vii).

3 Dashiell Hammett, *The Thin Man* (New York: Vintage, 1972), p. 27. All subsequent reference to this novel will be to this edition, with page references included parenthetically in the text.

4 William F. Nolan, in his casebook on Hammett, points out that John Guild was originally the hero of a detective novel begun in 1930 that roughly followed the general plan of *The Thin Man*. According to Nolan, this character "combined the businesslike Agency approach of the Op and the ultra coolness of Spade" (p. 75). One of the characters in this uncompleted novel calls Guild "bloodless" and a "ghost of a man" who is "unreal, untouchable." It seems important that this extension of utter neutrality and grim professionalism was abandoned by Hammett and replaced by the more human character, Nick Charles.

5 Throughout *The Thin Man*, for example, Hammett has Nick make references to the Russian Revolution and the Stalinist Five-Year Plans; such specific political references are largely absent in the earlier novels.

6 Bazelon, p. 472.

7 In this respect, the portrayal is perhaps an idealized one; in Nick, Hammett may have created a fantasy version of what he wanted to be: a man who could drink as much as he wanted and yet be free of the debilitating effects of alcohol. Thus, those critics who closely identify Hammett's own life with his fictional character should take into account that Nick may be closer to an idealized version of Hammett than a true reflection. Nick is not, as argued by Bazelon, a symbol of any degeneracy in Hammett's life; he is rather a figure who manages to transcend the personal problems that plague his creator.

8 Christine Doudna, "A Still Unfinished Woman: A Conversation with Lillian Hellman," *Rolling Stone*, Feb. 24, 1977, p. 56.

7. Conclusion

1 Gertrude Stein, *Everybody's Autobiography* (New York: Vintage, 1973), p. 4.
2 Hammett, *Knockover*, p. 352.

Bibliography

—◡—

Auden, W. H. *The Dyer's Hand and Other Essays.* New York: Random, 1962.

Bazelon, David T. "Dashiell Hammett's 'Private Eye.'" *Commentary* 7 (5): 467–72.

Cain, James. *Three of a Kind.* New York: Knopf, 1943.

Cain, Paul. *Fast One.* New York: Doubleday, 1933.

Cawelti, John G. *Adventure, Mystery, and Romance.* Chicago: Univ. of Chicago Pr., 1976.

Chandler, Raymond. *The Big Sleep.* New York: Ballantine, 1975.

———. *The High Window.* New York: Vintage, 1976.

———. *The Little Sister.* New York: Ballantine, 1976.

———. *The Long Goodbye.* New York: Ballantine, 1953.

———. *Raymond Chandler Speaking.* Boston: Houghton, 1977.

———. *The Simple Art of Murder.* New York: Ballantine, 1977.

Chesterton, G. K. *The Spice of Life.* London: n.p., 1967.

Coxe, George Harmon. "Murder Mixup." In *The Hard-Boiled Omnibus*, edited by Joseph T. Shaw. New York: Simon and Schuster, 1946.

Daly, Carroll John. "The False Burton Combs." In *The Hard-Boiled Detective.* New York: Vintage, 1977.

———. *The Hidden Hand.* New York: Grosset, 1929.

———. *The White Circle*. New York: Edward J. Clode, Inc., 1926.

Dent, Lester. "Tropical Disturbance." In *Murder—In Spades*. New York: Pyramid, 1969.

Doudna, Christine. "A Still Unfinished Woman: A Conversation with Lillian Hellman." *Rolling Stone*, Feb. 24, 1977.

Edenbaum, Robert I. "The Poetics of the Private Eye: The Novels of Dashiell Hammett." In *Tough Guy Writers of the Thirties*, edited by David Madden. Carbondale: Southern Illinois Univ. Pr., 1968.

Grant, Maxwell. *The Living Shadow*. London: New English Library, 1976.

Hammett, Dashiell. *The Big Knockover*. Edited and with an introduction by Lillian Hellman. New York: Vintage, 1972.

———. *The Continental Op*. Edited and with an introduction by Steven Marcus. New York: Vintage, 1975.

———. *The Dain Curse*. New York: Vintage, 1972.

———. *The Glass Key*. New York: Vintage, 1972.

———. *The Maltese Falcon*. New York: Modern Library, 1934.

———. *The Maltese Falcon*. New York: Vintage, 1972.

———. *Red Harvest*. New York: Vintage, 1972.

———. Review of *The Death of Cosmo Revere*, by Christopher Bush. *New York Evening Post*, May 24, 1930, p. 3.

———. *The Thin Man*. New York: Vintage, 1972.

Hellman, Lillian. "Introduction." In *The Big Knockover*, by Dashiell Hammett. New York: Vintage, 1972.

———. *Pentimento*. New York: Signet, 1973.

———. *Scoundrel Time*. New York: Bantam, 1977.

———. *An Unfinished Woman*. New York: Bantam, 1974.

Knox, R. A. *Literary Distractions*. New York: Sheed, 1958.

Layman, Richard. *Shadow Man: The Life of Dashiell Hammett*. New York: Harcourt, 1981.

Marcus, Steven. "Introduction." In *The Continental Op*, by Dashiell Hammett. New York: Vintage, 1975.

Murch, A. E. *The Development of the Detective Novel*. Port Washington, N.Y.: Kennikat Pr., 1968.

Nolan, William F. *Dashiell Hammett: A Casebook*. Santa Barbara: McNally, 1969.

Nye, Russel. *The Unembarrassed Muse: The Popular Arts in America*. New York: Dial, 1970.

Paterson, John. "A Cosmic View of the Private Eye." *Saturday Review* (Aug. 22, 1953).

Review of *Red Harvest*, by Dashiell Hammett. *New Statesman*, July 27, 1929, p. 500.

Ruehlmann, William. *Saint With a Gun*. New York: New York Univ. Pr., 1974.

Shaw, Joseph T., ed. *The Hard-Boiled Omnibus*. New York: Simon and Schuster, 1946.

Smith, Martin Seymour. *Who's Who in Twentieth Century Literature*, New York: McGraw, 1977.

Spanos, William. "The Detective and the Boundary: Some Notes on the Postmodern Literary Imagination." *boundary 2* 1 (Fall 1972):147–68.

Spillane, Mickey. *My Gun Is Quick*. New York: New American Library, 1950.

Stein, Gertrude. *Everybody's Autobiography*. New York: Vintage, 1973.

Stewart, Donald Ogden, ed. *Fighting Words*. New York: Harcourt, 1940.

Symons, Julian. *Mortal Consequences*. New York: Schocken, 1973.

Thompson, George J. "The Problem of Moral Vision in Dashiell Hammett's Detective Novels." Diss., Univ. of Connecticut, 1971.

Whitfield, Raoul. *Green Ice*. New York: Knopf, 1930.

Wolfe, Peter. *Beams Falling: The Art of Dashiell Hammett*. Bowling Green: Bowling Green Univ. Popular Pr., 1980.

Index

—━▿━—